CORNBREAD NATION

John T. Edge, General Editor

D0188100

THE
UNITED STATES
OF BARBECUE

Edited by Lolis Eric Elie

Published in association with the

SOUTHERN FOODWAYS ALLIANCE,

Center for the Study of Southern Culture,

University of Mississippi,

by the

UNIVERSITY OF NORTH CAROLINA PRESS

Chapel Hill and London

CORN BREAD NATION 2

This volume of *Cornbread Nation* was underwritten,
in part, by a gift from the Atticus Trust.

Library of Congress Cataloging-in-Publication Data
Cornbread nation 2: the United States of Barbecue /
edited by Lolis Eric Elie.
p. cm.
"Published in association with the Southern Foodways Alliance,
Center for the Study of Southern Culture, University of Mississippi."
Includes bibliographical references.
ISBN 0-8078-5556-1 (pbk.: alk. paper)
1. Barbecue cookery—United States. 2. Food habits—Southern
States. I. Elie, Lolis Eric. II. Southern Foodways Alliance.
TX840.B3C67   2005
641.5'784—dc22   2004013682

08 07 06 05 04   5 4 3 2 1

CONTENTS

Introduction, 1
　Lolis Eric Elie

THE BARBECUE
. . . .

A PORTRAIT OF THE
DELICACY AS A YOUNG DISH,
OR THE EARLY YEARS

The Land of Barbacoa, 11
　Bárbara Renaud González
Barbecue Service, 14
　James Applewhite
Caribbean Connection, 16
　Jessica B. Harris
George Washington and
　Barbecue, 19
　Mary V. Thompson
An Ode to the Pig: Assorted
　Thoughts on the World's Most
　Controversial Food, 23
　Bethany Ewald Bultman
The Georgia Barbecue, 30
　Maude Andrews

TRADITIONS AND DISPUTATIONS

Dixie's Most Disputed Dish, 37
　Rufus Jarmon
Texas Barbecue in Black
　and White, 48
　Robb Walsh

The Rhetoric of Barbecue:
　A Southern Rite and Ritual, 61
　Stephen Smith
Politics and Pork, 69
　Jim Auchmutey
Barbecue Sociology:
　The Meat of the Matter, 78
　John Shelton Reed
In Xanadu Did Barbecue, 88
　Ripley Golovin Hathaway
We Didn't Know from Fatback:
　A Southern Jewish Perspective
　on Barbecue, 97
　Marcie Cohen Ferris
By the Light of the Moon:
　The Hash Pot Runneth Over, 104
　Saddler Taylor
The Ribs Hit the Fan, 108
　Max Brantley

THE CURRENT SCENE

Cheer Up Mama, 113
　Peter Kaminsky
When Pigs Fly West, 121
　Lolis Eric Elie
Whole Hog, 130
　Jeff Daniel Marion
Kicking Butt, 135
　Matt McMillen

Real Barbecue Revisited, 138
  Vince Staten
To the Unconverted, 141
  Jake Adam York

THE PEOPLE
· · · · · · · · · · · · · · · · ·

In the Kitchen, 145
  Linda Parsons Marion
Willodene, 146
  Juliana Gray
Creole Contretemps, 151
  Brett Anderson
The Viking Invasion, 160
  Molly O'Neill
Never Give a Child
  an Artichoke, 171
  Jenine Holmes
The Power of Memory
  and Presence, 172
  Randy Fertel
The Hamburger King, 181
  William Price Fox
End of the Lines?, 186
  Pableaux Johnson
Catfish People, 199
  Earl Sherman Braggs

THE PLACES
· · · · · · · · · · · · · · · · ·

And the Band Played On:
  Taylor Grocery, Mississippi, 203
  Sarah Thomas
Open House, 205
  John T. Edge

Learning and Loafing at Tennessee's
  Oldest Business, 211
  Fred W. Sauceman

THE TRADITION
· · · · · · · · · · · · · · · · ·

Roadside Table, 219
  Michael McFee
What Abby Fisher Knows, 220
  Sara Roahen
Ice Cream Dreams, 223
  Eddie Dean
For the Love of Mullet, 233
  Diane Roberts
Boiled Peanuts, 239
  John Martin Taylor
The Fruits of Memory, 246
  Amy E. Weldon
Missing Links: In Praise of the
  Cajun Foodstuff That Doesn't
  Get Around, 250
  Calvin Trillin
Women Who Eat Dirt, 257
  Susan Allport
Rich and Famous, 270
  Julia Reed
Love, Death, and Macaroni, 273
  Pat Conroy

Contributors, 277
Acknowledgments, 281

Illustrations appear after
pages 120 and 216.

Introduction

LOLIS ERIC ELIE

I was born happily in New Orleans. I was only dragged into the South thirty-some years later unwittingly and uneasily by the Southern Foodways Alliance.

The difficulty was not a matter of geography. One of the advantages of living in New Orleans is that you can hop in a car or on a plane and in a matter of hours, you've traveled from the northern Caribbean to the southern United States, from sugarcane to cotton, from crawfish to catfish. Indeed, I had visited the South many times and even spent three years of my youth exiled in that region's capital, Atlanta. No, the difficulty was a matter of identity, or more precisely, a matter of navigating the long list of identities available in America to find that one that best correlated with my own personal set of idiosyncrasies.

I suppose in those pre-Southern days, I was something of a Creole. Neither of my parents would embrace the term, but that was no impediment to my appropriation of the birthright. The Africans and Europeans whose cultures combined to form Creole identity were often less than wild about their café au lait progeny. Thus the Creole credo has always been that the great, grand whole is infinitely superior to the sum of the little parental parts. So whenever there was a North-South debate about culture, sports, or politics, I lofted above the fray, confident that New Orleans was superior in all matters that mattered—food, music, architecture, and, of course, attitude. I was a New Orleans nationalist, utterly convinced that my city-state and certain other choice morsels of southern Louisiana territory should be considered in their own separate sphere. I believed that certain self-evident truths needed to be re-examined, namely this notion that the American Purchase of the Louisiana Territory was such a great deal. (While the Americans have profited handsomely from the transaction, try as I might, I have failed to see any advantage in it for my people.)

In 1998 I was invited to speak at the second annual Southern Foodways Alliance symposium. The topic of that year's event was Creolization, and I couldn't wait. We were to talk and learn about the various clashes of cultures that have created the South. My mouth watered at the prospect of brand new heathens, freshly unwashed and poised to hear the good news of the Creole gospel. I was prepared to speak from the subject, "As to Escoffier's Silence in the Matter of Gumbo." (Though others may consider the matter long settled, I intended that talk to be a Declaration of Creole Independence from France in the guise of a paean to my nation's signature culinary perfection.)

I knew I was in trouble when I heard the first speaker, Jessica Harris, Ph.D. She proceeded to define, dissect, and describe my region and my people in a series of languages other than English, all of which are crucial to an understanding of Creole identity but none of which I speak. Imagine my amazement to learn that she's native to one of the New York provinces (Queens, I believe) and scarcely came into contact with Creole civilization until she was a full-grown adult. Then Ronni Lundy, a Kentuckian, described her homeland, in a talk that was in turns hilarious and touching. She made it clear that mine isn't the only distinct area joined by geography and fate to the American South. She also rendered it utterly impossible for me to toss around the word "hillbilly" with any confidence that the epithet will neither hit nor hurt anyone of consequence.

The Southern Foodways Symposium is held in the heart of Dixie, at Ole Miss, the rebel university that sought to insure that the twentieth century would never darken its door. That place captured the otherness of the South for me. Its history epitomized the South I had no wish to belong to. But much about it was familiar: Leah Chase finding a Catholic sanctuary in that Baptist town and attending mass Saturday afternoon; Kathleen Purvis inviting us to come by her room for a little Kentucky cognac so that we might be properly fortified for the ten-block walk to the place where the festivities awaited. That year, I was converted to John Egerton's vision of the South and the Southern Foodways Alliance's role in it.

His book, *Speak Now Against the Day: The Generation Before the Civil Rights Movement in the South*, chronicles the prehistory of his ideal. He will detail this philosophy from the podium, but he articulates it best for you at Ajax Diner or Off Square Books after he has feasted well in the company of old friends and we have all drunk deeply from the Jack Daniels bottle. He will tell you that ours is a large table stretching from the Gulf of Mexico to Washington, D.C., from the Atlantic Ocean to the Mexican border. He will tell you that this coming together at our table and the breaking of our various breads is an act of defiance. It is a speaking now, mouth full and spirit nourished, against the days when certain feet, those deemed too dark or too dirty, were violently separated from this supper. He will tell you that this fried chicken, these sweet potato pies are related to regular food in much the same way as communion hosts are related to regular white bread.

And even if he doesn't say it that way, you will hear it that way.

If you are privileged to hear this, you will return to Oxford. You will return thinking you know something about grits, then rethink your knowledge at a Sunday brunch, after tasting the way Anson Mills and its miller, Glen Roberts, have restored this dish to its previous glory. You might return confident in the knowledge that South Carolinians can't make good biscuits, only to have Charleston chef Louis Osteen make last-minute changes to his menu so as to effectively rebut an anti–South Carolina biscuits remark he heard during a lecture. You might return to feel something of that fellowship you used to witness in those impatient moments after church when you were hungry and young and ready to go but your grandmother insisted on greeting everybody from the pastor on down as if "time for small talk and socializing" appeared as an item on the order of worship.

In putting together this anthology, I have sought to evoke the warm fellowship that glows in the South of the Southern Foodways Symposium. This volume shares with other anthologies the goal of bestness, the hope that we have combed the pages of potential inclusions and found those that exemplify the highest standards of literature and scholarship. But I am also hoping that the selection of these pieces is a step toward the crafting of a Southern geography so precise and nuanced as to be beyond the capabilities of any cartographer. So this anthology is about the South of tradition, in which funerals and food naturally go together, as in Pat Conroy's "Love, Death, and Macaroni." It is the South of John Martin Taylor's boiled peanuts, a region that extends up to Harlem but doesn't include Jim Auchmutey's Atlanta. It is a place where the celebrated chefs are not always men in toques, but old Southern cooking women as in Sara Roahen's "What Abby Fisher Knows." It is the South of women like Ruth Fertel, who parleyed her technique and talent beyond the kitchen and into broader culinary economy (Randy Fertel's "Power of Memory and Presence"). It is about a place with traditions so old and otherworldly as to be scarcely recognizable to many of us (Susan Allport, "Women Who Eat Dirt"). It's also about a new South, leading the nation, as exemplified in Molly O'Neill's "Viking Invasion."

Barbecue occupies a place in this anthology much like the one it occupies in the pantheon of American food—large and cherished. We take our subtitle, "The United States of Barbecue," from Jake Adam York, the poet whose work

"To the Unconverted" appears here and whose poems often serve as invocations at SFA events. Like cornbread, barbecue is a food that unifies the vast expanse of the American South, an ever larger portion of the American mainstream. Though the various versions of barbecue differ from each other as much as cows differ from sheep, or as much as tomatoes differ from mustard seeds, the common themes of wood and smoke, meat and sauce, family and fellowship, transcend regional rivalries and recipe differences.

Other foods cover the geographic expanse of this nation, just as barbecue does. You can find fried chicken, hamburgers, hot dogs, and pizza from coast to coast. But none of these foods enjoy the great regional variation that barbecue does. None of them exemplify the competing themes of American unity and diversity as barbecue does. You don't hear heated arguments about the fundamental differences between the hamburgers in Albuquerque and those in Altoona. Hamburgers just ain't that deep. As John Shelton Reed reminds us in "Barbecue Sociology: The Meat of the Matter," "Southern barbecue is the closest thing we have in the U.S. to Europe's wines or cheeses; drive a hundred miles and the barbecue changes."

As the United States has weaned itself from the European culinary orbit in recent decades, the trained and celebrated chefs at the fancy restaurants have looked increasingly to the South for domestic inspiration. So barbecue and barbecue techniques show up on menus in places where real Southern food has long been alien. And as traditional slow-cooked barbecue becomes more difficult to find even in its homeland, folks in barbecue country have come to a greater appreciation of the preciousness of this food.

While books purporting to be about barbecue are popping up on bookstore shelves with increasing regularity, few of them approach the subject with any appreciation of the seriousness of barbecue history and sociology. While these books start off from the assumption that barbecue is a saleable subject, they often fail to recognize the extent to which any serious study of barbecue must of necessity contain within it a wide range of insights about American history and culture. So this anthology contains information that, while not necessarily new, is often overlooked.

If there were any doubts about the formative role barbecue has played in American history, they are laid to rest in Mary V. Thompson's essay linking the nation's first president with its preeminent food. Barbacoa, the slow-smoked cow's head delicacy of southern Texas, provides us with some of our earliest evidence of an American barbecue tradition. In her essay, "The Land of Barbacoa," Bárbara Renaud González gives us an update on the dish, informing us of the role such beef still plays in the memory of little girls. Just as the themes of race and religion have been pivotal in the formation of American identity, so have they been pivotal in the formation of barbecue culture. Even a casual student of barbecue knows that there are racial implications in any discussion of this food's origins and techniques, but in "Texas Barbecue in Black and White," Robb Walsh brings into question some of the assumptions cherished even by barbecue experts. And for those who thought that all adherents to the religion of barbecue were Christian, Marcie Cohen Ferris destroys that tenet in her essay about the Southern Jewish perspective on the subject.

With "In Xanadu Did Barbecue," a revision of the author's Vassar College senior thesis, Ripley Golovin Hathaway charts the growth of barbecue's popularity in the American mainstream. But in an 1896 essay in *Harpers' Weekly* ("The Georgia Barbecue") that her research unearthed, we see that barbecue has been a topic of interest to the readers of national magazines for more than a century. And Rufus Jarmon, in his 1954 *Saturday Evening Post* essay, "Dixie's Most Disputed Dish," demonstrates that this food was the subject of intense argument long before Max Brantley's ribs hit the fan in the pages of the *Arkansas Gazette.*

This book is but the second in what we, the members of the Southern Foodways Alliance, fully expect will be a long series of annual anthologies. Things change. By the time we get to volume 10 or 20, our people and our place will be different, changed by the loss of the older generations and the influx of new foreign forces from places like Cambodia and Ethiopia and New Jersey. There's no way to predict the impact of bagel bakeries and sushi bars on our traditional diet. So we present this volume to you as a State of the Southern Culinary Union. A snapshot. A reporting on how it is now. We offer it to you with the full knowledge that, even as you are reading this, our region will be remaking itself into something we hope and pray will be a more perfect union, a better reflection of our best selves.

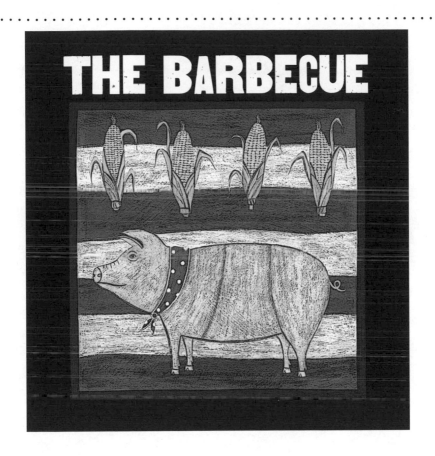

THE BARBECUE

A PORTRAIT
OF THE DELICACY
AS A YOUNG DISH,
OR THE
EARLY YEARS

The Land of Barbacoa

BÁRBARA RENAUD GONZÁLEZ

Daddy dreamin' 'bout it all the time.

When he isn't talkin' 'bout the War and all those dirtyjaps he killed in the jungle. "Three years . . . you know how long that is?"

No, vieja, no quiero arroz! Slanty-eyed.

Daddy won't touch my mother's cilantro rice. "Jap-food." Strictly a meat and potatoes man. Vegetables were a dirty word to him, "are you kidding?" Slab of lettuce, a thick slice of fresh tomato, hand picked from the rancho he worked as a sharecropper in the Texas Panhandle. A cool chunk of one of his fat cucumbers, maybe, but "don't forget the thousand-island, vieja!" Hot-Dam! Now that was a salad, "told you we know how to eat in Texas!"

My father's family's always been here. "How long?" Ask Daddy, not telling him about the white kids in first grade who are chasing me, yelling at me to go back to Mexico. And the crying later. "Forever, I reckon." Daddy's proud that our people settled Texas in the 1700s, and "then those thieving King Ranch people stole our land!" After the U.S.-Mexican War, he means. Never talks about the lynching and the way his grandfather was killed, but my mother says it's why Daddy's so mean sometimes.

That's how my father became a sharecropper working in the Panhandle, on this side of Oklahoma. No land left, you see.

People say he looks like one of those spaghetti-thin cowboys from the movies, a rougher Clark Gable type with a sleepy voice like Nat King Cole's. "Verdád que parece negro, comadre?" Only Daddy speaks Spanish and English so well that he doesn't need translation—all one song to him.

Daddy's grandfather had been a *real* cowboy. "Had to, no place to go—remember the Alamo?" "How can we forget, por amor de Dios, we lost!" dice Mami. Without land, the men went to work on the cattle drives—from their homes on the Texas border all the way to the Canadian. Six months to get to Chicago with God's help, before the snowstorms hit.

When Daddy's talking like this, the Tejano in him plucks a guitar from somewhere out of the summer's blue sky, his baritone voice exploding with a song in the cotton fields surrounding us, making us see the cowboys beside him, right here on this land, singing their corridos with dust in their throats. Burning despite the snow.

Cuando salimos de Kiansas
con la fuerte novillada
ay que trabajo pasamos

"Damned hard work . . . not like the movies! What they don't tell you is that Mexicanos were real cowboys, not like the gringos."

My mother's really tired of his stories. Her family lost their land too, but in the Mexican Revolution. "Wasn't ours to begin with. . . . The land belongs to everyone! That's what Zapata said, and what does your father think happens to those who steal it anyway? Cabrones!" Mami's in the kitchen, and she calls Daddy names under her breath cause he lets the gringos make him say jes-ser! and no-ser! and she wants him to be like Zapata and stand up.

My mother is pura Mexicana. "Don't forget that! Head to toe!" She's not even five feet tall, and though at twelve I'm already bigger than her, she still uses the belt on me. Hijos de María Morales! But Daddy's six feet tall, and he laughs at my mother's smallness, her poetic bullets whizzing by, her politics, for sure.

"You had to cross that border to eat, didn't you?"

Mami says that Mexico is paradise and that Texas is puro hell. Un pinche infierno. She says that over there across the river there are mountains and volcanoes, orchids, chocolate and dancing at the plaza on Sundays. Explains that Mexico's problem is she's like a beautiful woman who everyone wants to possess. Like land. But nobody can have her, she doesn't belong to men.

I don't understand this, but Mami sure doesn't let Daddy boss her around.

She wants him to leave the rancho and get a real job in town. But Daddy's expecting a good harvest this year, making up for all the bad years before. Already know this 'cause I heard them arguing late into the night about all the money they're owing for school clothes, for my brand-new flute and the sewing machine from Sears that Mami wanted so that she could help Daddy pay the bills.

Then the harvest finally, really, came. Daddy's humming Hank Williams, pinching Mami's nalgas when he thinks nobody sees. We're going to the town barbecue! With all the big gringo ranchers and everything! Daddy himself slaughtered a cow so that there's gonna be plenty of good comida. Everybody smackin' their lips, because the barbecue out-smells the cotton gin any day.

Better than Christmas with those chili-beans, mashed potatoes and coleslaw, peach cobbler and buckets of iced tea. Daddy's harvest. And of course, miles of barbecue extending like rich, jagged acres of brown-sauced dreams.

Daddy remembers the way his family used to cook their meat in a special pit in the ground lined with stones and mesquite wood. Now that was a party! Bautismos! Birthdays! Easter! Welcome Home! Slow-cooking a whole cow's head until, after several days, "it would melt in your mouth and make you forget all your penas!" Those barbacoa days with his family kept him alive during the worst days of the Big War, he said.

Reminds us that the cowboy's barbecue comes from the vaquero tradition. How it was the sweet and spicy dribbling from the handmade corn tortillas all the way down to the elbows at his grandfather's wedding fiesta. Staining his French great-grandmother's linens with the red chile salsa before that and the fringes of his Indian great-great grandmother's rebozo way before that.

"Who cares if I didn't get a Purple Heart." This barbacoa proved that he was a good man after all. Even if he didn't have land anymore.

But the bossman stole his harvest anyway. Mami and Daddy divorced a few years later, and I never had barbacoa again.

Until I moved to San Antonio. And here, every Sunday morning, there are lines of cars outside places like Adelita's and Big Joe's. The kids are waiting at home and they've placed their order early with Daddy for pura carne, and they've never seen a whole cabeza bundled with maguey leaves in the ground, but they know what they like with their breakfast. Corn tortillas! Flour! Salsa! Gorditas! Refried beans! Papitas! Scrambled eggs! Sunny-side up! Pico de gallo! Avocado! Juice! Coffee!

A cold bottle of Big Red! Please, Daddy! Por favor, papi!

And all over San Anto, families gather round the table as the father brings home a carton of just beef or just cow's head, after getting up extra-early to be in line at six on Sunday morning. That's what a good father does.

And the hot meat is silky and juicy and, ay, how good it tastes, how the kids are laughing, and the grease delicious, like memories slipping from the mouth to the chin to the table. Staining us with the past. Like blood. Like the land.

Just like it did that summer when we were a family.

Barbecue Service

JAMES APPLEWHITE

I have sought the elusive aroma
Around outlying cornfields, turned corners
Near the site of a Civil War surrender.
The transformation may take place
At a pit no wider than a grave,
Behind a single family's barn.
These weathered ministers
Preside with the simplest of elements:
Vinegar and pepper, split pig and fire.
Underneath a glistening mountain in air,
Something is converted to a savor: the pig
Flesh purified by far atmosphere.
Like the slick-sided sensation from last summer
A fish pulled quick from a creek
By a boy. Like breasts in a motel
With whiskey and twilight
Now a blue smoke in memory.
This smolder draws the soul of our longing.

I want to see all the old home folks,
Ones who may not last another year.
We will rock on porches like chapels
And not say anything, their faces
Impenetrable as different barks of trees.
After the brother who drank has been buried,
The graveplot stunned by sun
In the woods,
We men still living pass the bottle.

We barbecue pigs.
The tin-roofed sheds with embers
Are smoking their blue sacrifice
Across Carolina.

Caribbean Connection

JESSICA B. HARRIS

Barbecue scholars tell us that the American barbecue belt runs through the Carolinas, but they often ignore the fact that a parallel belt runs among the islands of the Caribbean Sea. Certainly the conjoining of meat and flame has taken place for millennia, but it is the Caribbean region that first perfected the uniquely hemispheric cooking form and that gave it its name: barbecue.

According to barbecue historian Lolis Eric Elie's *Smokestack Lightning,* Gonzalo Fernandez de Oviedo's 1526 account, *De la historia General y Natural de las Indias,* is the first work to use the word "barbacoa" speaking of the Indians of Tierra Firme who roasted meat on sticks and then placed them in the ground, "like a grating or trivet over a pit." He was perhaps the first European to witness this method of cooking. It should be noted that the Spanish hidalgo uses the term to describe not a food or a method of cooking but the grill upon which the food was cooked.

This is borne out more than a century later in 1698 by the good Father Labat, in *Nouveau Voyages aux Isles de l'Amerique.* In this four-volume treatise on the customs of the islands, Pere Labat, a Dominican friar and a fair bon vivant, doesn't use the term "barbecue" but rather the word "boucan" to refer to the method of preparation. His description of the grill, though, mirrors that of Oviedo, and he devotes an entire chapter to his discussion of a pig boucan. (A turtle boucan is mentioned elsewhere in the work.) It is a sort of wooden grill upon which the entire pig must be cooked. One cuts for this purpose four forked pieces of the width of an arm and about four feet in length, and one plants them in the ground so that they outline a rectangle about five feet by three feet. Across the forked pieces are placed smaller branches that form the grill. All is tightly bound with vines. On this bed or on this grill the pig is laid on its back, stomach opened, spread out as much as possible, and held in this position by sticks for fear of its closing up when it comes into contact with the heat that will be placed on it. Labat goes on to say that the cavity of the pig was filed with lemon juice, salt, and hot chiles. When cooked, the pig was served with a dipping sauce in two strengths, mild or hot, along with the condiments that seemed to have consisted of a calabash of the sauce from the stomach of the pig and another of lemon juice, salt, pepper, and chile, from which the diners could prepare their own sauce. He concludes by stating that the wild hog is tastier than the domesticated one and, in an apostrophe that will bring joy to the hearts of 'cue lovers, reminds readers that a boucan necessitates drinking often. As he puts it, "the rules demand it and the sauce invites it."

The boucan that Labat describes with such gusto was perfected by the French sailors or boucaniers—the buccaneers. Indeed it seems that when not raping and pillaging, these brethren of the coast spent their few sober hours preparing wild pigs in this manner, which they would then sell to other sea-farers. This method of slow-cooking over smoke became particularly popular in Jamaica at a time when the English crown had Northern and Caribbean colonies. While the Northern form went on to become a major form of public and private entertainment, the Caribbean version has gone on to become synonymous with Jamaica.

When the abbot of Jamaica in 1611 wrote to the king of Spain about the products of the island, he suggested that apart from the town of Santiago de la Vega, there was nothing much except a large herd of swine raised in the mountains which were considered common property and which yielded a large quantity of lard and jerked pork. Bev Carvey, in *The Maroon Story*, suggests that the tradition of jerk in Jamaica is a direct continuation of the boucan of the French-speaking Caribbean, with the Jamaican Maroons, or escaped Africans who had been enslaved by the Spanish, learning the technique from the buccaneers and the Carib Indians with whom it may have originated. The Jamaican addition to Labat's recipe is allspice, the fragrant and flavorful berry of a tree indigenous to the island.

Certainly by the time of Maria Nugent, wife of the Jamaican governor general from 1801 to 1805, jerk was being served to the gentry, and she records in her diaries that on March of 1802 she visited the Moro, a part of Hordley Estate, and ate a dinner that was so copious that it bore inclusion in her notes. She noted in her diaries, "The first course was entirely of fish, excepting jerked hog, in the center, which is the way of dressing it by the Maroons." A note signals the connection between the buccaneers and the Maroons and even states that the Maroons were referred to as "hog hunters."

The tradition that goes from barbacoa to boucan to jerk has been documented in detail by scholars and gourmands from Labat to Zora Neale Hurston. Hurston writes a lengthy and rapturous description of a Maroon pig feed she attended in Accompong, the Maroon capital, in her anthropological study

Tell My Horse. "Towards morning we ate our fill of jerked pork. It is more delicious than our barbecue. It is hard to imagine anything better than pork the way the Maroons jerk it." The Maroon tradition of jerked pork is alive in the pork pits of Boston Beach in Jamaica, where it is served with a fried dough that is known as "festival." There, visitors are occasionally able to watch as pit men prepare the traditional pork as well as more recent additions of chicken and fish, slathering it with a marinade prepared of fresh thyme, lime juice, allspice berries, Scotch Bonnet chiles, and other ingredients including perhaps, as one pit man confided in me, some of the blood of the slaughtered animal. The meat is then slow-cooked over a smoky fire of allspice logs—the one missing ingredient in all North American jerk—with the pit men watching, poking, probing, and verifying until it is done to their satisfaction. Then it is served up on brown paper with panache parallel to that of their North American brethren. One taste connects all of the history from the Carib to the Buccaneers to the Maroons, Labat and Lady Nugent, Oviedo and Hurston; the only thing left to do is savor and smile.

JESSICA B. HARRIS

George Washington and Barbecue

MARY V. THOMPSON

One of the first things any staff member learns after coming to Mount Vernon is that the American public's idea of George Washington is primarily taken either from marble statues they have seen in museums and statehouses or from the portraits on the one-dollar bills and quarters they carry in their pockets. Unfortunately, the impression they have taken away from these sources, as well as the rather dry treatments of Washington in their history texts from school, is of a rather stiff, formal individual who was never any younger than about forty-five, was always busy doing great and important things, and never had any fun. Barbecue and George Washington are probably never thought of in the same breath—but maybe they should be.

George Washington was born in 1732 in the British colony of Virginia, where a popular form of summer entertainment was attendance at a barbecue. According to the *Oxford English Dictionary*, the word "barbecue" had come into the English language by the mid-seventeenth century from the Haitian word "barbacoa" and the Guianan Indian "babracot," which refer to a framework of sticks set on posts. By the time of the Revolution, the principal dish at a Virginia barbecue was roasted pig. The guests would ride or sail down from their respective homes to a prearranged gathering place. While the food cooked, fiddles and banjos would play and the guests would dance.[1]

A slightly earlier version of the eighteenth-century barbecue seems to have been very much like what we would call a potluck supper. Plantation owner Landon Carter mentioned in his diary in 1772 that he had just been to his third barbecue that year and found it an expensive entertainment: "I confess I like to meet my friends now and then, but certainly the old plan of every family carrying its own dish was both cheaper and better." By the time Carter wrote these words, the organization of the barbecues had changed; instead of bringing their own food, people paid money ahead of time, and those subscription fees were used to pay for the provisions. One of Carter's principal complaints about this newfangled way of doing things was that "many on the credit of their Su[bsc]ription brought eaters enough there, some 5 and 6 for one Subscription. So that they all eat at about the price of 15d a head, when others [presumably he himself] paid at least 7/ for themselves alone which I think is a very unequal disposal of money." Always somewhat touchy and thin-skinned, two years later he groused that "barbecues and what not deprived some of their senses."[2]

George Washington went to a number of these events in the years before the Revolution, taking part in barbecues held, generally on a Saturday, in the city of Alexandria as well as at the home of his brother-in-law, Colonel Fielding Lewis, in Fredericksburg and, closer to home, along the Potomac River at Accotink and Johnson's Ferry.[3] He seems to have hosted at least one, and possibly two, in 1773, noting in his diary that he went "to a Barbicue of my own giving at Accatinck." In May of the following year, his financial papers record that he had either sold or donated forty-five weight of flour in August of 1773 "for Barbecue."[4]

The barbecues were very social events. For instance, Washington recorded that at a barbecue held at the home of his sister and brother-in-law on August 4, 1770, there were "a great deal of other Company" in attendance and that he had "stayd there till Sunset." Among the company that day were his wife, Martha, her daughter, Patsy, then fourteen years old, and probably the family of his younger brother Charles.[5] Three years later, his stepchildren's former tutor and other unnamed members of the family seem to have accompanied him to a barbecue at Alexandria. In the spring of 1774, Washington took his almost twenty-year-old stepson, John Parke Custis, that young man's wife and sister-in-law, and a friend, James Tilghman Jr., with him to one barbecue.[6] In that year, as in others, he brought overnight guests home with him afterward; sometimes Washington himself was an overnight guest at the home of someone else.[7]

More may have been going on in the way of entertainment at these barbecues than just music, dancing, and socializing. Washington mentioned in his diary that there was a boat race at the barbecue at Johnson's Ferry in 1774. In all probability, a lively round of betting accompanied that race, possibly helped along by the forty-eight bottles of claret he supplied for the occasion.[8] George Washington is also known to have taken part in several types of outdoor games during his life, any one of which may have filled the time of the gentlemen waiting for the roasted pig to finish cooking. During Christmas of 1773, for example, he came outside to find a group of young men comprising his stepson and some visiting friends playing a game called "pitching the bar,"

MARY V. THOMPSON

which was probably similar to today's game of horseshoes. One of the men there that day later recorded that Washington

> requested to be shown the pegs that marked the bounds of our efforts; then, smiling, and without putting off his coat, held out his hand for the missile. No sooner . . . did the heavy iron bar feel the grasp of his mighty hand than it lost the power of gravitation, and whizzed through the air, striking the ground far, very far, beyond our utmost limits. We were indeed amazed, as we stood around, all stripped to the buff, with shirt sleeves rolled up, and having thought ourselves very clever fellows, while the colonel, on retiring, pleasantly observed, "When you beat my pitch, young gentlemen, I'll try again."[9]

A French officer who knew Washington during the Revolution described the American commander playing "ball for whole hours with his aides-de-camp."[10] Although he did not specify what type of game the men were playing, some of the possibilities include early forms of cricket, with variations known as trap ball or stool ball; "bandy," very similar to hockey; and a game called "fives," which is a version of the modern game of handball.[11]

Two other outdoor games are known to have been played at Mount Vernon and may or may not have been played by people at barbecues. The first, lawn bowling, can be documented through several means. After the Revolution, George Washington transformed the western approach to his home from a straight road through an avenue of trees to a serpentine drive through groves of trees on the edge of a large flat lawn, which provided a spectacular view both of the house and from the house toward the west. That lawn was known as a "bowling green." Among the objects housed in the nearby Circle Storehouse, an outbuilding on the edge of that bowling green, were two balls made of lignum vitae, a very heavy and hard tropical wood.[12] A second game, called "prisoner's base," was described by a visitor to Mount Vernon in 1798 who watched a group of about thirty slaves, divided into two teams, playing it one Sunday, their weekly day off from work. Prisoner's base was a well-known English game, popular in Virginia, which was rather like a team version of the modern game called "tag."[13]

Washington also mentions picnics as a summer activity, but these seem to have been smaller and more low-key than the barbecues. In August of 1772, four of his friends arrived at Mount Vernon on a Monday evening, and the next day the five men went fishing on the Belvoir estate, below Mount Vernon. They dined outside that afternoon, presumably on the fish they had caught earlier in the day.[14] On another occasion, he rode on horseback up to Johnson's Spring one Saturday, accompanied by Martha Washington's eighteen-year-old niece, Fanny Bassett, his own Canadian-born secretary, William Shaw, and a visiting gentleman, George Taylor Jr. There they rendezvoused with a group of friends from Alexandria, "dined on a cold dinner brought from Town by Water, and spent the Afternoon agreeably, returning home by Sun down or a little after it."[15]

NOTES

1. Jane Carson, *Colonial Virginians at Play* (Williamsburg, Va.: Colonial Williamsburg Foundation, 1989), 14.

2. Landon Carter, vol. 2 of *The Diary of Colonel Landon Carter of Sabine Hall, 1752–1778,* ed. Jack P. Greene (Charlottesville: University Press of Virginia for the Virginia Historical Society, 1965), 2:722, 900.

3. For Washington's attendance at barbecues, see George Washington, May 27, 1769; August 4, 1770; September 4, 18, 1773; and May 7, August 27, 1774, in *The Diaries of George Washington*, 6 vols., ed. Donald Jackson and Dorothy Twohig (Charlottesville: University Press of Virginia, 1976–79), 2:154, 261; 3:203, 204, 248, 271.

4. For the provision of flour for a barbecue, see "Cash Receive'd on Act. of Colo. Washington by L.W.," May 1774, Lund Washington Account Book (manuscript, W-693, Mount Vernon Ladies' Association; typescript, Mount Vernon Ladies' Association), 48.

5. Washington, August 2–4, 1770, *Diaries of George Washington*, 2:261.

6. Washington, September 4, 1773, and May 7, 1774, ibid., 3:203, 248.

7. For Washington bringing home guests after a barbecue, see Washington, September 4–5, 18, 1773, and May 7, 1774, ibid., 3:203, 204, 248. For George Washington as the guest of others after a barbecue, see Washington, May 27, 1769, and August 4, 1770, ibid., 2:154, 261.

8. Washington, May 7, 1774, ibid., 3:248, 248n.

9. Artist Charles Willson Peale, quoted in ibid., 3:221n. See also Carson, *Colonial Virginians at Play*, 79–81.

10. The Marquis de Barbe-Marbois, September 12, 1779, in *George Washington as the French Knew Him: A Collection of Texts*, ed. and trans. Gilbert Chinard (Princeton, N.J.: Princeton University Press, 1940; reprint, New York: Greenwood Press, 1969), 75.

11. Carson, *Colonial Virginians at Play*, 81–84.

12. The 1799/1800 inventory done shortly after George Washington's death is published in Eugene E. Prussing, "Appendix II: Inventory of Contents of Mount Vernon," in *The Estate of George Washington, Deceased* (Boston: Little, Brown, 1927), 401–48; the reference to the lignum vitae balls can be found on p. 438.

13. Carson, *Colonial Virginians at Play*, 44; Merilyn Simonds Mohr, *The Games Treasury* (Shelburne, Vt.: Chapters Publishing, 1993), 310–11.

14. Washington, August 10, 11, 1772, *Diaries of George Washington*, 3:124.

15. Washington, September 10, 1785, ibid., 4:192. For the identities of Shaw and Taylor, see ibid., 4:158, 158n, 190n.

An Ode to the Pig

Assorted Thoughts on the World's
Most Controversial Food

BETHANY EWALD BULTMAN

Many will argue that it is the Southern cook's prowess with hog by-products that is our region's culinary signature. Indeed, the pig in all its manifestations has put its stamp on much of our culture. After all, in the South it's a compliment to say someone lives "high on the hog." When Southerners make white beans or greens, they are more like pork stew (pork being so necessary we don't mention it). Despite the expression, "to sweat like a pig," pigs only have sweat glands in their snouts and have inefficient systems to regulate body temperature. (Humans are actually the sweatiest of all animals, with horses a close second.) Yet one of the great geological mistakes of all time is that as the continents shifted, swine ended up in all temperate regions of the world except North and South America.

It wasn't until 1493, when Christopher Columbus deposited a Spanish hog in Cuba, handpicked by Queen Isabella, that pigs arrived in the New World. Twenty-seven years later Admiral Alonso Alvarez de Pinana may have lost some of his porkers around Mobile, but it was when Hernando de Soto and his six hundred armor-clad men traversed the Gulf Coast in the early 1540s that swine officially made landfall in our region. Pigs would arrive in the Gulf South at a time when the consumption of pork was a Christian duty for every Spanish-speaking Catholic. Reay Tannahill reveals in *Food in History* that during the Spanish Inquisition (1478–1834) it became obligatory to have pork simmering in a cauldron or *chorizo*, dried pork sausages, hanging from the rafters as a sure proof that no Jew or Muslim dined in the Christian home. De Soto certainly performed his Christian duty when he deposited fifteen hogs in Florida: within five years this herd had multiplied to more than seven hundred pigs.

Despite the popular misconception, the purebred, long-snouted, bristle-backed wild boars (*Sus scrofa*), kissing cousins of the domestic hog, did not make the transatlantic journey to our shores until about four hundred years after Columbus deposited pigs in the New World. Full-blooded wild boars are aggressive and clever, weighing between four hundred and six hundred pounds, making them popular prey for sportsmen. (Young boars are considered mildly palatable, while a mature boar is so tough that even the French won't eat any of it, except perhaps the head.) The Eurasian wild boar, which hails from Russia, first appeared in North America in 1890 when it was introduced to Sullivan County, New Hampshire, by a hunter.

With the advent of World War I, American hunters were no longer able to tramp through the hills and dales of Bavaria tracking wild boars. (Wild boar was so overhunted that it became extinct in the British Isles by 1683.) Thus, in 1912 a group of hunters imported a stock of wild boars from Europe to the mountains of Tennessee and North Carolina. This breed tipped the scales at a hefty six hundred pounds. Before you could say "oink-oink," these porkers had run amuck, rooting, foraging across seventeen states, and spreading trouble. They are predators of wildlife such as nesting songbirds and wild turkeys. They promote erosion, damage fences, and transmit diseases such as hog cholera and tuberculosis to domestic pigs and sheep. The U.S. Department of Agriculture considers all wild boars and feral hogs to be pests.

While there is relatively little controversy regarding pork consumption in the American South, in much of the world pork is the most controversial of foods. Muslims and Jews are forbidden from eating pork by religious law. In other places, the culture frowns on pork consumption. The relatively new science of paleoethnobotany fills in some of the gaps about what was prepared on the now-silent stone hearths of our respective ancient ancestors. At the same time, it does little to explain why civilized people evolved into diverse cultures, happily munching certain foods while disdaining others. Obviously the prime reason for the consumption of some unsavory animals has to do with simple necessity. The French must be applauded for their culinary ecumenicism. For example, *Cooper's entrecôte à la bordelaise* is the haute name for rat grilled with a little oil and shallots. According to Prosper Montagne's *Larousse Gastronomic* (1961), "Rats nourished in the wine stores of the Gironde were at one time highly esteemed." There is speculation that bordelaise sauce was actually created to overpower the musky rodent taste of rat. The Aztecs did not have pork, but they roasted the hairless *xquintli*, a dog still bred in Mexico, in a tomato-and-chili sauce similar to our barbecue sauce. While the consumption of rat and dog may make us squeamish, there is no nutritional consideration that engenders more cultural and religious taboos than that highly intelligent, cloven-hoofed domestic mammal, the swine. Deer are also cloven-hoofed, but it is only the hog associated in mythology with the devil and Pan.

Ethnoanthropology reveals that peoples of the Holy Land had been dining on hogs for more than five thousand years before pork became taboo. Tannahill concludes in *Food in History* that the precise date when the antipork regulations were instated is debatable, but that there is a clear correlation between their implementation and the arrival of nomadic invaders to eastern and western Asia about 1800 B.C.E. (Second Millennium). These pastoral tribes had been herding goats and sheep for thousands of years. "They seem to have an almost pathological hatred for the pig—a wayward beast with little stomach, a constitutional objection to being herded and a tiresome inability to live on grass," notes Tannahill. Hebrews arrived in Egypt at the end of the seventeenth century B.C.E., where they remained for more than three hundred years until the thirteenth century B.C.E. The first known Hebrew writings date from c. 1000 B.C.E. In the Old Testament, Yahweh is quoted in the Book of Genesis and again in Leviticus as condemning the pig as being so unclean it pollutes if touched. Deuteronomy 14 specifically dictates to the children of God which animals they may consume: oxen, sheep and goats, "the hart, and the roebuck, and the fallow deer, and the *pygarg*, and the chamois. Nevertheless we shall not eat of them that chew the cud, or them that divide the cloven hoof as the camel and the hare and the *coney* (rabbit): for they chew the cud, but divide not the hoof; therefore they are unclean to you. And the swine, because it divideth the hoof, yet cheweth not the cud, it is unclean unto you: ye shall not eat of the flesh, nor touch their dead carcass." (Also on the "unclean menu" are eagles, owls, hawks, swans, pelicans, storks, and bats.) But in Acts 10:15 of the New Testament, God tells Peter, "What God has cleansed, you must not call unclean."

Allah instructed his prophet Mohammed some fifteen hundred years later that the followers of Islam must follow the same divine pig-shunning practice of the Jews. Mohammed warned that pigs had been spawned from the excrement of elephants that had piled up on Noah's ark. Theories abound that perhaps it was a sound ecological strategy for Yahweh and Allah to ban the pig in their dry, arid lands. Pigs would have been the ultimate luxury, competing with man for scarce grains and fresh water. A few historians speculate that the ban on swine came to define the very barriers of Islamic expansion. They note that the Islamic religion spread rapidly out of Arabia in the seventh century C.E., yet its spread halted in China, the Balkans, and Spain, three pork-passionate regions. Early Christians closely followed Jewish regulations in prohibiting contact with hogs. But by the third century C.E. the bishops of Antioch had decided that perhaps old Yahweh might have been mistaken. European proponents of the omnivorous hog appreciated the efficiency with which hogs convert grains, tubers, and just about any garbage it is fed to high-grade fat and protein. By destigmatizing the pig, the early Christian church was also greasing the way for a smooth spiritual path for the conversion of barbaric northern European hog-loving tribes.

Thus by 597 C.E. Benedictine monks had brought the word of God to the hog-worshipping Celts in the British Isles. For peoples from the ancient Celts to many Asian cultures and the natives of New Guinea, hogs are both sacred and succulent. Pork was consumed on all-important occasions from birth to death. Pigs were sacrificed and gorged upon to enlist the help of the gods in times of war, to honor warriors in thanksgiving for victory, and to mourn ancestors. In ancient Norse mythology pork was what the warriors of the Norse god Odin dined on in Valhalla.

As to the French passion for pork, culinary legend insists that Louis XVI literally lost his head in 1793 over pork. The story goes that had the fleeing thirty-nine-year-old Louis XVI not demanded that his driver let him stop at a tavern famed for pigs' trotters in garlic sauce, he would have succeeded in his escape from house arrest in 1791.

History tells us that the earliest Europeans also held pork in the highest esteem. Posidonius, the Greek who made the first ethnographic study of the Celts in 70 B.C.E. noted, "When the hindquarters of the boar are served, the bravest man claimed the finest cut for himself, and if someone else wanted it, the two contestants stood up and fought to the death." Perhaps those infamous Appalachian families the Hatfields and the McCoys were but replicating that ancient ritual when they engaged in their infamous feud, a war that had its roots in the alleged theft of a pig. By the time it was over more than twenty people had been killed. Contemporary pork-related competitions such as the Swine Time Festival in Climax, Georgia, the Chitlin' Strut in Salley, South Carolina, the Big Pig Jig in Vienna, Georgia, and Hillsborough Hog Day in North Carolina rarely lead to death.

The tens of thousands of fans of the University of Arkansas's football team may "call the hogs" in unison, and Arkansas may grow more rice and hogs than Louisiana does, but Louisiana has jambalaya (named for the Provençal version of paella called *jambalaia*, from *jambon*, French for ham) and more hog-related celebrations than any state in the union. There are Uncle Earl's Hog Dog Trials (named for three-time governor of Louisiana, Earl Long [1895–1960]) in Winnfield, the Cracklin' Festival in Port Barre, the Louisiana

Swine Festival in Basile, the Cochon de Lait Festival in Mansura, the Festival de la Viande Boucanée in Ville Platte, the Boudin and Cracklin Festival in Carencro, and Le Grande Boucherie in St. Martinville . . . and that is just the tip of the sow's curly little tail. According to Tim Page at the LSU Agricultural Center, Louisianans eat more pork per capita than people in any other state in the union.

Pork consumption did not come naturally, however, to many of the first West African slaves who arrived in Louisiana in 1719. Dr. Gwendolyn Midlo Hall noted in her *Africans in Colonial Louisiana: The Development of Afro-Creole Culture in the Eighteenth Century* (LSU Press, 1992) that by the eighteenth century C.E. Islam had come to Senegambia, where most of Louisiana's early slaves came from. "The blacks living on both sides of the Senegal River and in the lands to the east and south were Muslims," reports Hall. The Mandigas in particular were noted as "missionaries of Mohammedanism" and were most certainly not pig-eaters. Conversion to Christianity would have been the necessary first step many Africans had to make before they adopted the European addiction to salt pork.

According to Sam Hilliard's book, *Hog Meat and Hoecake: Food Supply in the Old South, 1840–1870*, each year between 1840 and 1860 an average of two hogs were raised for every man, woman, and child below the Mason-Dixon Line. According to one study, it was recommended that each field hand be fed a minimum of between two and five pounds of pork per week. From the eighteenth century to the early twentieth century and the advent of fences and roads, many rural South farmers would mark their hogs' ears and let them roam free to dine on crabs, roots, and acorns. Once a hog was fattened up, the farmer would track it and chase it home for the slaughter. On most Southern farms the first cold snap harkened the end of summer vegetables and the annual hog slaughter. Livers, cracklins, and chitterlings (small intestines) were eaten immediately. (Another favorite post-boucherie supper was brains and onions along the Côte des Allemands of Louisiana.) Globs of hog fat were boiled in a gigantic black pot to be rendered into lard. Scraps of meat were ground up for sausages. Ribs were slowly steamed (as in the method recommended by Confederate general Stonewall Jackson, who oversaw the pork preparation for his boys in gray). Sides of bacon, hog jowls, shoulders, and hams were cured in salt for weeks. Then they were hung in the smokehouse along with a variety of sausages, ham hocks, and knuckles to be smoked over hickory or pecan wood, peanut shells, or corncobs (known as meat cobs). Some farmers cured their meat with red pepper to prevent infestations of fly larvae in the era before refrigeration.

While the gourmands in history may debate the merits of butter over olive oil, most cooks who stooped over Southern hearths employed a cheaper, more accessible, all-purpose fat. The Spanish had long elevated lard (41 percent saturated fat) to a fat as cherished as olive oil. When I encountered Carl A. Brasseaux's statement that "butter was practically unknown to the Acadians" in his book, *The Founding of New Acadia: The Beginnings of Acadian Life in Louisiana, 1765–1803*, I initially was skeptical. How could these seventeenth-century refugees of butter-eating Brittany and Normandy not have butter, especially when they kept cows in Nova Scotia and Louisiana? The answer seems to be simply that Acadians preferred the taste of pork.

Lard is so vital, in fact, that not one of the people of Acadian ancestry I interviewed could ever even remember eating butter prior to World War II. Even those who had ice boxes didn't eat much butter. "What would we use butter for?" reasoned a friend's Cajun, French-speaking great-grandmother from Villa Platte. "We cooked with bacon fat and lard. We put my fine fig preserves or cane syrup on our bread!"

"Butter was rare in our house," says Frances Aubert Hebert Richard, daughter of a turn-of-the-century rice farmer in Meaux, Louisiana. "Even though we had cows, I think churning butter was just too time consuming. Especially when we didn't have a cool place to keep sweet butter fresh."

"The only thing we used the milk from our Jersey cow for was to make *caillie egouté*, a type of cream cheese we ate with sugar," says Willie Schutz, past president of the Acadiana Herb Society and a fifth-generation native of New Iberia. "Butter was not predominant in our home, though." Her mother, Anna Mae Darce (b. 1923), grew up on Pebbles Plantation between New Iberia and Loreauville during the depression. Mother and daughter both follow an old family tradition and cook with only one cooking oil—hog lard. "When a hog was butchered in the cold months, the meat was stored in gallon syrup cans," recalls Schutz. "The lard was rendered to be used for piecrust and to sauté with."

Dr. Gabou Mendy is a Louisiana physician who was born and raised in Gambia in West Africa says, "The reason why foods made with rice, chicken, black-eyed peas and okra taste so different in Africa than they do in Louisiana is the fats which they are prepared with. In West Africa we traditionally cook with palm oil because it is the most available." Palm oil (51 percent saturated fat) is by all accounts the very soul of fat in the diets of many postcolonial cultures on both sides of the Atlantic.

Palm oil, unlike okra, rice, and West African one-pot cooking techniques, did not, however, leave its mark on Southern cuisine. To discover what our

BETHANY EWALD BULTMAN

gumbos and jambalaya could have tasted like had palm oil been consumed in Louisiana, we must travel to Brazil, where it remains a sensory cornerstone. Gastro-ethnographically speaking, we know that palm oil came to the New World with the West African slaves transported by the Portuguese to Brazil, where the palms they transplanted took root to create a cuisine similar in taste, look, and pungency to their homeland foods. It is West African palm oil, known in Portuguese as *Dendé*, that adds a potent red-yellow color and robustness to many Brazilian foods. With little oinkers gleefully languishing in the Gulf South's muddy environs, lard and its more flavorful smoky sister, bacon grease (40 percent saturated fat), provided the earthy punch closer in taste to palm oil than either butter or olive oil.

As the rural poor in the South relied on pork to sustain them, affluent urbanites sought gentrification through culinary Americanization. In 1877, *Godey's Lady's Book* advised readers that pork and ham were difficult to digest and unwholesome. As the Midwestern beef-and-potato diet become identified with post-industrial revolution American wholesomeness, pork fell from favor. Even Lafcadio Hearn's 1885 *La Cuisine Creole: A Collection of Culinary Recipes* reflects the trend toward nice, plain dishes. His book is filled with recipes for veal, calf head, stewed kidneys, and mutton. Pork is hardly mentioned.

While the consumption of pork from the late nineteenth to the mid-twentieth century may have been dictated by one's social status, it was the dependence upon pork that saved the South's gastronomic bacon from the mire of bland middle-Americanization. As Steve Juneau, the founder of the Jambalaya Festival in Gonzales, Louisiana, points out, "I don't recall ever tasting jambalaya or gumbo made with beef. Even during really hard times people may make their jambalaya out of lima beans and coon, [but] they'll stick in some government surplus bologna just to get that pork taste in there." Necessity and innovation wed to transform the French *boudin* (blood sausage) into Louisiana boudin, which is actually more like jambalaya finger food.

The consumption of this much pork fat may condemn Southerners to early graves, but we push back from the banquet of life with a grateful smile on our lips. In the rest of the country pork may be considered "the other white meat," but down here pork rules.

The Georgia Barbecue

MAUDE ANDREWS

Editor's note: This essay originally appeared in *Harper's Weekly*, October 24, 1896.

When Julian Ralph found "the best cook in the West" in New Orleans he had not made the acquaintance of the Sheriff of Wilkes County, Georgia. He did not, therefore, know of the succulent mysteries of that most popular of Southern institutions, a Georgia barbecue. The barbecue is one of the institutions of the South. To have known it means happiness; not to have known it means that a link in the chain of life has been lost.

The Sheriff of Wilkes is the patron saint of barbecue as it is known in Georgia. Just what are the duties of the Sheriff of that grand old county, which knew the Toombs, the Crawfords, Alexander Stephens, and others of the famous families as her own, might to the outsider seem a little indistinct, for the principal function of the Sheriff of Wilkes under the present régime—and that régime dates back almost to that time when the memory of man runneth not to the contrary—consists in the creation of a dish that brings joy to the heart of the Georgian and his brother, whether born under sunny Southern skies or the more frigid zones of North-land.

The word "dish" is used in a metaphorical sense. The barbecue gets its name from the method of cooking the meats that form its principal substance. It is a pagan feast. Its home is in the woods, by some clear running brook, and when found upon its native hearth such modern conveniences as knives and forks, tables and chairs, are not known. One of the exposition spots that the Northerners are sure to seek out is the shed near the Manufactures and Liberal Arts Building, over which this same Sheriff of Wilkes presides, and where, at all hours of the day, the good cheer which is so closely connected with his name is dispensed. The shed is rather a rough place, for the barbecue with the modern conveniences and the delicacies of Delmonico's would lose its flavor. The chinaware is the old ironstone variety, known principally for its thickness. You get knives and forks, it is true, and paper napkins,

30

but the table at which you sit is innocent of linen. You order a dinner. There is brought before you a half-dozen kinds of meats, steaming hot, the aroma of which is most pleasing to the appetite if you have one to start on; and if you have none, it is sure to create one for you. Then there is a mysterious dish which the Sheriff calls stew, and pickles and bread and butter and a cup of not-too-good coffee are furnished "on the side." The stew is a concoction of many vegetables, and, for some reason not altogether clear even to its maker, bears the mysterious name of Brunswick. It is a necessary adjunct to the dinner, and when it is made sufficiently hot by a sufficient quantity of pungent peppers, it is indeed a rare appetizer.

It is, however, in the meats that the virtue of the barbecue lies. The consistency of them, after they have gone through the barbecuing process, is of that rare degree described only in the old-time phrase "They melt in your mouth," and the seasoning that comes through the basting process adds the aroma and taste that make you its slave forever.

To be initiated into the mysteries of barbecue methods is the desire of everybody who has enjoyed communion with the product.

To the back of the eating-house, there, we follow the massive Sheriff, until we come to the great roasting pit. The Colonel (every Georgian is a Colonel) folds his arms with the pride of Alexander after his conquest of the world.

"That's the way we cook 'em," he says.

The scene is quite unique and picturesque. Above the pit is a box of dried leaves that, with the fragrance of the hickory bark beneath the carcasses, mingles an aromatic odor with the smoke from the roasting meat. At the head of the pit is a great brick oven with three tremendous pots as were used for boiling the bacon and cabbage for the field hands in slavery days. Two of these pots are filled with water for cleaning and scalding the meat and in the other is that barbecue stew for which every barbecue boss has his own receipt.

"How is it made?" we ask the tall, black Negro boy who stands stirring the concoction with a long hickory pole.

He grins from ear to ear, and then begins to elucidate the matter, leaving us not much wiser than at first.

"Well, yer see, yer jest takes de meat, de hog's head, an' der libbers, an' all sorts er little nice parts, an' yer chops it up wid corn an' permattures an' injuns an' green pepper, an' yer stews an' stews tell hit all gits erlike, an' yer kain't tell what hits made uv."

"Turn dat pig over, an' put er little mo' fire under his back," says a big fat Negro behind us, who, like the Georgia Colonel, looks as if he had been fed for a lifetime on barbecue.

Two men take hold of the clean hickory poles that are run through the crisp carcass, give them a turn, and the pig's back begins to frizzle.

"Lor' chile, hit makes me hungry ter see dat meat!" says a fat old Negro cook as she stands watching the performance with her arms akimbo. "Hit seems like pig an' possum is jest made fur fat niggers," and she gives a laugh as olly and jolly as her round black face.

In a big pot to one side of the pit, a half-grown Negro boy is ladling out the gravy to the waiters who come with plates full of carved meat. He is the thorough type of that regular country darky who in his childhood wears one shirt all summer and supplements it in winter with a pair of trousers and one suspender. He croons a song to the measure of his dips into the gravy:

An' we shell have some rabbit stew—
  Chillun, chillum, foiler me—
An' nice fried onions dipped in dew.
  Halle—halle—halle—hallellujah!

The darkies, gnawing barbecued bones on the outside, smack their lips in approbation of the refrain.

The singer of the company is the great brawny black man whose duty it is to keep the fires burning in the coal-pit and to replenish the coals in the roasting-pit.

"He de leader in de singing on de boss's plantation," says the gravy-boy.

And one well might believe it, for like the notes of a great ebony organ arises his deep resonant voice, and so religious and solemn are his refrains that as he lifts the great logs into the pit one might fancy him some barbaric high priest feeding sacrificial fires:

De sun went down in de purple extreme,
De moon changed inter glow,
Ef I git dar afore you do,
King Jesus dewilder me.

This is the curious refrain set to such splendid music. And after its solemn cadences comes something lively in a regular jig-time, and all the helpers, the roasters and stewers and gravy-makers, and even the bone-gnawers on the outer circle, put aside their occupation to pat their feet and hands and join the melody:

Satan am er liar, hallelujah;
Drive old Satan away;

Drive 'im in de briar-patch, hallelujah;
Drive old Satan away.

This bright scintillant atmosphere grows jubilant with the melody, until one can fancy that every microbe is having more than his measure of fun in witnessing the rout of the devil.

Yes, the picture is one well worthy to keep within the memory, for the Georgia barbecue is one of the few remaining feasts of antebellum days left to the present generation—a feast typical, indeed, of that lavishness not elegant perhaps, often barbaric, indeed, but proffered with the generosity and magnificence of monarchs.

The Georgia Sheriff will tell you all about how he begins and completes the preparation for his day's roast.

The roasting-pit is filled with live coals at daybreak, for just as the sun kindles a light in the sky do these black children of light and heat begin to kindle the fires for their feast. By seven o'clock the ground is hot through for several feet; then more coals are put on, and the carcasses are pierced through with clean hickory poles and laid across the pit. Their cooking refutes the old phrase that a watched pot never boils, because the meats are carefully tended during the entire time; for to make them crisp and tender without burning they must be turned every fifteen or twenty minutes.

All sorts of game are roasted over the pit—partridges, young wild turkeys, ducks, squirrels, and rabbits; and now that the winter season has come, the darkies have a possum supper for themselves every Saturday night. They stand greedily around and watch the roasting of the animal, which is sweeter to them than any other that lives. In the ashes they roast their sweet potatoes, and when it is all done and they sit there jabbering amid their crude surroundings, the firelight falling athwart their black faces and gay garments, a visitor to the exposition might well fancy himself at the feast of an African king.

TRADITIONS AND DISPUTATIONS

Dixie's Most Disputed Dish

RUFUS JARMON

By each mid-July the great wrath of summer's heat has enveloped the state of Georgia. Clouds of gnats and mosquitoes arise with steam from the moss-draped swamps near the coast. Farther inland the area of wire grass, palmettos, and towering pine trees cooks under a terrible sun that cracks the paint from buildings, boils the sap out of lumber, and causes asphalt highways to swim beneath waves of heat. Northward, in the clay-hill country, the red dust becomes shoe-top deep, as hot as new ashes; in the distance the low, gently sweeping outline of the Blue Ridge seems to quiver in the smiting atmosphere of noontide.

As a gastronomic influence, this is weather that inclines most people toward cooling drinks and light meals of chilled fruits and raw vegetables. But in Georgia it signals the arrival of the season of barbecues—Gargantuan feasts alfresco, held by the hundreds as come-ons for all sorts of political, religious, social, and family occasions. Literally tons of hot pork are served up with a tongue-searing sauce and accompanied by Brunswick stew, a highly seasoned, rich conglomeration of meats, vegetables, and sauces simmered many hours in big iron pots over outdoor fires. In size, barbecues range from a big one the Ku Klux Klan gave several years ago in Atlanta's Piedmont Park, where 20,000 or more Knights of the Invisible Empire did away with 16,000 pounds of meat, on down to rustic soirees of half a dozen or so backcountry families. People may gather in the woods to cook a shoat simply because they are lonely for company and tired of their regular menu—grits, greens, and sowbelly. Some groups go at the meat with their hands and get grease in their ears. In more polite circles the crooked little finger, held elegantly beneath a deftly manipulated fork handle, is not unknown, and there is frequent, delicate use of paper napkins.

The average attendance at public barbecues is probably around 300. They are usually held in a grove where the air is still perfumed by the sweet, burned aroma of roasted meat and the penetrating, acid odor of hardwood smoke. A thin spiral may still be curling up from the pits where whole carcasses of pigs, now and then a goat or lamb, but almost never beef, were cooked throughout the preceding night. Guests feed from long, shelflike wooden tables, built from tree to tree and piled high with baker's bread, vats of pickles, tubs of lemonade, or maybe iced beer. Sometimes there are jugs of corn likker stashed out in the woods. It all makes up a powerful fare that would dismay many Northerners even on a winter day. But Southerners, from field hands to debutantes, can eat frightening amounts of 'cue and stew on the hottest day of summer without visible damage to their systems.

Instances are cited of ulcer victims who could digest barbecue better than other solid foods. And there was the time down at Brooks, Georgia, when Old Man Martin Turner became so feeble that he could eat nothing but Brunswick stew. He subsisted for several years on that alone.

On the other hand, there was a tragic outcome several years ago down in southern Georgia at the big annual barbecue given on his birthday by Frank Oliff Miller, mayor of Pembroke, Georgia—population, 1,282—and publisher of the *Pembroke Journal* ("Liked by Many, Cussed by Some, Read by All"). The most enthusiastic guest on this particular day was old Judge W. F. Slater, a renowned eater from over near Eldorado. His wife had died a year before, and the judge had been batching. He hadn't had a square meal in several weeks, being a poor cook. He fell to at Miller's barbecue with such abandon that he took sick that night and died.

Another unfortunate, but less tragic, result of eating barbecue befell one of the "Tree-Climbing Haggards of Danielsville" at one of the late Eugene Talmadge's speakings. Among Talmadge's entourage of bucolic camp followers and stooges were Old Man Haggard and his eight sons. They dressed like "Ole Gene," in suits of rusty black with wide-brimmed hats and red galluses, and they would climb to the tops of nine tall pines in each speaking grove to shout down encouragement and cues to Talmadge, according to a carefully rehearsed script.

"Tell us about the schoolteachers, Gene!" a Haggard would cry from a treetop.

"Oh, yes," Talmadge would respond. "I'm glad you brought that up, brother." He would then carry on with remarks about pedagogues until a Haggard in another tree would croak, "Tell us about the old folks, Gene!"— his cue for remarks about pensions.

One time when Talmadge was speaking at Quitman, about three o'clock on a hot afternoon, one of the Haggards, having eaten heavily of barbecue earlier, fell asleep on his perch. When the time came for his cue, he fell out of the trees, causing much amusement among the onlookers. Talmadge forgot what he'd been discussing. It should be added that the Haggards had not eaten the barbecue at Quitman, but at a town up the road where Gene had given a noon speech. On political occasions the barbecue is never served before the speaking.

It is generally agreed down South that barbecue will not hurt anybody when properly cooked, and that the secret of proper barbecuing is patience and more patience. Good barbecue cannot be hurried; it should be allowed to cook and drip for twelve hours over an outdoor fire of hardwood coals. Then it is done throughout. The excess grease has dripped off into the fire after permeating the meat during the cooking. Every true barbecue chef—and every Georgia community has at least one locally celebrated amateur—agrees that no flame should be tolerated in the pit. Some say only half-burned-out coals, whitening with ash, produce heat delicate enough for fine barbecue. Most cooks also agree that pork is the ideal meat. As Uncle Harry Powers, celebrated cook around Rocky Mount, North Carolina, explains it, "Even after he gutted, a pig is so full of blood and water and fat dat it keep him nice and moist through all them hours it take to cook him. You take and barbecue a yearlin' and if you ain't keerful, he turn as black as a hat. No matter what you do, he goin' to be tough."

Some authorities say that the word "barbecue" derives from French, *á barbe de queue,* meaning "from beard to tail," and refers to cooking whole carcasses. Others claim that it comes from a Haitian word, *barbacoa,* meaning a wooden framework, referring to spitting the meat on poles over the pit. Still others say it derives from "buccaning," the process by which the buccaneers of Santo Domingo and St. Christopher cured by smoking on a wooden frame the meat of wild cattle and hogs. They sold the food as provisions to shipmasters of the Spanish Main three centuries ago. It is thought that Negro slaves picked up the barbecuing art in the Caribbean; they brought it to the Southern states. Almost all barbecuing was done by Negroes in past years, and much of it still is. The traditional time for a Georgia barbecue is when crops are "laid by," when cultivation is finished and the farmer has only to wait for the harvest. Since early days it has been customary for plantation owners to entertain their retainers and neighbors each year at gigantic, almost pagan, festivals of meat eating.

Of course, barbecues have not been confined to Georgia. They have flourished from Virginia to Texas for 200 years. Most authorities, however, seem to feel that Georgia is the home of barbecue. "Get ten people together," one student of the custom has written, "and where the Irish would start a fight, Georgians will start a barbecue." A food authority of the last century declared, "The barbecue is to Georgia what the clambake is to Rhode Island, what a roast-beef dinner is to the English, what canvasback duck is to a Marylander, and what a Saturday night pork-and-beans supper is to a Bostonian."

The first known Northern barbecue was held in connection with the presidential election of 1876. On the morning of October eighteenth, two oxen were paraded through New York to Myrtle Park, Brooklyn where they were slaughtered. By eleven o'clock that night one ox, weighing 983 pounds, was roasting on a spit beside an outdoor coke fire. It was declared done at eight the next morning and removed to cook, while the second ox was put on the spit. By noon several thousand curious persons were on hand. The feast began at one o'clock, after 800 loaves of bread had been made into barbecued-ox sandwiches. The crowd was so enthusiastic about the meat that in twenty minutes only the skeleton was left. The second ox was served up that night. The two animals didn't begin to feed the 50,000 persons the affair attracted.

Nowadays barbecuing, or something so called, has spread throughout the land. These days it isn't politics so much as the popularity of backyard cookery that promotes barbecuing. Countless men in chef's caps and fancy aprons, with their eyes reddened by smoke, regale their guests with burnt and raw flesh. Many Georgia epicures insist that this is an insult to the honorable name of barbecue. They assert that, statements in various magazines to the contrary, you cannot barbecue hamburgers, roasting ears, potatoes, onions, tomatoes, wieners, or salami, and it is a shame and disgrace to mention barbecuing in connection with such foolishness.

These purists are even more dismayed by the thousands of "Bar-B-Q" stands that line highways from Maine to California. There exists in Atlanta an organization sworn to boycott any roadside stand displaying the hated "Bar-B-Q" sign. Members say such a sign is usually a tip-off that the "barbecue" will be an underdone pork roast served with a sauce so hot and bitter that the victim can't tell what he is eating. One member swears he once saw a sign made of painted pictures of an iron bar, a honeybee, and a billiard cue. He can scarcely control his emotions when describing this ghastly sight.

Southerners cannot agree even among themselves about proper barbecuing practices. In one Georgia county they claim that oak is the best barbecuing wood. Another county will advocate hickory. Pecan wood is favored somewhere else. In one community the custom is to baste the meat all through the cooking with a sauce made of vinegar, butter, and pepper. In the next community they baste with salt water and do not sauce and salt the meat until it is ready to serve. Georgians, who like their barbecue served in thick, juicy slices, regard as dreadful the North Carolina method of cooking the meat very dry, then mincing it into small, thin particles.

Southerners are even more horrified by certain barbecuing practices of the North, East, and West. Dr. J. G. Woodroof, of the Georgia Agricultural Experiment Station, near Griffin, was shocked to learn that in Michigan barbecue consists of pressure-cooking the meat, "then letting a little smoke filter through it at the last minute." He was even more appalled to find that in California a barbecue is cooked over coke. One Georgia epicure swears he found a Boston cookbook recipe calling for barbecuing chicken by dredging it in flour, then cooking it in a closed pan in an oven.

Many Georgians feel that Brunswick stew is even more abused and less understood than barbecue. In 1946, during observance of Georgia Week at the national capital, one Washington restaurant billed on its menu something called "Brunswick stew." Every Georgian who sampled it was outraged, especially members of Congress from Georgia, who, as a class, are more vocal and excitable than other people. "I wish you could have seen the mess they were serving under that sacred name," Rep. Henderson Lanham, of Rome, told the press. "It might as well have been creamed chicken, with a few pieces of liver and lamb and a scattering of green peas."

Both Georgia and Virginia claim to have originated Brunswick stew. Some Georgians say it was first made from wild game and vegetables in the mid-1730s, when followers of John and Charles Wesley, founders of Methodism, were converting the Indians near the present site of Brunswick, Georgia. In 1946, the *Atlanta Journal* reported another theory: that the stew was first made on July 2, 1898, by a mess sergeant for a company of soldiers on guard duty at Gascoigne Bluff, St. Simons Island, which is also near Brunswick. The sergeant was said to have had no particular recipe, using only a hodgepodge of meats and vegetables he had at hand. It turned out to be so luscious that Negroes of St. Simons preserved his formula.

There seem, however, to be more grounds to believe that the first stew, so called, came from Brunswick County, Virginia. It is said to have been developed around 1828 by "Uncle Jimmy" Matthews, retainer of Dr. Creed Haskins, of Mount Donum, on the banks of the Nottoway River. Uncle Jimmy, an inveterate squirrel hunter and a celebrated cook, made squirrel stews for picnics and public gatherings in that area all his life. When he died, Dr. Aaron Haskins became the area's stew chef, to be succeeded with the passing years by Jack Stith, a relative, and finally by Colonel Thomas Mason, of Redoak, Virginia.

Uncle Jimmy never called his dish anything but squirrel stew, but when residents of the area moved elsewhere and made something like it, their stews were called "Brunswick" for identification purposes.

Uncle Jimmy's stew contained no vegetables except onions. The Georgia version calls for liberal use of chicken, hog head and other meats, tomatoes, corn, and other vegetables. Thus, it is quite possible that the Brunswick stew of Virginia and that of Georgia are completely different items and always have been. In any case, the old recipe for a small mess of Uncle Jimmy Matthews's stew follows:

> Take six squirrels, put them in cold water, parboil one hour. Take up and scrape free of all scum. Then put them in a pot of boiling water with a pound of good bacon cut into inch cubes. Add one quart of sliced onions, salt, red and black pepper. Cook slowly, stirring well until the meat is done and will come to pieces (about four hours). Then add a little butter and stale bread crumbs until the stew is no longer watery, but not too thick.

By contrast, a typical Georgia Brunswick stew recipe for feeding 3,500 people is 850 pounds of the meat of fat hens, boiled until it falls from the bones, sixty gallons of chicken broth, 200 pounds of chopped lean beef, 200 pounds of chopped pork, sixty gallons of tomatoes, twenty-five gallons of creamed corn, eight gallons of vinegar, fifty pounds of butter, forty bottles of ketchup, forty bottles of Worcestershire sauce, twenty bottles of A-1 sauce, ten bottles of chili sauce, ten boxes of paprika, twenty boxes of black pepper, ten boxes of red pepper, juice from twenty dozen lemons, and five boxes of salt. This particular stew was cooked from eight o'clock on a Friday night until eight Saturday morning in fifty-gallon iron pots. Legend says these pots were stolen by natives of North-Central Georgia from Sherman's army, which had used them as soup kettles. There are still a dozen or more in Bartow County, Georgia.

At crop laying-by time last summer I went to Georgia to attend several barbecues. One was the sixtieth-birthday shindig of mayor and editor Frank Miller of Pembroke. His birthday celebrations over the past sixteen years have developed into one of the best-known annual eating events of South Georgia. A few days later in Atlanta I attended a barbecue given by Mayor William B. Hartsfield for some friends, and a couple of days after that, one given by Fulton County commissioners to dedicate a convict camp. Next I rode with Governor Herman Talmadge to a barbecue served in an old barn near Elberton during the dedication of a state park.

One Sunday I attended at Brooks, Georgia, a barbecue that has been given yearly for three generations by J. B. Mask, his father and grandfather before him, on their 5,000-acre farm beside a lake. The whole community is always invited, and the ladies bring along cakes and pies for dessert. Mask is one of the few who have made a commercial enterprise out of a tradition. Back during the last war some Brooks people canned Brunswick stew, according to the Mask recipe, and sent it to their stew-hungry sons and brothers in the armed services. It was received so enthusiastically that people urged Mask to go into the stew-canning business. He did, shortly after the war, with his brother-in-law and his nephew, W. M. Gay Sr. and Jr. Now they gross $500,000 a year, presumably from people who can't stand the wait from one barbecue to the next.

Perhaps the most interesting, colorful, and traditional of the barbecues I attended was the seventieth annual feast near Cartersville, Georgia, of the Euharlee Farmers Club, said by the United States Department of Agriculture to be the oldest farmers' club in continuous operation in the world. It hasn't missed a monthly meeting since its organization in 1883 in the Euharlee community. Its constitution requires its member to conduct agricultural experiments on their separate farms and report findings back to the membership—an early form of agricultural extension work. The club has always had twelve regular members, all leading farmers of Bartow County, and now it has three honorary members—the president of a Cartersville bank and editors Milton Fleetwood, of the *Daily Tribune-News*, and W. Ryan Frier, of the *Bartow Herald*. Members remain with the club until death. Then the other members spend several months selecting a worthy successor. The Euharlee club has been identified with some of Georgia's most progressive agricultural strides, including formation of the university's College of Agriculture, improvement of cotton culture, diversification of crops, and raising of livestock. But to most people in that part of the state, it is probably best known for its annual barbecue. This is an invitation affair for about 300 guests, including the leading farmers and businessmen, the best families and prettiest girls in that part of Georgia.

Their last barbecue was held at Malbone, the antebellum home of member Robert M. Stiles. His family has owned this land since his great-grandfather, who later became U.S. chargé d'affaires in Austria, was awarded the property in 1835 by the government for negotiating the treaty whereby that area of Georgia was bought from the Cherokee Indians. This estate and several like it lie along the course of the Etowah River—Cherokee for "muddy water"—in a three-mile-wide valley of fertile bottom lands and timbered areas of black walnut, oak, poplar, cedar pine, and hickory. In the distance can be seen the smoky outlines of the Blue Ridge.

The main house on the Stiles place has twenty-inch walls of brick made and laid by slave labor. There are twelve-foot ceilings, oval-topped windows, and heavy old mahogany furniture, including an old-fashioned planter's desk, used to keep plantation accounts back before the War between the States. There are marble-topped bureaus, immense old wardrobe chests, porcelain doorknobs, and ornate, heavy furniture brought from Austria by the first owner. A banquet table capable of seating about forty fills the old dining room. The library is notable for an old Franklin stove and for the fact that during the campaign for Atlanta a company of Sherman's cavalry used it for a stable. They put horse troughs in the twenty-inch-wide sills of the tall windows, and used the family's bound set of Congressional Records for flagstones to make a path to the well. The Stiles family was not present for this performance, having refugeed to Terrell County in covered wagons. They had buried their glass and silver in a pit near the river. It was never found by the Yankees, and it now adorns the old dining room.

Most barbecues are noon affairs, but the Euharlee party started at six P.M. At the first pinking of dawn on the big day, barbecue chef Robert Auchmutey, a Cartersville fireman, and his chief assistant, "Uncle John" Pendergrass, an elderly Negro, were on hand to get things started. A barbecue pit eight feet long, four feet wide, and two feet deep had been dug under the shed of the old log barn. On the walls nearby hung old-fashioned farm implements—harvesting cradles, hoes, plows, ancient work-mule harness, and even an old wooden yoke for oxen. In such an atmosphere one almost expected to see Uncle Remus, Br'er Rabbit, Br'er Fox, and "de yudder critters" emerge through the early-morning haze out of a blackjack thicket across the cotton patch.

Three pork carcasses and two whole lambs had been cooling through the night in the springhouse. Uncle John and several Negro helpers brought them to the pit and began sticking two iron rods through the shoulders and hindquarters of each animal. A "stretcher stick" of hickory was inserted horizontally to spread the sides and keep the carcass open. Supported by their rods on either side of the pit, the carcasses were placed inside down, where they would cook for eight hours before being turned to brown evenly and to finish dripping over the slowly cooling coals.

Meanwhile chef Auchmutey was seeing about his fire. Stacked nearby were several cords of oak and hickory limbs, four feet long, five inches in diameter, and still containing some sap. Auchmutey mixed some pine for kindling in with the hardwood. He soon had a leaping fire going. It would be fed all day so a supply of coals would always be available. Roscoe Tatum, the local Brunswick stew specialist, who had his iron pots in place by now, put logs under them from the big fire, which by this time had also produced coals. The acid smoke began stealing up through the pale meat. It caught up the odor of roasting and drifted down the valley, informing everybody who could smell that a barbecue was now on the fire.

Another school of barbecue fire makers, headed by J. B. Mask, decries the use of coals from a supplementary fire. Mask advocates a pit three feet deep, floored with hickory logs twelve inches in diameter. The top of the pit is filled with pine, which is burned for five hours before the barbecuing starts. By then the pine is gone, but the hickory logs, their aromatic bark still intact, are glowing with heat that will hold all during the hours the cooking requires.

As the day wore on, men began to gather by twos and threes at the Stiles barn. Some were Euharlee club members come to help set up tables and do other chores. Others came just to enjoy watching the meat and stew cook. "A man ought to be on the grounds three hours ahead of time to really enjoy eating barbecue," one spectator observed. "As he absorbs the aromas of the cooking meat and the wood smoke and watches the other preparations—the turning of the meat, the stirrings of the stew, and the laying out of bread and pickles under the trees—his system responds. His gastric juices flow, and his digestion is so stimulated that he can eat 'cue and stew all day, and it won't hurt him a bit."

As often happens, two or three barbecue cooks not employed on this job paid courtesy calls at the Euharlee club pit during the afternoon. They entertained with some stories of famous barbecues of the past. Pat Wofford Jr., of Atco, Georgia, was asked about the chicken he was unable to cook for Brunswick stew the time he superintended a big barbecue near Cartersville.

"That was the world's toughest chicken," Wofford laughed. "We had killed two hundred chickens, thinking they were all fat hens. But one turned red and wouldn't cook. We cooked this bird three hours under fifteen pounds of steam in a pressure cooker. Then we threw it in the pot and boiled it four hours, and it would still bounce like a rubber ball when dropped on a table. The Negro help named it 'Ole Abe.' They tied a string to his leg and hung him on a pole like a flag for everybody to see. I really think it was an old rooster whose crowing had been disturbing that end of the county for years. Looking back, nobody could remember seeing or hearing him since a couple of days before our barbecue."

Another barbecue historian present in the Stiles barn mentioned that the man who probably did most to put Georgia barbecue on the map was the late Sheriff John West Callaway, of Wilkes County. He had the barbecue concession at the Cotton States Exposition in Atlanta in 1895. At his stand, purposely made rural and crude, with Negroes crooning over the pits in the background, Sheriff Callaway fed as many as 500 people at a sitting, including the president of the United States and other visiting dignitaries. When the exposition ended, Sheriff Callaway was much in demand to superintend barbecues all over the nation.

His stand was the forerunner of a number of famous barbecue places, such as the stand at Rocky Mount, North Carolina, of Cap'n Bob Melton. He is an eighty-two-year-old, 250-pound, old-time barbecuer. His restaurant serves nothing but barbecue, Brunswick stew, coleslaw, boiled potatoes, and corn bread, and it is known as far away as California. Or there is Sprayberry's place, at Newnan, Georgia, famous as an eating oasis for travelers heading southwest from Atlanta. Posse's, in Athens, Georgia, is held in such high regard by the barbecue-eating University of Georgia football players that they sometimes hold their annual banquet there. In Nashville, Tennessee, Charlie Nickens, who started out twenty years ago in a shack in the slums, has built a big restaurant and probably a fortune from his barbecue, which is cooked over green-hickory blocks.

Perhaps the most interesting aftermath of Sheriff Callaway's barbecuing triumphs, however, is the tradition he started for sheriffs of Georgia counties. They all seem to become barbecue cooks. Sheriff A. B. (Bud) Foster, of Fulton County, is known as the leading barbecuer in the Atlanta area at present.

The tale-spinning around the pit in Stiles's barn came to an end about four-thirty, when the meat was taken off the fire and a crew began "cutting up" for serving. An hour before eating time, most of the guests began arriving. The meat was brought to the serving tables in big washtubs. Pork and lamb were kept separate, and each guest was asked which he preferred or how much of each. Each cardboard plate was heaped high with meat. The Brunswick stew was poured into a smaller division, leaving some room in the middle of the plate for bread and pickles. Several big tubs of ice-cold lemonade, stirred by young Negro women in white aprons, stood handy, so that guests might cool off their throats after parching them with hot barbecue.

The eating began after a prayer by a local minister and a few words of welcome from host Stiles. Little time was wasted on talk. In less than an hour everybody had finished. Most of the guests sat around to digest their food, to enjoy watching the coming of night, and to tell stories about the Civil War—still a favorite topic of the area.

Meanwhile, the fifteen members of the club were following their custom of dividing equally among themselves the leftover barbecue. In this case it was only half a pig. Also according to tradition, the ten gallons of leftover Brunswick stew were sold to guests at a dollar a quart. There were more people eager to buy than there was stew to sell.

As the last guests were leaving, a big full moon had come up, tinting with silver the tops of the cotton stalks that come right up to the edge of the big old yard. Out across the valley a mist was rising from the river, and from the thickets whippoorwills had begun to call. A day like that makes it easier to understand why Georgians regard their barbecues with such reverence.

Texas Barbecue in Black and White

ROBB WALSH

Cowgirls are taking turns climbing onto the stage and turning around to display their denim-clad derrieres to the audience and judges. It's the "Miss Blue Jeans Contest" at the Houston Rodeo Barbecue Cook-off. When a frisky female undulates provocatively, the men wave their cowboy hats in the air and roar in approval. The girls are all white. And so are the hundred or so males standing in front of the stage. The guy next to me is wearing Confederate flag Mardi Gras beads.

I make my way through the grounds checking out the contestants. In front of one booth, there's a huge wooden sign with the team's name, "Confederated Cookers," carved across the stars and bars. Right around the corner, I stumble upon four members of the Skinner Lane Gang, who are busy taking barbecue off the smoker. I stand there staring at them, awestruck. They are the first all-black barbecue cook-off team I've ever seen.

And this isn't the Skinner Lane Gang's first big rodeo. They won the overall championship trophy here in 1994. And they hope to win it again this time, they tell me. First, I sample a healthy pile of their brisket and a few excellent ribs. Then I start asking questions.

"How many black teams are entered this year?" I ask Louis Archendaux, the team leader.

"I think there's two or three," he says.

"Out of how many?" I ask.

"A little over three hundred."

The main reason blacks don't enter barbecue cook-offs is money, says Archendaux, who runs his own chemical company in Sugarland. "You've got to know somebody. We don't have any sponsors—except for friends and relatives who help us out with a few bucks here and there. We have one of the littlest booths out here. We are barely getting by with $5000 or $6000."

The team's booth is furnished with a few picnic tables and a small bar.

There are about a dozen people of various races sitting around eating barbecue and drinking beer. I ask the team members who gets invited in to eat.

"We set up folding chairs outside the booth here and watch for hungry people who don't have wristbands," chuckles Reginald Wilson. "You can tell by the look on their face that they have no idea what's going on. So we bring them in and give them some barbecue."

Anyone foolish enough to purchase a five-dollar general admission ticket to the Houston Rodeo Barbecue Cook-off without a corporate wristband gets a pathetic chopped barbecue sandwich, a scoop of industrial coleslaw, and some tasteless beans served on a Styrofoam plate at the public tent. Then they get to walk around and peek into the invitation-only tents. Sponsors entertain and raise money for worthy causes, and that's where the competition-quality barbecue, live bands, and open bars are.

For barbecue buffs who lack corporate connections, the Skinner Lane Gang booth is a tiny outpost of real-world charity. I take a second helping of brisket, which is very tender and cut into irregular chunks. I am curious about how it will fare in the judging. But Archendaux tells me the brisket they will enter is sliced completely differently.

"Do you change your cooking style for the competition?" I ask.

"You have to," says Archendaux. "If you get it really tender, you can't slice it perfectly. And appearance is very important to the judges.

"Are any of the judges black?" I wonder.

"Probably not," he says. A visit to the judging booth confirms Archendaux's suspicions. All the judges I see are white.

Texas isn't the only place where barbecue cook-offs are divided along racial lines. Jim Auchmutey of the *Atlanta Journal-Constitution* attended a Georgia cook-off called the Big Pig Jig in 1994. "Only a few black teams registered, an imbalance that's typical of the cook-off circuit," he wrote. Although organizers would like to see more black teams, the Caucasian block-party atmosphere drives them away, Auchmutey reported. One sign he saw read, "Redneck Mardi Gras." And that sums up the cook-off atmosphere pretty well, he tells me on the phone.

Confederate flags were much in evidence at the Georgia event. "The flag is a big issue at these things," he says. "If you fly even one, that puts out a signal to black people that this isn't our scene."

"Two years ago, when that flap was going on over in South Carolina, barbecue teams started flying Confederate flags here in Houston," says Archendaux. "Somebody complained, and the Livestock Show folks told the teams to take down the flags." Confederate flags are still banned at the Houston Rodeo Cook-off.

But Archendaux couldn't care less about the flags. The Skinner Lane Gang has been breaking the color barrier at Texas barbecue cook-offs for going on twenty years now. "We were the first black team at the Fort Bend County Cook-off in 1984," Archendaux says. "They had Confederate flags flying all over the place."

"Did anybody give you trouble?" I ask him.

"There's always a few assholes," shrugs Archendaux. "But we are kind of rowdy. If you want to take it there, we can help you out. We never minded a little scrape."

The BP World's Championship Bar-B-Que Contest at the Houston Live-stock Show and Rodeo, as it is officially known, doesn't discriminate against blacks, its white organizers, white corporate sponsors, and white judges will tell you. If very few blacks choose to participate, well that's just the way things work out.

But the white-dominated contest is symptomatic of a larger racial divide that runs through the middle of Texas barbecue with far more serious conse-quences. This division wasn't the result of intentional racism either. It's just that, according to Texas mythology, barbecue belongs to white people.

The pork shoulders have been smoked over hickory until the meat is as soft as applesauce. I eat mine on a sandwich bun with vinegary sauce. Supervising the cooking is a famous pit master named Devin Pickard who has flown in from Centerville, Tennessee, for the occasion. "Barbecue: Smoke, Sauce, and History" is the name of this three-day symposium sponsored by the Southern Foodways Alliance (SFA), an affiliate of the Center for the Study of Southern Culture at the University of Mississippi.

The SFA brings together a diverse group of scholars, journalists, and restaurant folk. Founding members include African American food authority Jessica B. Harris and Southern cooking's television belle, Nathalie Dupree. The meals at this symposium are being catered by some of the most famous names in Southern barbecue—black and white.

Paper plate in hand, I find a spot at one of the tables that have been set up under the tall shade trees of the quadrangle, an open space in the middle of the Ole Miss campus. The sandwich is delicious, although it's hard for a Texan to comprehend that this mushy pork on a bun is considered America's purest form of barbecue. Anyway, it gives me something to talk about in this shady grove, where a couple hundred barbecue experts have assembled to brag, debate, and pontificate on their favorite subject.

The consensus here is that barbecue is an icon of the American South held equally dear by blacks and whites. And as several speakers explain, in the Deep South it is sometimes the common ground that brings the races together, and sometimes the battleground on which they clash. The case of Maurice Bessinger is a prime example of the latter, and a topic much discussed at the symposium.

Shortly after the Confederate flag was removed from the South Carolina statehouse a couple of years ago, Bessinger lowered the giant American flags he used to fly over his nine Piggie Park barbecue restaurants and raised the stars and bars. It wasn't the first time Bessinger had taken a rebel's stand. In the early 1960s, Bessinger refused to integrate his barbecue joints until, in the oft cited case of *Newman v. Piggy Park Enterprises,* he was forced to by the courts.

Given this history of discrimination, and the fact that Bessinger also passed out religious tracts in his restaurants claiming slavery was justified by the Bible, the usual "regional pride" defense of the Confederate flag didn't wash. And so blacks started protesting Bessinger's racism. As a result, national chain stores removed his popular barbecue sauce from their shelves. Bessinger sued, claiming his right to free speech was being violated. "This is part of my exercising my beliefs in Christ and putting out the word," Bessinger told CNN in explanation of his views.

The way in which barbecue and race are emotionally intertwined in the Old South is among the most fascinating topics in food history. Among the deeply held convictions on the subject are opinions as to whether the true progenitors of barbecue in the American South were whites or blacks.

Based on the etymology of the word barbecue, most scholars agree that the cooking style came from the Caribbean, or at least that's where it was first observed by Europeans. The word first appeared in print in the English language in 1661. In 1732, Alexander Pope was already writing about the craving, "Send me, Gods! a whole hog barbecu'd."

In Colonial times, barbecue had become common in the Carolinas and Virginia. Cooking whole hogs over smoldering coals in long pits was the usual methodology. By the height of the plantation era, no political rally, religious revival, or civic celebration in the Deep South was complete without a barbecue. Whites obviously did the organizing, but who did the cooking?

In the heart of Dixie, evidence suggests that African Americans did the work. "It was said that the slaves could barbecue meats best, and when the whites had barbecues, slaves always did the cooking," writes a former Virginia slave in the *Autobiography of Louis Hughes*. But there are also Southern barbecue traditions, in the Appalachian Mountains of North Carolina and elsewhere, where whites were always in charge. So, what's the verdict?

"Did blacks create Southern barbecue?" I ask Lolis Eric Elie, the black author of the widely acclaimed barbecue book, *Smokestack Lightning*, and a staff writer for the *New Orleans Times-Picayune*.

"You can't draw a straight line between black and white contributions to Southern culture," Elie says philosophically. "But you can't ignore the fact that the South is distinct from the North because of the presence of so many black people. And many white Southerners are still afraid to acknowledge the African influence that flows through their food, their music, their manner of speech, and their attitude toward life."

The origins may be hazy, there can be no doubt that barbecue became central to black identity in the South after the Civil War. Black barbecue stands on the side of the road became the first barbecue restaurants in the Old South. And because of the fame of black barbecue, "whites, in a strange reversal of Jim Crow traditions, made stealthy excursions for take-out orders," according to the *Encyclopedia of Southern Culture*.

But a combination of forces conspired to take the barbecue business away from its rural black roots. Urbanization, new sanitary regulations enacted during the Progressive Era at the turn of the century, and strict segregation laws gave white-owned barbecue businesses major advantages.

At the symposium, we watched a documentary called *Smokestack Lightning: A Day in the Life of Barbecue*. In the video, Lolis Eric Elie asked the owner of Charles Vergos's Rendezvous, perhaps the most famous barbecue joint in Memphis, about the origins of the Southern barbecue tradition.

"Brother, to be honest with you, it don't belong to the white folks, it belongs to the black folks," Vergos said. "It's their way of life; it was their way of cooking. They created it. They put it together. They made it. And we took it, and we made more money out of it than they did. I hate to say it, but that's a true story."

Racial controversy is part of the culture of Southern food, and the sfa has never shied away from it. In fact, the association's 2004 symposium will be devoted entirely to racial influences in Southern cooking. After all, promoting diversity and multicultural understanding is part of the association's charter.

Which is why the sfa's "Taste of Texas Barbecue Trip" ran into problems in the planning stage. The idea was to bring food writers, scholars, and barbecue lovers from across the country to the Lone Star State for a barbecue tour in June of 2002. But SFA officials were dismayed to discover that all of the barbecue spots selected by a committee of Texans were white-owned.

The SFA asked for a list with more diversity. The Texas barbecue experts insisted that the state's most emblematic barbecue was produced by Czech and German meat markets. When officials insisted that any SFA program about barbecue in the American South must be multiracial, one Texan accused the SFA of "inserting a racial agenda" where one didn't belong. In a compromise, a few black and Hispanic-owned barbecue joints were eventually added to the tour.

But the conflict put the widely held assertion that Texas barbecue is a white tradition under the microscope. And considered in the larger context of racial issues discussed at the Ole Miss symposium, the matter raises some troubling questions. "The Bessinger controversy has given barbecue a starkly political dimension," wrote Brent Staples in the *New York Times*. "The pulled pork sandwich you eat is now taken as an index of where you stand, on the flag, the Civil War and on Maurice Bessinger."

Last summer, the *New York Times* picked the top four barbecue joints in Texas: Kreuz Market, Louie Mueller's, Cooper's, and the Salt Lick. All of them are white-owned. The article, entitled "Stalking 4-Star Barbecue in the Lone Star State," appeared on Wednesday, July 24, 2002. A barbecue survey that excluded black establishments anywhere else in the South would have no doubt drawn angry charges of racism from Brent Staples.

So why is Texas barbecue different?

In the myth of Texas that most of us know, the state was settled by brave Anglo pioneers and rugged cowboys. And since they were there all by themselves, Texas barbecue must have been invented by Anglos too. Lacking any specific details, many creation stories have emerged. In all of them, the inventors of barbecue are white Texans.

In the proposal for *The Chuck Wagon Cookbook of the Lyndon Baines Johnson Ranch*, author Jane Sherrod Singer wrote:

> In the cattle-raising country of Texas, each owner of a ranch brands his calves with his own insignia, a Texas kind of heraldry. Legends says that in the early days, a cattle owner, a Mr. Bernarby Quinn, used a branding iron with his initials B.Q., with a straight line under the B. He also served the best steaks for five hundred miles around. Thus the Bar-B-Q is synonymous with excellent cook-out foods.

The Bar-B-Q ranch story is also recounted in Jane Butel's 1982 cookbook, *Finger Lickin' Rib Stickin' Great Tastin' Barbecue*. Only in Butel's version, the rancher is named Bernard Quayle.

In the early 1940s, the Texas Writers Project submitted material for a book called *America Eats*, a collection of food folklore from around the country that was never published but can still be found in the Library of Congress. The liberal writers were staunch defenders of the rights of minorities. But they evidently had no idea that barbecue even existed in the Old South. The Texas chapter had this to say about Texas barbecue history:

> Precisely when and where a barbecue was first served in anything like its present form falls within the realm of folklore. Texans concede that some simple form of barbecuing meat doubtless came from below the Rio Grande—or perhaps from French Louisiana—but believe that its present form is a Texas development. Wherever it came from, and whatever in the beginning may have been its recipes and customs, the barbecue fell into friendly hands when it met the Anglo-American pioneers who were settling in the Southwest.

Until the friendly hands of Anglo-American pioneers got ahold of it, Texas barbecue was just Mexicans burying cow heads, the logic goes. But of course, nobody believes those old creation stories anymore. Now it is widely held that it was old German butcher shops that date back to the turn of the century and before, like Southside Market in Elgin and Kruez Market in Lockhart, where the current form of Texas barbecue was invented.

When I started writing the *Legends of Texas Barbecue Cookbook*, I believed these meat markets were the birthplace of Texas barbecue, like everybody else. But there were a few problems with the story. For one thing "barbecue" isn't a German word or a German concept. So how did wurst and *Kassler Rippchen* suddenly turn into Texas barbecue?

Several old-timer pit bosses tipped me off. It was the hoards of black and Hispanic cotton pickers who once roamed the state that started calling German smoked meat barbecue, they said. So I combed through Texas libraries and museums looking for archival material about black cotton pickers and barbecue. What I found were narratives in which former slaves talked about cooking barbecue on Texas cotton plantations before the Civil War and turn-of-the-century photos of blacks cooking barbecue in earthen pits.

It wasn't what I was looking for. In fact, it ruined my whole neatly organized book outline. If blacks were cooking barbecue on cotton plantations in

Texas in the early 1800s, then how could I write that German meat markets invented Texas barbecue half a century later?

And how did it happen that we forgot blacks used to cook barbecue in Texas in the first place?

"African Americans have been completely erased from the meta-narrative of Texas history," University of Texas history professor Neil Foley told me. Foley is the author of *White Scourge: Mexicans, Blacks, and Poor Whites in Texas Cotton Culture*. I was intrigued by a couple of paragraphs in the book's introduction about the way Texas reinvented its history after the Civil War. So I called Foley to see if he could help me understand the strange disparities in Texas barbecue history I was running into.

"Between 1880 and 1920, Texas cotton farmers lost ownership of their land and became tenant farmers and sharecroppers," Foley summarized. Nobody was proud to be a cotton farmer anymore. Meanwhile the cattle business had taken off, and although it didn't employ that many people, it provided Texans with an image.

"You want to hang your mythological hat on something you can be proud of. The image of the rest of the South was cotton, the Confederate flag, overalls, and mules," Foley said. "But Texas had something no other Southern state had—the Alamo. Texans were the men who won the West, the men who defeated the Mexicans."

"So in the early twentieth century," Foley says, "Texas started to consciously reshape its history." The melancholy Confederate symbolism was swept away in favor of the mythology of the cowboy. Of course, Anglo Texans didn't actually invent the cattle culture, as some American history texts claim.

"What did Moses Austin from Connecticut know about cattle?" Foley chuckles. "There was already a thriving cattle culture in northern Mexico before the Anglos ever got here. But there's nothing new or unusual about this sort of thing, it's been going on forever," he says. "You expropriate the cultural material of the people you subjugate and then repackage it as part of your own culture."

And so it was with barbecue. Whites and Mexicans have struck a Faustian bargain in Texas, the historian suggests. Mexican Texans play the role of the colorful minority, and in exchange, Anglos acknowledge that much of the state's heritage is actually Mexican. Everyone agrees that Mexican barbacoa was probably common in South and West Texas long before open pit barbecue arrived.

But blacks were an inconvenient reminder of cotton and slavery and poverty. So their contributions were expropriated, and they were left out of the story. "Once the myth becomes accepted history," Neil Foley tells me, "nobody questions it anymore. College-educated people from all over the country still see Texas as the wild West. There's a reason for that. Tourists come to Texas to see San Antonio and the Alamo. There are no African Americans in the Alamo scene."

The German meat market story is the current white creation myth. "[While] the ultimate roots of barbecue can be traced back to the Stone Age . . . it's more immediate Texas origins date from one hundred or so years ago, when meat markets cooked and smoked their surplus stock," said *Texas Monthly* in May 1977. *Gourmet* magazine's Jane and Michael Stern credit "East European immigrants" for definitive Texas barbecue. (November 2000).

I called the author of the *New York Times* article, Steven Raichlen, an acquaintance of mine who has published many books on the subject of barbecue. I asked him if he had ever been to a black barbecue joint in Texas and how he came to pick his winners.

He said he had visited a few black places, but that the white-owned barbecue joints he'd chosen were classic examples of the Texas style. "When you're in Florence, you go see the Michelangelos," he concluded.

It's a Saturday afternoon carnival at Burn's BBQ on De Priest Street in the Acres Home neighborhood. There's music coming from a jam box out front and more music coming from the cars in the parking lot.

"What's good today?" my companion asks a woman in gray sweats climbing into her car with a pile of styrofoam containers.

"This time I got ribs," she giggles. "But this is my second trip. It's all good, and they really pile it on!"

Outside the front door, a guy in a black Oakland Raiders shirt and matching hat is standing at a card table, selling 3-for-$18 CDs. There are lots of Marvin Gaye, Temptations, and Stevie Wonder albums, along with a little rap. Inside, there are twenty customers waiting in line.

I find Roy Burns, the patriarch of Burn's BBQ, sitting in a plastic chair in the back. Burns, sixty-five, grew up in Midway Texas. He's been selling barbecue for over twenty years. "I used to set up a smoker on the side of the road, but my arthritis got to me," he says. So he settled down and opened a restaurant and brought in some family members to help. He has been at this location for the last twelve years.

We eat at a picnic table under a canvas tent in the front of the restaurant. The ribs are well done, but the meat holds together under a sweet subtle glaze of sauce and smoke. They are among the best ribs I've tasted. The brisket falls apart on the way to your mouth, it is as soft and wet as pot roast.

"That's the difference between white and black barbecue," Houston artist Bert Long once told me. "White people don't cook it as long. And they doctor it up with marinades. Blacks cook everything to death." At Goode Company, one of the most popular of Houston's white-owned barbecue places, every piece of meat is served in a perfect slice, he says. In the black East Texas style, they don't mind serving you a messy pile of meat debris.

As I learned at the barbecue symposium, the epitome of Deep South barbecue is pork, slow smoked to stringy mush. In the black East Texas barbecue style, this original Southern cooking tradition is preserved, but with the substitution of beef, which was cheaper and more plentiful here.

"Need no teef to eat my beef," is a favorite slogan of black Texas barbecue men. If the beef isn't falling apart, then it simply isn't done enough, according to this way of thinking. Black Texas barbecue has its own aesthetic. If you are judging it by the standards of white barbecue, then you don't get it. Put some of that falling apart brisket on a bun with barbecue sauce, pickles, and onions and think of it as Texas's answer to a Carolina pulled pork sandwich—suddenly you'll understand.

Except for my friends and I, everybody at Burn's BBQ is black. And everybody seems to be having a very good time. The cars in the parking lot remain long after the sandwiches are eaten, and there is a basketball game shaping up on asphalt nearby.

A plume of rising oak smoke liberally scented with spicy meat has long been the beacon of black celebrations in East Texas. "We ate barbecue at every wedding, funeral, and family reunion I can remember," says Gary Reese, a local black writer who grew up in Conroe. "My uncles would stay up all night cooking the meat."

Whites also held huge barbecues in Texas. In Texas, barbecues attended by thousands of people for which whole herds of cattle were slaughtered marked major occasions of all varieties. But the open pit cooking style used at these events and the traditions of barbecue as a civic gathering came to Texas with the cotton culture. And the people doing the cooking, in the Old South and in East Texas, were black.

"My grandfather, Emmett Turner, had a pit in the backyard, and I mean a hole in the ground," remembered Bill Bridges, a seventy-seven-year-old food writer and photographer from Palestine, when I asked him to describe old-fashioned white barbecues in East Texas. "This would have been around 1930. He used to barbecue a quarter of beef; he wouldn't bother with anything smaller. We'd go to the butcher shop and poke around until he picked one. Then he'd pick up a colored guy named 'Lijah who actually came and did the work. Grandpa would sit in the shade and drink beer all day and tell 'Lijah what to do, 'Time to turn it over, 'Lijah, time to mop it.'"

When the facts as you understand them don't fit into the existing meta-narrative, you write a counter-narrative, a different version of history, Neil Foley told me. Based on oral traditions and other evidence, African Americans can present a convincing counter-narrative of Texas barbecue history.

"After the cotton was all picked, the slaves were given meat, whole steers and pigs, to barbecue. It was a big party at the end of the harvest," Louis Archendaux explained when I asked him what he knew about the origins of the Texas barbecue tradition.

The evidence suggests barbecue was as common on Texas cotton plantations as it was elsewhere in the South. "De sarvants had lots ob picnics an ole Marse ud gibe us meat fer barbecue," former Texas slave Winger Vanhook of Waco told an interviewer. The WPA Slave Narratives, a series of interviews with over 2,300 former slaves conducted in the late 1930s by writers working for the Works Progress Administration, contain several references to black barbecue by former Texas slaves and their offspring.

"I kin remember w'en I was jes a boy about nine years old w'en freedom cum's [June 19th, 1865] . . . w'en we commenced to have de nineteenth celebrations . . . an' everybody seem's like, w'ite an' black cum an' git some barbecue," former Texas slave Anderson Jones remembered.

Steve Williams, a slave in Goliad County, described life after being driven away from the plantation. "So we jes' scatters 'round, here and yonder, not knowin' zactly what to do. Some of us works on one farm and some on another for a little co'n or some clothes or food. Finally I works 'round 'til I comes to San Angelo, Texas, and I cooks barbecue (at a barbecue stand) for a long time 'til I jes' finally breaks down."

Tamale salesman, barbecue sellers, and outdoor food vendors of all varieties began to disappear in Texas, as in the rest of the country, when sanitary regulations were introduced around 1910. As food service establishments came to be licensed and inspected, whites brought Texas ethnic food traditions into restaurants. Mexican food went from street corner chili stands to Anglo-owned establishments like the Original Mexican restaurant in San Antonio.

Since African American pit barbecue was still cooked in a hole in the ground at the turn of the century, roadside stands had little hope of complying with sanitary laws. The German and Czech butchers, on the other hand, smoked meat in brick enclosures and were already subject to whatever sanitation regulations various Texas counties chose to enforce.

In the 1920s, a Beaumont barbecuer named Joe Burney came to Houston and taught the local blacks how to construct cinder block pits that would pass inspection, old-time Houston barbecue man Harry Green explains. Of course, black barbecue restaurants were segregated and restricted to black neighborhoods. But during the era of segregation, they were quite successful. The Fifth Ward alone supported six outstanding black barbecue joints at one time. But once integration arrived, blacks deserted the old neighborhoods, and by the early 1970s, black-owned barbecue joints began to disappear.

"In East Texas, white barbecue is served in restaurants. You get nigger barbecue from a stand by the side of the road—usually about the size of an outhouse with a hand-lettered sign," Bill Bridges, a white Texan, told me on the phone from his home in Palestine. "In the old days, white barbecue was brisket, the same as it is now. Black barbecue was hot links and the stranger parts of the animals."

Bridges is a very likable and knowledgeable guy, and he doesn't consider himself a racist. But he was born in 1925 and can't break certain lifelong habits. Although his use of the N-word is deplorable, ironically, he is one of the few white Texans I've talked to who understands the key role blacks have played in Texas barbecue history.

"Nigger barbecue isn't a derogatory term in East Texas," Bridges says when I ask him about his use of the word. "It's like calling Brazil nuts 'nigger toes.' If anything, the term is used with affection."

Smoke billows from a camper trailer parked in a vacant lot on the side of the road. I have been hearing about this particular trailer and the barbecue brisket sandwiches that get handed out of its little window for quite some time now. I park my car, walk up to the window, and stick my head inside. There, I see William Little, a middle-aged black guy sitting in a plastic lawn chair watching television.

We exchange a few pleasantries, and I ask for a sandwich. Little ambles up to the front and opens the steel doors of a smoker that has been improbably welded right into the trailer's frame. When the sweet-smelling smoke abates, I see foil-wrapped packages and charred hunks of meat waiting to be sliced. The doors of the smoker open into the camper's kitchen, which has a multi-compartment sink, counter space, and a refrigerator. The firebox is fed from the outside. The back of the pickup truck that pulls the trailer is loaded with oak and pecan logs. William Little has been working out of this trailer six days a week for the last fifteen years.

I first tasted Little's brisket when I begged somebody who was going to Dickinson to bring me back a sandwich. I had heard he had some of the best brisket in the Houston area. I wasn't disappointed. The meat was incredibly smoky and very tender, and the sandwich was loaded with a huge amount of the meat. Barbecue sauce had been drizzled on the bun, and the whole thing was topped with raw onions and dill pickles. It was so good, I decided I better track the man down.

Little usually parks on Highway 3. But some days he goes to events, like the rodeo in Pasadena. "Did you ever think of entering the Houston Rodeo Cook-off?" I ask.

"Nah, I can't afford it," he scoffs, but he doubts he would win anyway. "Black people know how to cook brisket, but the rules for judging are not really about how it tastes. It's all about how pretty it looks. I've eaten brisket cooked by a team that won, and it was nothin' special," Little says as he hands the coveted sandwich through the tiny window. I eat it over the trunk of my car.

"That's some smoky brisket!" I mumble with my mouth full.

Black East Texas barbecue joints don't need any help from affirmative action, I reflect as I wipe the sauce off my chin. An unbiased opinion and a map drawn on a napkin will do just fine.

The Rhetoric of Barbecue

A Southern Rite and Ritual

STEPHEN SMITH

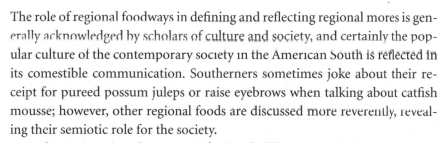

The role of regional foodways in defining and reflecting regional mores is generally acknowledged by scholars of culture and society, and certainly the popular culture of the contemporary society in the American South is reflected in its comestible communication. Southerners sometimes joke about their receipt for pureed possum juleps or raise eyebrows when talking about catfish mousse; however, other regional foods are discussed more reverently, revealing their semiotic role for the society.

Barbecue is serious business in the South. The fervor which characterizes the membership of the barbecue cult becomes obvious as the field researcher attempts to define the topic. The scholar will immediately encounter definite and differing attitudes, depending upon the individual informant, with regard to the rites and rituals of barbecue. Areas of disagreement include: (1) definition of the South; (2) definition of barbecue; (3) correct spelling of the word; (4) type of meat; (5) type of cut; (6) ingredients for sauce; (7) type of pit; (8) type of wood; (9) wet versus dry cooking; (10) the highest shaman; (11) the preparation ritual; and (12) the design of the temple.

In many respects, barbecue is taken as seriously as religion. In fact, the barbecue cults throughout the region often display a hostility to criticism and an intolerance to opposing beliefs that have characterized certain religious groups. Folks in these parts, observed Max Brantley, "don't just eat barbeque. They spend hours perfecting home recipes; they burn tanks of gasoline searching for it; they argue about it. Emotions run high. Nothing I've written stirred more comment, or brought down more abuse, than a series of articles about barbeque six years ago. . . . For my opinion, I was branded a socialist by a Malvern woman—no kidding—and drew letters of criticism from two states." The analogy between barbecue cults and religious sects becomes even more clear when one looks beyond the present manifestations of name-brand religious denominations to try to define the essence of religion. The definition of religion offered by one scholar could be applied as easily to the barbecue cult as well. Religion, suggested Melford Apiro, is "an institution consisting of culturally patterned interaction with culturally postulated superhuman beings," and it is an attribute of social groups, comprising a component part of their cultural heritage. These symbolic, but definitely instrumental, activities constitute, of course, a ritual, or symbolic action system. While some might challenge the validity of that paradigm, this essay accepts Joseph Pieper's contention that "culture depends for its very existence on leisure," and that one's leisure activities—whether one chooses to participate in worship of the sacred or the profane—can tell us much about the cultural assumptions and the cultural heritage of a people.

In trying to define "the South," historians and sociologists have quibbled with each other and among themselves, but the plurality seem to include the eleven states of the old Confederacy and sometimes Maryland, Kentucky, and Oklahoma. barbecue aficionados contend that the true South is coterminous with real barbecue. One critic advised, "If you don't like barbecue, don't move to the South; in some sections, you might starve. If you can't find a barbecue joint in the phone book, you're not in the South." Empirical evidence confirms this hypothesis: the Atlanta directory boasts twenty-eight barbecue locations, while there is not a single entry under barbecue in the twenty-six pages of restaurant listings in the Boston area Yellow Pages.

There are probably more barbecue joints than Baptist churches in the South, but the exact number in existence is unknown, since the census bureau does not identify restaurants by their specialty fare. One newspaper editor in Arkansas suggested, "it's safe to say that no incorporated municipality lacks at least one barbecue man." He conceded, however, "No precise number can be known. There's no Arkansas Rib and Loin Association with an executive secretary to lobby for exemptions from state health regulations and for tariffs on imported barbecues."

Field research indicates that the Barbecue South lies between the 30th and 37th north parallels and between the 77th principal meridian on the east and U.S. Highway 69 on the west. Some informants will label this heresy, but it appears valid. Parts of Kentucky and Virginia will argue that the 37th parallel is too far south; however, Kentucky was disqualified because its best "barbecue" is said to be mutton, and Virginia was eliminated after a Washington-based Southerner testified that the closest edible barbecue was on the North Carolina line. Texans will complain that the western boundary excludes Dallas and Houston; however, only northeast Texas qualifies, because the rest of the state has a strange fascination with beef and mesquite. In Oklahoma, the line is drawn through Muskogee between Slick's, which is included, and My Place, which is out but has a large flock of devotees. South Florida, the Gulf coast, and the Atlantic counties of North Carolina will not protest their exclusion, but a splinter sect in Kansas City will stage a sit-in at Arthur Bryant's.

The repartee involving barbecue goes beyond cartography to include lexicography as well. One reader of a language column recently asked the columnist to settle a domestic argument. "My wife contends that the correct spelling of a certain process for preparing pork is *barbecue*, the spelling always used in your newspaper. It's is her contention that the word is derived from the Spanish word *barbacoa*, which Spanish explorers of the 1660's got from the Taino tribe of Haiti, where it meant a framework of sticks on which to roast meat," he wrote, "I believe that the correct spelling is *barbeque*. For one thing, you see far more signs advertising B-B-Q that B-B-C. For another, since pork is the only true source of barbeque, and hogs were not native to Haiti, I maintain that the word comes from the French phrase *barbe a queue*, meaning beard-to-tail, derived from roasting whole pigs." As a final argument, the reader said, "Stuart Berg Flexner and Noah Webster, both Yankees, seem to agree with my wife, which is another reason I think I'm right. Yankees don't know any more about spelling barbeque than they do about how to prepare it." Another reader wrote in support, "Never mind the etymology, opinion hereabouts is firm, the final syllable-*que* represents the swine's tail as in *queue* (pigtail); a visual onomatopoeia, so to speak."

The columnist, though hedging on the answer, agreed with one point, "that the only real barbecue, or barbeque, is pork. To deny that would be to sanction what goes on in Texas, and the only people who know less about this subject than Yankees are Texans." The point made here is that the Southern barbecue purists insist that both meat and ribs must be pork or the product is not barbecue. Max Brantley, the leading authority on the subject, has suggested that any charlatan who serves beef ribs rather than pork probably waters the beans as well. Perhaps the best stated formal definition is found in the "Official Rules and Regulations" of the Memphis in May International Barbecue Cooking Contest, a regional affair held on the banks of the Mississippi River at the foot of Beale Street: "Barbecue is defined by the sponsors as pork meat (fresh and uncured) prepared on a wood or charcoal fire, basted or not, as the cook sees fit, with any non-poisonous substance and sauces as the cook believes necessary."

Brantley also advances the argument that pork meat alone does not constitute barbecue. In refuting the claim of Arthur Bryant's Barbecue at Eighteenth and Brooklyn in Kansas City as the King of Ribs, Brantley said, "Dear hearts, smoked meat is *not* barbecue, unless you're a Texan. Barbecue is sauce, never mind the dictionary. No matter how long Bryant ages the peppery stuff he slaps on his meat as an afterthought, it's not fit to baste a Wonder bun at most Arkansas barbeque shacks." Katherine Zobel, writing in *Southern Exposure*, discovered during her research that "like religious tenets, barbecue sauces are touted as being essential while, at the same time, being unknowable," a belief supported in practice. J. D. McClard, who "gets up at 4:30 A.M. each day to cook thirty gallons of [his] mixture down to a thick fifteen gallons," has been using the same recipe his father acquired in 1928, and the original is kept in a bank lockbox. Charles Ballard, who learned his trade twenty years ago under the legendary Elmo Johnson, insists that the sauce is the real secret to success, adding, "Every barbecue man knows that, and he ain't going to tell you what's in it."

One food editor, attending a barbecue cook-off with 200 teams, discovered that "despite their gregarious proclivities, not a one was willing to share a sauce recipe. The majority said they used secret formulas derived from 'grand-mother.'" Unlike the truths of revealed religion, the formula for the perfect barbecue sauce is more akin to a magic spell. As Malinowski observed, "The spell is that part of magic which is occult, handed over in magical filiation, known only to the practitioner. To the natives, knowledge of magic means knowledge of spell, and . . . it will always be found that the ritual centers around . . . the spell. The formula is always the core of the magical performance." In his analysis of the cultural impact of magic, he also provides insight to the function of the high braggadocio associated with the barbecue ritual. Magic, he said, serves "to ritualize man's optimism, to enhance his faith in the victory of faith over fear," and to express "the greater value for man of confidence over doubt, of steadfastness over vacillation, of optimism over pessimism." Perhaps the magic of the barbecue ritual is the perfect antidote for overcoming the pessimism and sense of failure inherent in the burden of Southern history.

These sauces are not for the weak of stomach, for almost all the sludge-bottom cooking cauldrons start the day filled with vinegar, black and red pepper, salt, lemons, onions, sugar, water, and in some versions tomato puree. When Lipton decided to test-market Wish-Bone Western Style Barbecue Sauce in a plastic squeeze bottle, the company chose Kansas City, Milwaukee, and St. Louis for their trial balloons, wisely avoiding the South, where the doctored ketchup would have failed regardless of the packaging.

Other arguments most frequently arise over whether the pork should be sliced, chopped, or torn; whether the pit should be dug into or built above ground; whether the wood should be mesquite, oak, sassafras, or hickory; whether the meat should be rubbed before or basted during cooking; and whether it is a sacrilege to include tomatoes in the sauce base. The prevailing wisdom seems to support torn, dug, hickory, rubbed, and tomatoes.

As with all things religious, there are those who seek financial gain from mass audiences, and barbecue is no exception. Luther's Bar-B-Q, Inc., is the Southern culinary equivalent of the Southern televangelists. Founded in Houston nine years ago, Luther's is now a regional "cafeteria-style" barbecue chain with approximately fifty stores in fourteen states. Acquired by Diversifoods, formerly Chart House, of Itasca, Illinois, in 1981, Luther's corporate headquarters has been moved to Atlanta, but that does not disguise the carpetbag philosophy behind the chain's marketing strategy to expand to 700 stores during the next four years. Ron Crews, marketing vice president, projected a $10 million annual advertising budget and said, "It's a total research and a total positioning job . . . the barbecue segment is not very developed. We feel we're creating a new segment." No real barbecue proprietor would talk like that nor suggest spending that kind of money to paint smiling pigs on their signs when RC will provide them for free.

Generally, even successful barbecue joints have difficulty expanding to a second location without losing something in the process. In a review of one establishment's efforts at expansion to an "underserved" area, Brantley gave the fare a favorable rating, then added, "But, there is a but and this is it: Stubby's is a West End barbecue stand. That is, it sells middle-of-the-road barbecue aimed at a large audience. There's none of the one-of-a-kind, take-it-or-leave-it funkiness in either the sauce or the surroundings that you find on the other side of town at such legendary places as Sims' or Ballard's."

Taking note of the ritualistic nature of barbecue, an article in *Southern Living* suggested that Southerners "revere legendary haunts as if they were shrines," and most seem to prefer the rectitude found in "barbecue eateries identified by torn screen doors, scratched and dented furniture, cough syrup calendars, potato chip racks, sometimes a jukebox, and always a counter, producing an ambiance similar to a county-line beer joint." When a longtime barbecue landmark was threatened with closing by the state health department, one zealot protested the action and complained that "anyone with a lick of sense knows that you can't make good barbecue and comply with a health code."

As advice to the novice, one old hand recommended a parking lot survey to the neophyte seeking the Holy Grail of pork ambrosia. "If you can spot an equal number of Mercedes sedans and Ford pickups, you've found a good place. Too many expensive new cars and the joint is likely to be fake; too many pickups and it's liable to be a dive. Balance is the key word. Beware of new buildings. Everything in a barbeque joint, including the help, should be old. It takes a certain amount of seasoning to get good barbeque, and that goes for the building as well as the food."

The high priests of barbecue, both the self-anointed and the popularly acclaimed, labor vigorously to maintain their reputations. One restaurant in Dallas houses a "Barbecue Hall of Fame" to honor famous white Texans who hosted gargantuan feeds for multitudes of followers, but it seems to have selection criteria based upon the quantity served rather than the quality of the product. John R. Wills Jr. of Memphis, two-time winner of the Memphis in May Barbecue Contest and recipient of *Memphis* magazine's "best sandwich" award, decorated his restaurant with pig portraits (not intended to resemble the Stations of the Cross) and barbecue trophies (not intended to resemble religious icons). No Southern barbecue professional would make application for the Hall of Fame, for as Brantley observed, "The barbecue man doesn't have the time for conventions. He's up early to tend his fires and on his feet up to sixteen hours a day, smoking his meat, brewing his sauce and serving his creation. He is surrounded by family members and precious few others. The barbecue man, even the mediocre one, is serious about the secrets of this trade, and a grunt is the standard reply to questions on a potion's ingredients. The majority of barbecue men, if not barbecue stand owners, are black."

The status of mythic hero, or superhuman, conferred on black barbecue artists contributes, at least subconsciously, to the erosion of past patterns of racial discrimination and leads to genuine interracial communication and understanding in a context unrivaled by the prevailing practices in most Southern churches. That is not, however, to suggest that the religious analogy fails here. One of the shrines of barbecue in Arkansas, Lindsey's, in North Little Rock, was founded in 1955 by AME bishop D. L. Lindsey, and in the tradition of hereditary succession, it is still operated by his descendants. The *Arkansas Times* award for best barbecue in the state was recently given to Sim's Barbecue, and establishment started by Allen Sims, high priest of barbecue and "purveyor of pork nonpareil," and presently managed by his nephews, Ronald and Russell Settlers. Sims's dedication and devotion to preparing his fare is legendary; he "is the man who once told a reporter after a man and woman shot each other in his dining room, 'I didn't see nothing. I was just basting my ribs.'"

One of the most obvious religious parallels is between the old-time camp meeting and the contemporary barbecue cook-off contests, exemplified by the Memphis in May festival in Memphis, Tennessee, "Pork Barbecue Capital of the World," where 295,000 people from fifteen states came to watch 200 teams compete for the 1983 title. At this famed event, the 1984 contestants included such teams as Trichinosis Terry and His Borderline Swine, Sooie and the Piglets, and the River City Rooters. The Hog Doctors wore scrub suits, dispensed their sauce from an intravenous bottle, and donned surgical gloves to cut their ribs entry on an operating table for the official judging.

Such antics were not unheard of at the frontier camp meetings of old. As one historian of the South, Dickson Bruce, noted,

> So much has been made of the camp-meeting's frontier origins as well as its more sensational qualities that one often loses sight of its religious character and the content of its religious appeal. For many observers, then and now, the secular role of the camp-meeting has far overshadowed whatever religious significance the practice might have had. Recognizing the hard character of frontier life, these writers have shown that the plain-folk greatly needed the kind of social occasion afforded by camp-meetings. Gatherings provided an opportunity, usually right after harvest time, for people to get together for several days of unencumbered social activity, and in a region where population was sparse and work was hard, such an opportunity must have been greatly appreciated.

Despite the perceived misplaced emphasis, he suggested that the camp meetings provided a ritual which nurtured close personal relationships, cooperation, reflection, and Southern hospitality. Dickson acknowledged, however, that "the gathering took on the form of a 'holy fair' or 'religious holiday' because the whole community turned out, religious and irreligious. But as with any fair, holy or otherwise, all of the activities of the campground were not of the variety desired by church leaders."

It is not coincidental that most contemporary barbecue contests are held either at a spring "hoedown" celebration or at harvest time. Corresponding festivals are also prominent in major religions. Malinowski contended that the "festive and public character of the ceremonies of cult is a conspicuous feature of religion in general. Most sacred acts happen in a congregation. . . . This public character, the gathering together of big numbers is especially pronounced in the annual or periodic feasts held at time of plenty. . . . Such feasts allow the people to indulge in their gay mood, to enjoy the abundance of crops or quarry, to meet their friends and relatives, to muster the whole community in full force, and to do all of this in a mood of happiness and harmony." Specifically supporting the thesis of this essay, he concluded, "there can be no doubt that religion demands the existence of seasonal, periodic feasts with a big concourse of people, with rejoicing and festive apparel, with an abundance of food, and with relaxation of rules and taboos."

In many ways, the Barbecue Eucharist serves as the perfect metaphor for understanding contemporary Southern society. The catechism contains a reverence for tradition and the heritage of the past, the vestiges of rural camp meetings, a chorus of regional chauvinism, a pulpit for oratory, and opportunity for community participation, appreciation for the vernacular, equality of opportunity, and subtle interracial respect.

Charles Brightbill suggests that recreational activities have historically been related to religion, and the barbecue ritual is an excellent example of this relationship. Both, he said, "are engaged in voluntarily, occur during leisure, provide a chance for gain, balance, and perspective, provide the opportunity to express and satisfy our inner desires, place us at the center of our own destiny, recognize the supreme worth of the individual, [and] provide for us the exercise of free will." Developing that analogy, he held that "with some people, under certain circumstances, recreation can become a substitute for religion—just as religion sometimes becomes a form of recreation."

The community values represented by the high-priest cooks and the dedication of their congregations suggest that the rhetorical ritual of barbecue, characterized by hyperbole and boastful humor among friends, may also serve to further human understanding and humanitarian values among the faithful. As such, it is a regional community ritual worthy of our academic analysis as well as our voracious appetites. Brightbill's conclusions about recreation in general are applicable to the rites of Southern barbecue as well, especially his observation that in "this kind of recreation, we can find those things which aid our self-respect, self-confidence, and individual dignity. As we follow these pursuits, we can also learn something about how to live well and get along with others. We can learn to shape material with our hands, compound ideas with our minds, and establish good neighborly relations with our hearts. Consideration of the rights of others and a fuller realization of our own obligations and responsibilities are reasonable outcomes to expect."

Amen.

STEPHEN SMITH

Politics and Pork

JIM AUCHMUTEY

Anyone who has spent much time in the South knows that barbecue and politics go together like fat and flavor. But that kinship isn't always obvious to newcomers. I realized this a few years ago when the dining critic at my newspaper, the *Atlanta Journal-Constitution*, asked me to go along with him to check out a popular pit, Williamson Brothers.

John is from the Northeast, and while he truly loves barbecue, he doesn't fully appreciate the culture of it the way most of us who grew up flicking gnats away from sauce-smeared paper plates do. John liked the ribs and the chopped pork. He was feeling pretty good about the food, then he excused himself to visit the men's room. He came back with a sick expression on his face.

"Have you seen the photos in the hallway back there?" he asked me. I'd seen them. Like a lot of people in the Atlanta suburbs, the Williamsons support conservative politicians. When the local congressman, Newt Gingrich, was elected speaker of the house, they went to Washington to do a barbecue for the Republican revolutionaries who were taking over the Capitol, vowing to cut all the pork out of government. There are some pictures of Newt in the back hall near the restrooms; with those big nostrils and fleshy jowls, he looked like something the Williamsons might have spread-eagled over the coals. John is definitely not conservative in his politics, and his sensitivities were on edge since the Monica Lewinsky affair was just busting out, so when he came back to the table looking like the ribs were disagreeing with him, I assumed he had seen Newt grinning down from the wall.

He asked me, half-joking, "How can you eat in a place like this?" I told him it was easy: In the South, we try to remember that the pigs are nonpartisan.

Every political party from the Whigs and the Mugwumps to the Republicans and the Democrats has used barbecue as a way to gather voters, thank supporters, and pass the hat. It's an old tradition in our politics, right up there with stump speeches and influence peddling. In some states, like Georgia and

69

North Carolina, barbecues are an almost expected part of the election season. I believe it was a Raleigh newspaper editor who observed that "no man has been elected governor of North Carolina without eating more barbecue than was good for him." Low cholesterol or high voter approval ratings? Southern politicians have been trying to work out that dilemma for years.

We've had barbecue people who become politicians. Until recently, the mayor of Augusta, Georgia, was a man named Larry Sconyers, whose principal claim to fame was that he ran the city's best-known barbecue joint. He might have been the only mayor in America who wore a gold pig ring and a gold pig necklace and drove a car with a license tag that read "No. 1 Pig." A little farther east, in Columbia, South Carolina, they've got Maurice Bessinger of Maurice's Piggie Park, who ran for governor and lost, and more recently lost a lot of business by wrapping himself in the Confederate flag.

We've also had politicians who became barbecue people. After he made his reputation as a field general for Ronald Reagan and George Bush, Lee Atwater used his fame to do what any red-blooded Carolina boy wants to do: he started playing guitar in a band and opened a chain of barbecue restaurants called Red, Hot and Blue.

We've had august bodies of lawmakers turn their energies to the important task of ensuring the quality of barbecue. In 1986, South Carolina legislators passed a "truth in barbecue" law requiring restaurants to disclose whether they used authentic hardwood smoke or attempted to hoodwink the public with gas. This was a case of worthwhile government regulation.

We've also had barbecue restaurants figure in important legal precedents. Isn't it curious that the two most conspicuous challenges to the Civil Rights Act of 1964 involved eateries that specialized in the South's two most renowned dishes? In Atlanta, it was Lester Maddox refusing to serve fried chicken to black folks at his restaurant, the Pickrick, and then chasing them away with pick handles. He rode the notoriety all the way to the governor's mansion. In Birmingham, it was Ollie McClung and his son filing suit against the U.S. government rather than serve pig meat to blacks in the dining room at Ollie's Barbecue. The McClungs won a ruling in federal district court but lost an appeal before the U.S. Supreme Court. Unlike Lester, who closed his restaurant rather than desegregate, Ollie had the good sense to remain open. I stopped by a few years ago and witnessed a bustling interracial crowd at lunchtime.

This intermingling of barbecue and politics isn't a story just for people who grew up saying "y'all." Take Newt Gingrich. As you probably know, Gingrich is an adoptive Southerner, "an army brat" who grew up mostly in Pennsylvania. When he moved to Columbus, Georgia, as a teenager, he developed a keen interest in politics and apparently absorbed the local conviction that pulled pork is one of the surest ways to a voter's heart. Isn't it funny how newcomers to the region become some of the most devoted practitioners of its folkways?

Gingrich began his career as a history professor at West Georgia College and soon became one of the most popular faculty members, in part because of the barbecues he threw for students at his house. Sometimes he'd even dig up part of the yard to cook a pig. Clearly this was a man who craved approval. Is it any wonder that when he became House speaker he celebrated with a big pig-pickin' catered by his favorite Republican pit masters?

Like the pigs, most barbecue joints are nonpartisan. But there are exceptions—restaurants whose owners have such obvious leanings that they become known as much for their political loyalties as for their sliced pork plates. I ran across a dramatic example of the phenomenon in the town of Ellijay, in the Blue Ridge Mountains of Georgia. Ellijay is small, population 1,200, but it has not one but two political barbecue joints. One is unabashedly Democratic, the other stridently Republican. They sit about six miles from each other beside the Appalachian Highway, which was renamed for a politician, naturally; it's now the Zell Miller Mountain Parkway.

The Republican place is Poole's Bar-B-Q and Pig Hill of Fame. You may have seen a photo of this establishment. Behind the restaurant, there's a hillside studded with plywood pigs with names painted on them. The first time I drove past, I thought it was some folk artist's idea of a barbecue graveyard, "an Arlington National Cemetery for pork," with little memorials to the pigs who made it all possible. The truth is more mundane: If you give the proprietor five bucks, he'll put up a pig with your name on it. The owner is Oscar Poole, a Methodist minister who retired to the mountains and tools around town in his Pigmobile, a 1977 Volare customized with a snout and pointed ears. That was good enough for the Gilmer County GOP, and they made Oscar their chairman. Every time Pat Buchanan rears up and runs for president, he goes to Ellijay and does an appearance at Poole's and cracks a few jokes about political pork.

The Democratic barbecue place is—and I'm not kidding here—the Pink Pig. Oscar Poole, who remembers the McCarthy era with great nostalgia, tells folks that it's actually the Pinko Pig. But barbecue aficionados know that the pinkness only refers to the smoke ring. The Pink Pig is run by a former truck driver named Bud Holloway. Over the years, he's cooked fund-raising barbecues for Democrats like senators Zell Miller, Max Cleland, and the late Herman Talmadge. But the Democrats he's closest to are Jimmy and Rosalynn Carter. Holloway moonlights as a carpenter and helped the Carters build a cabin in the woods nearby, where the former president liked to hole up and write. The Carters drop in with the Secret Service every now and then to eat barbecue. Holloway has photos of them in the restaurant, and he cannot bear it when customers occasionally are so boorish as to bad-mouth his friends. After Carter left the White House, Holloway told me, "people would come in and say ugly things about him, and I'd have to ask them to leave."

I was happy to see that when Carter won the Nobel Peace Prize, the Atlanta newspaper called Bud Holloway for a reaction. The owner of the Pink Pig was quoted right beside Andrew Young and Bishop Desmond Tutu. Two admirable men to be sure, but I wonder if *they* can cook a pig?

Probably half the men who have occupied our nation's highest office knew something about pig-pickins, starting with George Washington and continuing through to our current George, Dubya. Washington hosted barbecues at Mount Vernon and is known to have made one of the first American references to a public barbecue in his diary. He wrote that he was going up to Alexandria for three days for a barb-i-cue (he spelled it with an "i," setting a precedent for all the misspellings that would appear on restaurant signs in future generations). The diary entry is from 1763, so we can only hope that the father of our country still had his natural teeth and could enjoy gnawing the ribs.

By the time Andrew Jackson took office a few decades later, political barbecues had become a bona fide political institution. There's an editorial cartoon from the 1830s showing Jackson's enemies turning him on a spit. Old Hickory appears as a pig, complete with hoofed extremities and a curly tail. The cartoonist apparently knew that Tennesseans prefer pork.

The president who perfected the political barbecue was probably William Henry Harrison, a Virginia native who won fame as an Indian fighter at the Battle of Tippecanoe in the Northwest Territories. Every history student learns his slogan: "Tippecanoe and Tyler, too." It was the most honest part of his campaign. Harrison's candidacy in 1840 was a triumph of image-making. His handlers wanted to persuade voters that Tippecanoe was a man of the people like Jackson, so they staged enormous barbecues across the country, erecting log cabins as the centerpiece, to symbolize their man's humble roots. Never mind that Harrison grew up in a plantation manor. The barbecues were festive and entertaining, and voters loved them. Well, not all voters. One abolitionist minister, the Reverend J. D. Long, disapproved of what the spectacles implied about the values of the electorate: "There is not much difficulty in the South in raising money for a barbecue, or to buy whiskey for political purposes; but when the funds are wanted for a library, that is quite another question."

Many years after Harrison died in office, my hometown of Atlanta, always eager to suck up, tried to impress another president in a most peculiar way. William Howard Taft, our largest chief executive, visited in 1909, and the city threw him a banquet that was commensurate with the awesome presidential circumference. They served 600 people and had to hold it in the new Municipal Auditorium. Among the thirty-two dishes on the menu was barbecued possum. The record does not show whether Taft was impressed or horrified by this offering of smoked marsupial.

The modern president who made the most of barbecue—as food and symbol—was undoubtedly Lyndon B. Johnson. LBJ loved to show off his ranch for the same reason politicians of Harrison's time liked to claim a log cabin birth. The ranch advertised LBJ's roots in the dirt of the Texas Hill Country. As if that weren't enough to make the point, Johnson liked to take visitors out for a spin in his Lincoln Continental, driving so fast that he'd cover the speedometer with his Stetson so reporters couldn't see how high the needle was climbing. Some journalists said that he'd drink a beer or two while he was speeding and toss the cans out the window, but Johnson denied that. He said Lady Bird would kill him if she thought he was a litterbug.

In his five-plus years in office, Johnson hosted more than one hundred barbecues on the LBJ Ranch. One of the most memorable was the first one he staged for a visiting head of state, the chancellor of Germany, who came in 1963, a little more than a month after the Kennedy assassination. The media was quite amused by the prospect of such an event, coming so soon after the Eastern sophistication of the Kennedy years. One New York paper dubbed it "barbecue diplomacy."

There's a good retelling of this barbecue in a recent book, *LBJ's Texas White House,* by Hal K. Rothman. Before LBJ became president, his barbecues were usually pretty down-home affairs, with lots of gingham and fiddle music and corny comedy from an emcee by the name of Cactus Pryor, who reminded everyone of Will Rogers—it sounds to me like the scene from "Oklahoma" where they sing "The Farmer and the Rancher Should Be Friends." But now Lyndon Baines Johnson is the leader of the free world, and it dawns on his entourage that maybe they should strive for a more presidential tone. I mean, the chancellor wouldn't welcome them to Germany in lederhosen, would he? So Cactus Pryor, of all people, "the humorist" suggests that they show the world that Texans aren't a bunch of cowhands by inviting Van Cliburn down to perform. The acclaimed pianist had grown up in Fort Worth and quickly agrees to come. Only when he gets to the ranch, he finds out that they want him to perform in blue jeans and a red checkered shirt like the rest of the help.

Maybe they wanted to put him to work basting the brisket before he took the stage. Cliburn protested that he always performed in a tux. When no one could find a tux, he consented to wear a business suit. In the end, the barbecue and the concert were a tremendous success, "although it was probably the last time Cliburn ever played in a basketball arena." Because of the cold weather, the event had to be moved at the last minute from the ranch to the Stonewall High School gymnasium.

I was interested to see that our current president has tried to revive this tradition of presidential barbecues in Texas. In November 2001, George W. Bush had Vladimir Putin down to Crawford for a summit conference at his ranch. After the barbecue, some students were allowed to ask the Russian president a few questions, and one of them wanted to know his opinion of the mesquite-smoked tenderloin. Here's his answer, as provided by the translator: "I had a hard time imagining how could a living person create such a masterpiece of cooking." I'm a little concerned about that "living person" part. Do dead persons cook in Russia? If you ever get over there and see barbecue on the menu, perhaps you'd better take a pass.

As far as I can tell from this historical review, there is no correlation between presidential greatness and great barbecue. In fact, one of our most exalted presidents, Franklin D. Roosevelt, may have set the standard for the most pathetic attempt at alfresco state dining. In 1939 he actually served hot dogs to the king and queen of England. It was unimpressive food, but clever political imagery. FDR was trying to show America that our partner in the fight against Hitler was, if not a regular George, at least willing to eat like one from time to time. I would hope that the president knew enough from his extended stays in Warm Springs, Georgia, not to call his little weenie roast a barbecue. I wouldn't be so sure about Eleanor.

Tip O'Neill said that all politics is local. I think the same could be said of barbecue. Every part of the South has its distinctive traditions when it comes to political pork. In western Kentucky, office seekers flock to the mutton barbecue and burgoo feeds that the Catholic churches hold to raise funds. In North Carolina, anyone who wants votes around Charlotte knows to work the crowd at the Mallard Creek Presbyterian Church's annual autumn barbecue, which has been known to attract 20,000 people. In Tennessee, you wouldn't think of running for office without strolling through the tipsy multitudes at the Memphis in May barbecue contest. I saw a photo of Al and Tipper Gore eating ribs there a few years ago. It wasn't flattering; their teeth are bared like wolves ripping apart a small mammal. The wise politician probably ought to spend more time pumping hands than pumping his elbow.

The state that claims the largest political barbecue in history is not, as you might expect, Texas. It's Oklahoma. When he took office as governor in 1923, Jack Walton promised Oklahomans an old-fashioned square dance and barbecue the likes of which had never been seen. The menu sounded like the passenger manifest for Noah's Ark: 289 head of cattle, 70 hogs, 36 head of sheep, 2,540 rabbits, 134 possums, 25 squirrels, 2,000 pounds of bison, 1,500 pounds of reindeer, 15 deer, 1,427 chickens, 210 turkeys, 14 geese, 34 ducks, one antelope, and one five-year-old boy from Tulsa. (I just threw in that last part to see if you were paying attention.) By the time the festivities wound down, more than 50,000 citizens had been fed, and the decimated fields and forests around Oklahoma City were very quiet.

In Georgia, there's one name that's synonymous with politics and barbecue: Talmadge. It started back in the 1920s with Eugene Talmadge, a rural populist who was Georgia's version of Huey Long, without much of the substance. In barbecue terms, we'd say he was all sauce. Perhaps literally: Talmadge died of complications from cirrhosis of the liver. Ole Gene, as his followers knew him, was a colorful stump speaker who'd stand up there snapping his red suspenders, a flock of hair flying loose, and denounce the city slickers in the state capitol and "them lyin' Atlanta newspapers" that told on him. He liked to say that there were only three things that the poor dirt farmers of Georgia could trust: God almighty, the Sears Roebuck catalog, and Gene Talmadge.

Talmadge kicked off his first campaign for governor in 1932 with a huge barbecue that drew 10,000 people to his hometown of McRae, in middle Georgia. Farmers donated scores of pigs and goats and cows and chickens. A local man, Norman Graham, known as the Barbecue King, was appointed to oversee the cooking, which took thirty-six hours to complete. A crowd of townspeople came out to watch, as if the barbecuing and not the speechmaking were the point of it all. William Anderson, in his biography of Talmadge, *The Wild Man from Sugar Creek*, described the scene on the night before as they fired up the Brunswick stew pots: "Insects swirled and buzzed crazily into the string of naked light bulbs that wound over the pits giving a hard brightness to the cooking area." So many bugs flew into the kettles of stew, "drawn there by its sweet aroma, that no pepper had to be added for flavor." As one of the men explained, "Bugs was good spice."

This confirms many of our fears about the ingredients of Southern stews.

Talmadge rode his barbecues and conservative populism to multiple terms as Georgia governor. The *Atlanta Constitution*'s Celestine Sibley, who covered Talmadge at the end of his life, liked to tell a story about what happened to him during one of his campaign appearances. He was headed to a rally in south Georgia, "a fish fry, I believe," and asked his driver to pull over at the next farm so he could borrow the man's outhouse. "Gene goes in there to take care of business—I'm kind of hoping there was nothing to use but a Sears Roebuck catalog," and while he's sitting there a black widow spider bites him on his genitalia. By the time he got to the rally, his undercarriage had swollen up like a nursing sow and he wasn't able to do much but say hello, goodbye and get himself to the doctor.

Gene's son, Herman, followed him in the governor's office in the late 1940s and continued the tradition of Talmadge pork. Actually, it was more Herman's wife, Betty Talmadge. She started a business curing and selling Talmadge hams from their plantation in Lovejoy, south of Atlanta. She always claimed the house was the model for Twelve Oaks in *Gone With the Wind*. She just loved having barbecues on the grounds like the one that begins Margaret Mitchell's novel. Betty published a recipe book called *How To Cook a Pig*, in which she reminisces about a big barbecue she threw for the Carters during the 1976 presidential campaign.

The man who succeeded Herman Talmadge as governor figures in this survey if only for one folksy comment he made at the end of his career. Marvin Griffin was a small-town newspaperman editor of the *Bainbridge Post-Searchlight*, which has always been my favorite name in all the Georgia press. Being a newsman, he knew how to craft a quote. Unfortunately, he was also an awful governor. He spent most of his term in the mid-1950s defending segregation and a remarkably corrupt administration. Another newspaper said that Griffin's philosophy of government could be summed up by saying: "If you ain't for stealing, you ain't for segregation." It was on Marvin's watch that Georgia adopted the Rebel state flag that has caused us so much grief.

Georgia governors back then were restricted to one term at a time, so Griffin had to leave office in 1959. When he ran for another term in 1962, he pulled all the old tricks. He was still as racist as ever, vowing to put Martin Luther King Jr. "so far back in the jail that you'll have to pump air to him." And, of course, he used all the old-fashioned campaign tools, including Talmadge-style barbecues from one end of the state to the other or, as we say in Georgia, from Tybee Island to Rabun Gap.

But Griffin's opponent was more savvy. Carl Sanders was a handsome attorney from Augusta who didn't look or sound like the kind of man who would embarrass Georgia in the nation's eyes. Cufflinks Carl, they called him. He put his faith in TV commercials more than barbecues and stump speaking, and he won the Democratic primary.

Old Marvin seemed to realize that he was a victim of changing times. He told a reporter that he had been deceived by the size of his campaign crowds, which were easily larger than Sanders's. That may have meant something in the old days, but it didn't necessarily matter anymore. Here's the way he put it, and I love this quote: "Everybody that ate my barbecue I don't believe voted for me."

In the forty years since that election, the place of barbecue in politics has evolved considerably. You don't have many pig-pickins on the courthouse square these days. When politicians do a barbecue nowadays, it's usually a $500-a-plate fund-raiser where the party faithful can rub elbows with the candidate, or a catered affair to celebrate a triumph, like Newt's ascension as House speaker. Political barbecues are no longer campaign necessities. Like so many things in American life, they have become in large part self-conscious allusions to our shared heritage. Politicians used to believe they could sway votes with a dram of whiskey or a plate of pork. Now they do it with tax cuts and state lotteries. The barbecue was cheaper.

But that doesn't mean that this tradition is coming to an end. In fact, today there's a whole new field of political barbecue: the cook-off circuit. If you've ever been to Memphis in May or the Big Pig Jig in Georgia or one of the dozens of other barbecue contests throughout the region, you know that there's more going on there than a redneck Mardi Gras. These competitions are as political in their own way as anything the Talmadges ever did. Like the craftiest lobbyists on Capitol Hill, cooking teams do everything in their power to influence the judges. And like all but the most honest legislators, the judges can be influenced. It doesn't take cash under the table; usually a cold beer on a hot day is enough to grease the wheels of deliberation.

But after the lobbying and after the tasting, in the end it still comes down to a vote. And it is then that the conscientious judge realizes that Thomas Jefferson, that great American and quasi-vegetarian, was wrong: All ribs are *not* created equal.

Of course, one of the great things about this country is a person is free to support the barbecue of his choice. In the spirit of that freedom, I'd like to say, God bless the pigs; God bless the politicians; and God bless American barbecue.

Barbecue Sociology
The Meat of the Matter

. . . .

JOHN SHELTON REED

I've almost never before *set out* to write specifically about barbecue. I was only one of a couple of hundred judges at Memphis in May, and that was only because my sister knew the woman who picked the judges. But in the course of writing and talking about the South, I seem to have wound up writing and talking right much about Southern food in general, and smoked meat in particular.

To put some numbers on it, when my wife Dale and I wrote a book called *1001 Things Everyone Should Know about the South*, roughly 1 percent of the 1,001 things—eight of them—dealt with barbecue. And the second-most-quoted sentence I've ever written (I'm embarrassed to say that you can find out these things on the internet: it's like some pathetic day-trader watching his portfolio)—the second-most-quoted sentence I've ever written is this one, from a 1988 review of Greg Johnson and Vince Staten's *Real Barbecue*: "Southern barbecue is the closest thing we have in the U.S. to Europe's wines or cheeses; drive a hundred miles and the barbecue changes." (I'll get to the most quoted sentence I've ever written later.)

I don't think you can really understand the South if you don't understand barbecue—as food, process, and event. If you look at a map of restaurants affiliated with the National Barbecue Association, most of them are in the South. Now, of course, many of the best barbecue joints aren't the kind of establishments that would join—or even know about—something called the National Barbecue Association. Nevertheless, observe where the dots are concentrated.

For the time being, at least, barbecue is Southern. But, as the map shows, it has started to metastasize, popping up wherever large numbers of expatriate Southerners are found—no surprise, because that's who cooks it: Southerners who took their tastes and their techniques with them during the Great Migration out of the South in the first half of the last century.

Like those migrants, barbecue followed well-established migration paths, recapitulating in the process some of the internal divisions within the South that we've been hearing about and that I'll say some more about in a minute. In Oakland and Los Angeles and East Palo Alto you'll find pork ribs, to be sure, but also beef brisket and hot links and baloney—naturally, since most Southerners on the West Coast came from Texas and Oklahoma. Mississippians and West Tennesseans who went to Chicago and Detroit took Memphis-style barbecue—even "dry ribs"—along. And in the Northeast you'll find the distinctive barbecues of the Carolinas and Georgia, cooked and seasoned with techniques that came north on the Chickenbone Special. One of my favorite Northeastern joints, mostly because of its location, was the late Jake and Earl's in Cambridge, Massachusetts, run by Chris Schlesinger from Norfolk. Chris wrote *The Thrill of the Grill*, a pretty good cookbook (although the title contributes to Yankees' endemic confusion about the difference between grilling and barbecuing).

To be sure, barbecue, like jazz, has sometimes changed when it left its Southern birthplace. And, in my opinion, like jazz, not always for the better. A few years ago I read about a New York restaurant called Carolina that served mesquite-grilled pork on a bed of lettuce with Dijon mustard. And just last May Dale and I ate at the Arkansas Barbecue in East London's old Spitalfields Market. Although the proprietor has changed his name to "Bubba" and actually comes from Maryland, he cooks pretty good pulled pork and brisket. But he caters to local taste by serving them with mushy peas.

Anyway, barbecue may someday escape its native Southern matrix and become an all American institution, as Coca-Cola did a century ago, as NASCAR and country music and the Southern Baptist Convention may be doing today. But it hasn't happened yet. Even in the East End of London barbecue still retains its identification with the South. It's still not just *a* Southern food, but almost *the* Southern food.

Which makes it odd is that some conspicuous parts of the South are not especially good places to find it. South Louisiana, of course, but that's not what I'm talking about. I mean towns and cities that have got above their raisin'—or, anyway, want to get above it. You may know the country song by Clyde Egerton that goes "I'm a Quiche Lady in a Barbecue Town." Well, in some Southern towns there are a lot of quiche ladies—of both sexes, domestic and imported—so many in some places that they call the shots. What you get then is a quiche town.

Atlanta is one of them. You can still find good barbecue in Atlanta, but most of the joints are hidden away—off the beaten track, in obscure and sometimes unsavory neighborhoods. Harold's is one of the best—it's near the prison. There used to be a pretty good place on Peachtree Street, Wyolene's, but it closed. Even the Auburn Rib Shack, just down from the Ebenezer Baptist Church, went out of business a while back. It's almost as if downtown Atlanta is ashamed of barbecue—finds it too country, too low-rent.

In fact, it's more polite than accurate to say it's "almost as if they're ashamed." Damn it, they are ashamed. When the Olympics came to town, the fellow in charge of arranging to feed the crowds (a friend of mine from North Carolina) lined up a local African American concessionaire to welcome the world to Georgia with a wonderful array of Southern food—most definitely including barbecue. But the Atlanta Olympic Organizing Committee was desperately eager that visitors understand that Atlanta is a cosmopolitan place—a "world-class, major-league city," as a welcome sign at the airport once proclaimed. When the committee saw the proposed menu, they vetoed it—and hired a food-service firm from Buffalo to sell hot dogs and hamburgers.

Which brings me to the most quoted sentence I've ever written: "Every time I look at Atlanta, I see what a quarter of a million Confederate soldiers died to prevent."

One of the reasons I like Texans is their attitude toward barbecue. Go to Dallas: there's Sonny Bryant's smack downtown, not far from Neiman Marcus. Go to Houston: Goode Company's right out in public where people can find it. These places say: Welcome to Texas. Have some Texas food. We like it, and you will, too.

Yes, there are Southern cities with barbecue pride.

But the real home of real barbecue is in the small-town South. Not Charlotte, North Carolina, say, but Shelby, an hour west—where Dale and I go for supper when we're in Charlotte: barbecue as good as we've ever had at either of two wonderful establishments, Alston Bridge's or Bridge's Barbecue Lodge (I think the two Bridges are cousins or something).

Seriously, start listing great barbecue towns: Lexington, North Carolina (where Vince Staten found sixteen joints for 16,000 people), Goldsboro, Owensboro, Lockhart. . . . The only barbecue Mecca with over a 100,000 population—the only one over 50,000—is Memphis. The South's other cities may have barbecue, sometimes good barbecue, but it's not a religion. And, in many of them, the best on offer these days is at branches of barbecue chains. I don't approve of chain restaurants in general, and I dislike barbecue chains more than most. It was Rousseau who memorably observed the paradox that man is born free and is everywhere in chains. Expansion is not good for barbecue joints. That's a rule almost as reliable as Vince Staten's maxim that a place without flies is no good. (You should ask what the flies know that you don't.) I'm sorry, but Dreamland in Birmingham just isn't as good as Dreamland in Tuscaloosa. If the owner's not around to keep an eye on things, it's a pretty safe bet that both the food and the, ah, ambience will suffer. And it's especially sad when a chain imports somebody else's traditions to a place that ought to celebrate its own. I think about this every time I eat Memphis dry ribs at Corky's in Jackson, or Red, Hot and Blue in Chapel Hill. Which is often. Because when it comes to barbecue the truth is the worst I ever had was good, as Dave Gardner once observed on another subject. (At least I think he was talking about another subject. Sometimes it's hard to tell with Brother Dave.)

Anyway, I think places with local barbecue traditions should shun synthetic tradition, even if it comes from Memphis and tastes pretty good. When I have a choice I prefer the local product, ideally served up in a cinder-block building with a dancing pig sign out front. One reason I prefer it has nothing to do with the food; it has to do with community cohesion.

Go into one of these joints in or near a small Southern town and you're quite likely to find that it has brought all sorts of unlikely people together, just about everyone except quiche ladies: businessmen and construction workers, farmers and lawyers, cowboys and hippies, black and white and everything in-between and sideways, Protestants and Catholics. Even Jews. Some of you may know the Old Smokehouse Barbecue, in Anniston, run by Gershon Weinberg. You've heard the phrase "Root, hog"—well, this is sort of "Kashrut hog."

I once suggested half-seriously that if the South needs a new flag—as it surely does—we could do worse than to use a dancing pig with a knife and fork. You want to talk about heritage, not hate. . . . That represents a heritage we all share and can take pride in. Barbecue both symbolizes and contributes to community. And that's without even mentioning its noncommercial manifestations—for instance, in matters like fund-raising for volunteer fire departments. But there's another side to this coin. It's often the case, and it is in this one, too, that community is reinforced by emphasizing differences from and with outsiders.

There's no denying that barbecue can be divisive. Drive a hundred miles and the barbecue does change. The only constant is slow-cooking with smoke (and, yes, I know some places cook with gas only and call their product "barbecue," but I don't).

Suppose we go with the Southeastern majority and cook pork. Will it be shoulder, ribs, or whole hog? What kind of sauce—mostly vinegar, tomato, or mustard? How hot? How sweet? Will we baste or not? Or forget the sauce and go with a dry rub?

OK. The meat is done. What are the divinely ordained side dishes? Carolina hush puppies? Alabama white bread? Arkansas tamales? (Check out Mc-Clard's in Hot Springs.) Coleslaw is almost universal, but I've only seen boiled white potatoes in eastern North Carolina; rice only in South Carolina; jalapeños only in Texas and Oklahoma. The questions of what to cook, how to cook it, and what to serve with it are not resolved by the individual whim or creativity of the cook. Like Byzantine icon painters, barbecue cooks differ in technique and in skill, but they are working in traditions that pretty much tell them what to produce.

And those traditions reflect and reinforce the fierce localism that has always been a Southern characteristic, the "sense of place" that literary folk claim to find in Southern fiction, the devotion to states' rights and local autonomy that was an established characteristic of Southern politics long before it became a major headache for the Confederate States of America.

As I wrote once, barbecue is not like grits—in more ways than the obvious. Grits (if you'll excuse the image) glue the South together. Barbecue, on the other hand—well, you could say it pits community against community. This rivalry, this competitive aspect of barbecue, has been institutionalized in the formal contests that seem to have become a permanent feature of the Southern landscape. Last time I looked, something called the Sanctioned Barbecue Contest Network sponsored some thirty major contests a year, and the schedules in a fat newspaper called National Barbecue News suggest that there are enough minor-league contests to keep you busy most weekends if you're inclined that way, and some folks are.

One of the biggest and best-known of these competitions is at Memphis in May, where I got to be a judge a few years ago.

Memphis in May offers not just great barbecue but a complete barbecultural experience, including Elvis impersonators, vendors of plastic pig snouts, campaigning politicians, and evangelists distributing leaflets on "What to Do in Case You Miss the Rapture." Not a street mime in sight. Saturday night entertainment is provided by folks like the Reverend Billy C. Wirtz, boogie-woogie piano player and composer of such songs as "Mennonite Surf Party," "Stick Out Your Can ('Cause Here Comes the Garbage Man)," and "Your Greens Give Me the Blues."

The contest takes place in a park right on the banks of the Mississippi, and you can smell the hickory smoke a half-mile away. My year, there were 180-odd teams—some odder than others. One contestant called himself "M. C. Hamhock" and performed a rap number that went

Don't need no knife, don't need no fork,
Just wrap your lips around my pork.

(A couple of weeks ago in San Antonio I saw a sign that went that one better. It said "You don't need no teeth to eat Bob's meat.")

In Memphis, the teams compete not just for the best barbecue, but for the best "area." Some mom-and-pop operations make do with folding lawn chairs and funeral home tents, but other teams erect booths, pavilions, kiosks, huts, gazebos, and God knows what all else, some of them two- and three-story structures with lattice-work, decks, statuary, and hanging plants. Each team has a name, and many have mottoes such as "Hogs smell better barbecued," and "We serve no swine before it's time." Portable generators power everything from electric fans to fountains and neon signs, and over their constant drone mighty sound systems pump out music—mostly country, Cajun, or rap, but when I was there I also heard the Village People's "YMCA."

I saw smokers ranging from backyard Weber pots to an eighteen-wheeler-pulled behemoth billed as the world's largest portable barbecue cooker, but most were roughly coffin-sized, some obviously off-the-rack, but others homemade from fifty-five gallon drums and stovepipe. And everywhere you looked you saw the pig-totem of the People of the Swine.

Now, for years I kept a mental log of barbecue joint signs. I'd seen pigs reclining, running, and dancing; pigs with bibs, with knives and forks, with crowns and scepters. I'd seen pigs as beauty contest winners, pigs in Confederate uniforms, and pigs in cowboy hats (one with a banjo). I'd seen Mr. and Mrs. Pig dressed for a night on the town, and Mr. and Mrs. Pig as American Gothic.

But I had never seen pigs like I saw in Memphis. Pigs in chefs' hats and volunteer firemen's helmets. A pig in a Memphis State football uniform triumphant over some University of Tennessee pigs. A pig in a Superman suit rising from the flames. There was a pig reclining in a skillet; another on a grill, drinking beer. Two pigs basting a little gnomish person on a spit. Lots of pigs drinking beer and a whole trainload of partying pigs on the T-shirts of a team called the Rowdy Southern Swine from Kossuth, Mississippi. It's a hard call, but my favorite was probably some pigs with wings and halos, from a team called Hog Heaven.

For some reason, Italy was being honored by the festival that year, so a number of teams struck what they took to be Italian notes (although if any actual Italians were present to receive this hands-across-the-sea homage I didn't run into them). Some booths were decorated with hanging bunches of plastic grapes or simulated marble columns, and there were almost as many Italian flags as Confederate ones. T-shirts said "Ciao Down." And of course the pig signs got into the act. Pigs ate pizza. Pigs wore handlebar mustaches. Pigs reclined in gondolas. Pigs stomped grapes. Pigs posed in gladiator gear and togas and Mafia outfits.

Among the humans, some men wore overalls, Western clothes, or biker gear, but since it was well over ninety degrees in the shade, most wore shorts and T-shirts, revealing all too plainly what beer and barbecue can do to the male physique. Female attire ran to halter tops and cutoffs. The cutoffs had often been decorated with stickers lovingly applied to passing butts by free-lance inspectors in pig noses. The stickers said things like "HOT," "Can't Touch This," "Roman Hands," and "USDA Choice."

Professor that I am, I couldn't help but think of a grim "feminist-vegetarian" monograph I'd run across called *The Sexual Politics of Meat*. If its poor author had come to Memphis with me, she'd probably have been carried off gibbering. As a matter of fact, pig people seem to be politically incorrect on just about every score. I once saw a column in the *National Barbecue News* urging compassion for victims of HIV—high intake of vegetables.

Memphis in May teams also competed on "showmanship," based on musical routines with barbecue and Italian themes. "White boys can't dance" was my sister's summary of one of these efforts, but I reminded her that black ones probably couldn't either after drinking as much beer as some of these guys had. Shoot, they were doing pretty well to stand.

Inevitably, given the Italian connection, several skits celebrated the concept of barbecue pizza, which I gather is actually served as a regular thing at one Memphis restaurant. I ate some at the judges' reception, and it's not quite as vile as it sounds.

Anyway, I'd been worried that I was out of my depth, but the orientation session for the judges reassured me. Our instructor began with the basics ("If you don't eat pork, please let us know"), and he moved on to matters of deportment ("Stay sober until after the judging") and ethics ("If your ex-wife's boyfriend is on a team, you should disqualify yourself").

We were introduced to the rating scheme and told what to look for in the meat and sauce. I was a rib judge, and "on-site" as opposed to "blind," and there were so many of us judges because nearly two hundred teams were competing in three divisions (ribs, shoulder, and whole-hog). Each entry was to be judged by six of us, and each of us was to judge only three to six entries.

When the pork finally met the palate, the best ribs I had were cooked by those Mississippians from Kossuth. The smell made my mouth water. When I picked up a rib and examined it, I saw a crisp brown crust over moist, tender meat, pink from smoking, the color even from end to end. The meat came easily off the bone but kept its integrity (none of the mushiness that comes from parboiling). This meat had been cooked with dry, cool smoke, and lots of patience. A dry rub sealed in the juices, but most of the fat had long since melted and dripped away.

The rib tasted as good as it smelled: sweet and smoky; crunchy, chewy, and melt-in-your-mouth, all at the same time. As for the sauce. . . . Well, I can't describe it without sounding like an ad in *Southern Living*: "A symphony of Southern flavors: tart Sea Island tomatoes, mellow onions from Vidalia, sweet-and-sour molasses from Louisiana cane fields, and the Latin kick of peppers from South Texas. A sauce the color of Tennessee clay, with the fiery heat of an Alabama afternoon and the long, slow sweetness of a Kentucky evening." Or, worse, like a wine critic: "A sauce of great character and finesse. Bright claret color, with a complex, peppery nose. Lusty full-bodied taste: tomato catsup and chili the principal notes, with a definite garlic background and hints of—could it be grape jelly? Balance sustained throughout. An assertive finish and a pronounced afterburn." (I made all that up, actually, except for the grape jelly, which I'll bet anything was the secret ingredient in one sauce I tasted.)

In the end, none of the teams I judged even placed. The winners came— well, they came from Illinois, of all places, although they graciously pointed out that their hometown is only thirty-five miles north of the Mason-Dixon Line. Still, from Illinois! It just goes to show what Yankees can do when they put their minds to it. But I'll bet my guys had more fun, and I was pleased to find that I could discriminate intelligently among several first-rate plates of ribs.

Speaking of sauces, and of competition, leads me to the matter of what is another long-standing rivalry, as you're learning if you didn't already know: that between eastern and western North Carolina.

Just last month a writer named Carroll Leggett set off a new battle in that ancient conflict with a column in Raleigh's *Metro* magazine about the barbecue he was raised with: East Carolina–style chopped whole-hog, with a simple vinegar and red pepper sauce. Not surprisingly, he likes it. He even likes the surprises that chopped whole-hog offers. I'm going to quote him at length:

> At Eastern [barbecue] shrines kids sit in wonderment every meal and fish objects from their barbecue:
> "Hey, Mom, what's this?" they ask.

"That's just gristle, Antoine.

"That's just skin, Ashley.

"That's just a piece that cooked too long, Latonya.

"That's just a li'l ole piece of bone, Puddin.

"I don't know what it is, Sean." Whap! "Just shut up and eat it."

Now, if Leggett had just extolled his native style of barbecue, no one would have minded. No one would have noticed. But he went on to deprecate western, "Lexington-style" barbecue as mere "roasted pork shoulders chopped and mixed with a thick tomato sauce that masks the meat's flavor and textural sameness." He noted the absence of "ribs, tenderloin, and crispy skin" and complained about the lack of these "special parts to vie for"—even with its implication that there are . . . other parts.

Well, that put the fat in the fire. Within days there was a website where Tar Heels could vote their preferences for eastern or western barbecue, and I was getting email from friends, acquaintances, and total strangers across the state urging me to vote. (One pointed out that I was allowed to vote once a day, and begged me to do so.) I found it interesting that all these lobbyists apparently just assumed that I, like all reasonable people, share their preference.

In truth, I like both Tar Heel varieties—to paraphrase Will Rogers, I've never met a smoked pig I didn't like. I've never said in public whether I like eastern or western better. State employees are supposed to stay out of politics. Besides, I live in Chapel Hill, right on the border between eastern and western, and, anyway, even after thirty-three years I'm still a Tennessean, an outlander, so I tend to keep my head down when these intrastate battles flare up.

After many years in Chapel Hill I've come to love simple vinegar and red pepper. East Carolina minimalism. It respects the meat. But in Mississippi, out of the cross fire, I will confess that I really do like sweet, red sauce on my barbecue. Maybe this shouldn't be surprising, since East Tennessee, where I'm from, used to be western North Carolina—far western North Carolina.

Let me close by discussing the kind of barbecue *I* grew up with, the barbecue from a joint in Piney Flats, Tennessee, called, simply, the Ridgewood.

Now, when you think of great barbecue towns, Piney Flats doesn't come to mind. In fact, nowhere in East Tennessee comes to mind. But right outside Bluff City, midway between Johnson City and Bristol, a stone's throw from Kingsport (where Vince Staten and my wife and I grew up), is this modest-looking place that since 1948 has served what *People* magazine once called the best barbecue in the country—and therefore, obviously, in the world.

OK (I hear you say), but what does *People* magazine know about barbecue?

JOHN SHELTON REED

Well, try this: The Ridgewood is the only out-of-state establishment mentioned in Bob Garner's book, *North Carolina Barbecue: Flavored by Time.* Given Tar Heels' largely justifiable chauvinism in these matters, that's a testimonial indeed—although, to be sure, Bluff City is only some twenty-five miles from the North Carolina line.

When I was a lad, people drove a long way to eat at the Ridgewood, despite notoriously capricious hours and service that ranged from brusque to surly. That service was almost as legendary as the food. In *Real Barbecue*, Vince quoted a devotee who said that going to the Ridgewood was like going to the Don Rickles Restaurant.

Well, last month Dale and I went back there with Fred Sauceman, and the place has changed a bit. We were almost disappointed to have a waitress who was downright pleasant. We were also disappointed to find squeeze bottles of sauce on the tables. In the old days, the management had definite ideas about how much sauce to use: a lot. This nectar was poured over the thin-sliced pork before it was served. You ate what was put before you.

So, the times they are a-changin'. But so far the barbecue hasn't—good pork, well smoked, served with a fabulous sauce—and that combination is what has drawn folks to the Ridgewood for a half-century now. Like most sauces west of Raleigh, it's sweet, thick, and red. But the flavor is marvelously complex. Think of it as Overmountain Baroque. Think of it as what the catsup will taste like in heaven.

In Xanadu Did Barbecue

RIPLEY GOLOVIN HATHAWAY

Today's national enthusiasm for barbecue and its associated foods is the culmination of a 150-year evolution. While tradition and climate combined to help establish the barbecue as a Southern institution of long standing, the national adaptation of the food and the event were a bit longer in coming. It was a progression shaped and molded by changes in technology and world events.

As America approached the twentieth century, an outdoor movement burgeoned. The restraint and decorum of the Gilded Age gave way to a more relaxed style of living and entertaining. While the warmer climate of the South had made porches a necessity and outdoor dining a popular alternative, picnics and porches proliferated in places where they had been rarer before. People in the less temperate climates of the country began to reexamine their relationship to nature.

In the North, picnics were the precursor to barbecues. On all-day outings, perhaps to one of the facilities of the newly established National Park System, the picnic eliminated a trip home for lunch and enabled people to enjoy the outdoors for longer spans of time. It was a common-sense solution that was destined to become chic. By the early 1900s, picnics became extremely elaborate. Women prepared and served traditional food at these affairs: cold sandwiches, deviled eggs, and chocolate cake. As Americans' affinity for the outdoors increased, they also sought to enjoy the outdoors during the work week. The wide acceptance of sleeping porches at the turn of the century facilitated the movement from the dining parlor to the porch. As Charles Aked, writing for *Colliers* in 1910, put it, "Anyone who has not yet formed the habit of eating on the porch in summer has not yet fathomed the delights of warm weather."

The porch by the end of the nineteenth century had become a firmly established part of an American home. It marked simultaneously the beginning of the integration of the house and its surrounding environment and the differentiation of covered outdoor living spaces. The mass production of the car and the development of the bungalow in the teens furthered America's love affair with the country. Simultaneously, an informal and inexpensive home architecture that incorporated within it the natural environment sprang up in California. It was to be the precursor of the suburban home of the 1920s.

While developments in both architecture and automobile manufacture enhanced an American's independence, they sparked the demise of neighborliness and community. With these inventions life became more insular and families turned inward, giving birth to the small-family hot picnic.

In 1913 Henry Ford opened his Highland Park Assembly Plant and with it a new era of car manufacturing. Production rose and prices fell, both by more than 50 percent. No longer locked into railroad schedules, a city family could drive out to the country and have a picnic when they desired. By 1920, more than four million Tin Lizzies zoomed around the country, driven by the large new middle class that industrialization had created.

Auto-camps, which charged for the use of their grounds and cooking facilities, sprang up all over. There, people would fry bacon in a skillet over a fire or eat a picnic brought from home. A fireless cooker provided hot food, if needed. Heated and filled before leaving, this ceramic container cooked the food as people traveled to their picnic spot.

Gertrude S. Mathews wrote in 1915 of a precursor to the backyard barbecue, the bacon bat. Mathews perceived it as a campfire dinner of bacon, wieners, and chips held in one's backyard. As similar as a bacon bat may be to many people's conception of a barbecue, it lacked the emphasis on the process of cooking the meat that characterizes a true barbecue. Other articles of the period often discussed broiling steak but made no mention of cooking it over wood coals. Rather, they spoke at length about pan broiling in the oven.

During World War I, the auto manufacturers Ford, Leland, and Durant, turned their plants over to the war effort, producing aircraft engines, submarine chasers, tanks, helmets, hand grenades, and trucks. The housing industry ceased production as its supply of materials was redirected to the war effort. The pent-up demand for new homes in the early 1920s led builders to experiment with a new and inexpensive housing type—the bungalow.

The word bungalow, an Indian term for a small house, was applied to a modern house style, a style characterized by its single story and low roof. It was the architectural successor to the Victorian cottage popularized by prominent architect Frank Lloyd Wright. As Americans were pushed back from the woods, as the roads became clogged with cars, and as the new architecture thrust man into his surrounding environment, conditions had ripened for the birth of the backyard barbecue.

Eleven years after the mass production of autos began at Highland Park, Nell Nichols's 1924 piece, "The Backyard Barbecue," appeared in *Woman's Home Companion*. It was the first national magazine article on the subject. These early "barbecues" retained visible vestiges of the picnic. From the article's subtitle, "Just the right picnic for a big hungry crowd," to its thoughts on appropriate entertainment, the article presented the barbecue as "the unusual way to entertain informally during the late summer or fall." The menu presented would, with a few revisions, become standard in places that didn't have their own long-standing barbecue traditions of whole hogs or sides of beef.

> Considerable choice is offered in the meats to be barbecued, although beef and chicken are the general favorites. Thick steaks and chops of all kinds are delicious as are roasts of beef, mutton, and lamb. When the meat is cooked it is served without delay. A table on the lawn holds, besides dishes and silver, the other food, which may consist of potato chips or salad, sliced tomatoes or cucumbers, cottage cheese garnished with thin slices of sweet green pepper, sliced onion, rolls or bread, milk or iced tea, and fresh fruits or iced melons. Coffee may be made on the coals, and corn on the cob boiled in the kitchen or roasted in the ashes is an ever welcomed dish.

By 1926 Helen Powell Schauffler would write in her *Good Housekeeping* article, "Over the Picnic Fire," "food cooked out of doors is usually rather hearty and it is wasteful and unwise to make sandwiches with tempting rich fillings. You would not dream of serving olive and nut sandwiches with a broiled steak at your table so why do it out-of-doors?"

The nascent barbecue had yet to formally distinguish itself from the picnic. Charcoal as fuel was recommended for emergency purposes only; later it would become de rigueur for any decent barbecue. Readers were directed to cook the meats in a frying pan as one would do at home on a stove. The "cook picnic" resembled a new species. It was so changed that in a 1927 *Ladies Home Journal* article entitled "The Little Barbecue Makes a Super Supper," Hortense King proclaimed, "It is true that the well known picnic appetite is still present, also the little green bugs and the stand pat mosquitoes, not to mention the rain cloud that floats up and blows over just as the supplies are being set out. . . . But nothing else of the traditional picnic remains—not even a sign of the cold chicken and colder pies, the weighty meats and cheeses, the oozing layer cakes."

With 1927, articles first mentioning the presence of, and reasons behind, male cooks appeared. In a 1927 *Sunset Magazine* article entitled "Drive Right In," the owner of a California auto-park, where people came to picnic and cook on the fireplaces provided, observed that the men did most of the cooking. He theorized that men cooked because they felt they knew more about campfires and campfire cooking.

The advent of disposable plates, cups, and utensils meant that the barbecue could be more self-service. With everyone, including the children, participating to some degree in the preparation and cooking of the meal, the need for games or planned entertainment disappeared. The barbecue, unrushed, soothing—the antithesis of the workday world—brought people together on an informal basis.

A momentous year, 1929 saw the stock market crash and the appearance of the outdoor fireplace. Throughout the decade-long depression that ensued, the outdoor fireplace, around which the barbecue centered, multiplied. First created in California, it became a possibility for backyards nationwide as articles in women's magazines focused on the fireplace's adaptability and the appeal of outdoor fireplaces to the male appetite. Related articles on etiquette, furnishings, and little artistic touches conceived to enhance the barbecue accompanied these pieces.

In July of 1929, *Sunset Magazine*, with its West Coast middle-class readership, was the first publication to do an article on outdoor fireplaces. A year later an article in the nationally distributed *Ladies Home Journal* proclaimed: "Now comes the outdoor fireplace, with its companion table and benches, under intimate shade, to invite picnicking in one's own garden. Breakfast bacon served hot off the open air grill when the scent of flowers is fresh with the morning; a barbecued dinner away from the walls at the end of a hot summer day. . . . Here is an idea evolved by California and rapidly becoming a Vogue on the Coast, which begins as a highly practical contribution to kitchen economy and ends by becoming a decorative element in landscaping the garden."

Outdoor fireplace construction was either attached or detached. Both styles were massive affairs of brick, stone, or cement. At first the attached fireplace, adjacent to the house, with a common chimney but separate fireback and flue, was the most common. The detached grill built out in the garden away from the house would in time become the more popular of the two. Larger than the electric ranges now prevalent in the American kitchen, detached fireplaces usually dominated the space in which they sat. All had grills, metal racks placed at waist level over the pit area that held the fuel. Some even had spits and ovens.

The outdoor fireplace is of Spanish origin, descended from the *chimenea del patio* (patio chimney), which was often constructed on the patio in a hacienda-style home. That cooking apparatus had hooks from which a pot of beans could be suspended over the heat and a grill over which meat could be cooked, all alongside a beehive-shaped adobe oven on the patio of the California hidalgo's hacienda. This structure, and variations on it, would become so popular across the country that in a March 1, 1937, article for *American Home*, George Carpenter would write, "The home-owning class of people in this country consists of two groups; those who have outdoor fireplaces and those who wish they had them. Nothing in the way of home modernization in recent years has caught the public fancy like the outdoor fireplace and grills."

Ironically, the outdoor fireplace was popular with those who could afford it because it was convenient and inexpensive. No longer did one have to pack up food and travel to the campground, the outdoors could be enjoyed with the comforts of home—the real napkins, cold drinks, and comfortable tables and chairs. The upper-middle class of California and the suburban Northeast and Midwest invested time and money in their barbecues because in these places al fresco dining had come to be viewed as luxurious.

Outdoor cooking differed from its indoor counterpart in that the man presided over the grill. It was his. He commissioned it or maybe even built it himself. Thus articles like Harry Botsford's 1937 *American Home* piece, "Picnics Give a Man a Chance," began to appear. Cooking was an important two-part process involving the man and his wife. She bought, and he cooked.

During the Great Depression the barbecue outside the South remained largely an upper-middle-class affair. Who else could afford the fireplace, the steaks, and the magazines that talked of the barbecue and its paraphernalia? Articles in the women's magazines in the summers of 1939–41 sounded very much like those of previous years, impressing the reader with the barbecue's fashionableness—"This Year Give a Barbecue," *Woman's Home Companion* suggested. In 1939 President Franklin Roosevelt and his wife Eleanor served the visiting King George of England hot dogs grilled over their outdoor fireplace in Hyde Park, New York. The barbecue, though long fashionable, was now socially acceptable. Instructions for the novice on how to do it continued to be provided. *Reader's Guide to Periodicals* lists more than twenty articles on barbecue preparation during the period between July 1939 and August 1941. During the war years, the number of articles dwindled to five from September 1941 to September 1945.

Once America became involved in World War II, the forced rationing of food and petroleum products began. In order to buy these commodities, consumers needed not only the requisite number of dollars, but the requisite number of points as well. Now that citizens were allocated a mere three gallons of gasoline a week for their cars, barbecues became less frequent, and their menus were altered. The casual afternoon jaunt to the country ended. The response, as *House Beautiful* put it in June of 1942, was to use your "Backyard as Your Summer Home." *American Home* and other magazines began to sell patterns complete with "construction drawings and material specifications" for building an outdoor fireplace.

Steak once again dominated the menu. Americans had become so predisposed to this cut of meat that one 1947 article in *House and Garden,* after extolling the virtues of the good Western-style steak, discussed at length ten places where the reader could obtain the best steak and potatoes. All the restaurants were in California, and all but one, the Brown Derby, grilled their meat. James Beard's barbecue cookbook, *Cook it Outdoors,* was published in 1941, signifying the professionalization of this mode of cooking.

Urbanites, who lacked a yard but owned a penthouse, broiled their Fourth of July steak on a portable grill. The first portable grills appeared in the late 1930s and were homemade. In 1940, *American Home* published an article referring to an industry-constructed portable.

Men continued to cook, but they cooked less steak. A pound of porterhouse steak cost twelve points and would feed at most two people, while one pound of hamburger cost seven points and could feed twice as many people. Recipes for burgers with fillers such as bran and carrots proliferated.

In the postwar years, the general population of the country, and its middle class in particular, grew substantially. Immediately after the war, manufacturers began to mass produce new goods for the consumer, including the portable grill. Its mobility and low price quickly made it more popular than the outdoor fireplace. In 1946, in the summer after the war, magazine articles returned with renewed vigor to the barbecue. At least eight articles in magazines such as *House Beautiful, American Home,* and *Popular Mechanics* touted the portable barbecue. Constructed of aluminum, a technological by-product of the war, manufacturers produced many styles and sizes: rectangular and circular, with and without warming ovens, spits, and incinerators. Some had detachable legs that enabled them to be put in the trunk of the car. They ranged in price from as low as $8 for a small, no-frills model to as much as $39.95 for a twenty-one-inch grill on wheels without a spit.

Why did the permanent indoor barbecue become so popular in the 1950s? The technology had finally arrived as industry concentrated on manufacturing consumer goods with unprecedented intensity. America's real average income by 1956 was over 50 percent higher than in 1929. People could afford new products. The interior architecture of the house had changed. The kitchen had opened up. It flowed into the dining area and the dining area into the living area. "Rooms" and the walls that defined them disappeared.

Instead of adding more rooms, Americans added more patios. Often they had two patios, one between the carport and the bedroom and the other in the U hollow of the living room–dining room–bedroom area. The second terrace became the barbecue shelter. More articles were written about the barbecue in the 1950s, in particular in the years 1953 and 1954, than any other time before 1980.

The next addition to the barbecue equipment arsenal came in the late 1950s with the introduction of the Japanese hibachi. Technically, we imported the Japanese *hichirin*. By definition the hibachi does not have a separate charcoal bowl and is used exclusively for heating. Nevertheless, the hibachi, miniature grill, or brazier, operating on as few as six to eight charcoal briquettes, was inexpensive, economical, and fun — and therefore popular. Food could be cooked wherever people were.

When Henry Ford manufactured the first charcoal briquettes in 1924, supply exceeded demand. He made them from wood leftover from his Model T assembly plants. He chose the briquette's pillow shape because it decreased shipping bulk and improved quality. A company employee suggested cooking with it. Ford sent briquette shipments to all his dealers for two decades. This idea did not work. Early barbecue grills used wood, and, though later grills used charcoal, the method remained linked to a small class of people. In 1951, there were only four manufacturers of charcoal; by 1963, there more than fifty. The largest of these was the Kingsford Company, which in 1951 had bought out the old Ford Company. By 1963, 500 million pounds of charcoal would be used by 40 million cooks to prepare 1.5 billion meals a year.

The best indication of the growth that followed in the 1960s and 1970s is the history of the Weber-Stephen Company, a manufacturer of barbecue grills. The founder of the company, George Stephen, was in 1956 part owner of Weber Brothers Metal, a Chicago sheet metal factory. That year his desire for a smokeless, slow-cooking, evenly heated grill led him to design the first Weber grill, with its distinctive spherical bowl and cover. By 1958, Stephen left Weber Brothers and founded Weber-Stephen Products because of the demand. In 1964, he opened another factory to increase production. By 1976, the $80, 22½-inch kettle, with sales increases of 25 to 40 percent a year, had returned over $20 million in sales revenue from an international market of the United States, Europe, Australia, New Zealand, and Japan.

Weber equipment helped balconies beckon city dwellers to the grill. An integral part of apartment houses constructed in the 1950s, the balcony by the 1960s was perceived as "the sign of someone who could not afford to go away on weekends." Nevertheless this was the period when apartment dwellers who did not possess a penthouse first entered the barbecue movement. Weber had developed a kettle grill that attached to the balcony railing. It cost only $34.95. New York City's fire code, which prohibited open fires within the city limits, was ignored.

So taken with the barbecue were New Yorkers that Hammacher-Schlemmer showed increased sales of aluminum waterfalls and tents to protect the balcony barbecuer from the weather. City dwellers could barbecue year-round.

In the sixties and seventies, such traditional carriers of barbecue articles as *Ladies Home Journal, House Beautiful,* and *Better Homes and Gardens* significantly reduced their coverage of barbecue. However, magazines with a specialized readership—*Ebony, Seventeen, Esquire,* and *Fifty Plus*—began publishing such articles. Ironically, *Ebony* courted black readers, the originators of American barbecue. This trend reflected the tremendous assimilation of blacks into white American culture during the 1960s and 1970s. *Ebony,* founded in 1945, did not print its first article related to the barbecue, "Dishes for Patio Dining," until 1961. Photographed were Pork Kabobs and California Spare Ribs; lesser emphasis was put on a Lamb Chop Mixed Grill and Homestyle Hamburger. Three years elapsed before the magazine wrote its next article on barbecuing, "Budget Barbecue." In 1975, *Ebony* would run an article entitled "Barbecue is Favored by Blacks of all Classes." It was part of an issue devoted to the middle-class black: "Without doubt, the black middle class and the masses share one common posture. For barbecues are recognized as a graceful, informal way to entertain whether on a penthouse garden, or in the heart of the ghetto. Part of its popularity rises from the fact that there is no substitute for the true tangy flavor of barbecued meat."

The increased overseas travel by Americans made possible by fleets of jet airplanes that lowered the cost of a ticket created a consumer more sophisticated and international in his or her outlook. The new style revealed itself most conspicuously at the dinner table. Editors adapted recipes to the barbecue. The consummate culinarist, Craig Claiborne, a Mississippi native presumably raised on traditional Southern barbecue, paved the way in his September 3, 1961, *New York Times* magazine article, "The Last Best Barbecue." He included a recipe for Pork Satay, a barbecued pork dish of East Indonesian origin. Twenty-three months later, in an article entitled "Back to Basic Barbecue," he reversed course, stating, "The current mania for charcoal cooking has led outdoor chefs to indulge in some far-flung flights of culinary fancy. Sauces for the barbecue may contain ingredients that range from vin ordinaire to champagne, from lemon and lime to pomegranate juice."

Mr. Claiborne's call went unheeded. In the next fifteen years, articles would present barbecue recipes from Argentina, Pakistan, Australia, Armenia, Yugoslavia, Brazil, India, and Mongolia. The backyard barbecue, versatile and adaptable, became an American industry that continues to grow.

We Didn't Know from Fatback

A Southern Jewish Perspective on Barbecue

MARCIE COHEN FERRIS

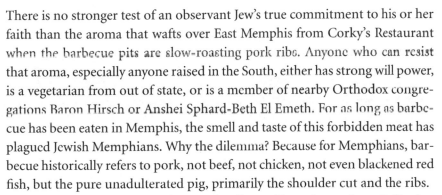

There is no stronger test of an observant Jew's true commitment to his or her faith than the aroma that wafts over East Memphis from Corky's Restaurant when the barbecue pits are slow-roasting pork ribs. Anyone who can resist that aroma, especially anyone raised in the South, either has strong will power, is a vegetarian from out of state, or is a member of nearby Orthodox congregations Baron Hirsch or Anshei Sphard-Beth El Emeth. For as long as barbecue has been eaten in Memphis, the smell and taste of this forbidden meat has plagued Jewish Memphians. Why the dilemma? Because for Memphians, barbecue historically refers to pork, not beef, not chicken, not even blackened red fish, but the pure unadulterated pig, primarily the shoulder cut and the ribs.

The taste of Memphis barbecue, the allure of its culture, the cult-like behavior of its followers, and its overwhelming presence throughout the city cause one to consider the irony that such a phenomenon coexists with one of the largest Orthodox congregations in the nation. Did a higher power place these Orthodox Jews in Memphis to test their faith? Is Memphis barbecue in some way responsible for the fact that one of the nation's largest Reform congregations is also located in the city? In the past, there was little middle ground when it came to Jewish observance in Memphis. Until the first Conservative congregation in Memphis was founded in the 1950s, Memphis Jews were either Orthodox or Reform. For four generations Memphis Jews have either embraced or rejected pork barbecue in their food traditions.

But times are changing in Memphis, and these changes reveal a Jewish middle ground and a new era of kosher barbecue. For the past thirteen years, the "World's Only Kosher Barbecue Contest" has been held in Memphis, sponsored by Orthodox congregation Anshei Sphard-Beth El Emeth. An equally significant development is under way at Jewish-owned Corky's, one of Memphis's most popular barbecue restaurants. Owners Barry and Don Pelts, longtime members of Reform congregation Temple Israel, are now selling a kosher version of their popular barbecue sauce. (They sell over a million bottles of their nonkosher sauce annually.)

John Egerton discusses Southern barbecue styles in his book, *Southern Food*, and quotes David Dawson's statement that pit barbecue in Memphis is "that element which binds us into a community. Barbecue is a social cause, something which gives meaning to our existence. . . . It is also a family affair, a church function . . . and in Memphis and west Tennessee, barbecue sometimes seems to take on the trappings of a state religion."

These sentiments toward barbecue and its importance within the community are clearly appreciated by Memphis Jews. They consider whether rejecting pork barbecue excludes them from the overall community. Or worse, does rejection of the city's "culinary religion" make Memphis Jews sacrilegious? Although the answer to both questions is technically "yes," white and black, Jewish and Gentile Southerners understand the significance of religious boundaries. Because Jews in the South have long been known by their Gentile neighbors as "a people of the book," their unusual dietary restrictions have been respected for generations.

Black and white Gentiles in Memphis not only acknowledge Jewish dietary practices, they also support Jewish efforts to maintain kashrut. In observant Jewish homes throughout the South, African American domestic workers mastered the Jewish dietary laws, often better than their Jewish employers. Memphian Fannie Kaplan recalls a conversation with Maggie McEwen, an African American domestic worker from Mason, Tennessee, who came to work for her family in the 1940s. "Where do you keep your milk things, your meat things, your *pareve* things?" asked McEwen. "Why do you need to know?" asked Kaplan. "This is going to be my kitchen, and I need to know," replied McEwen, who had learned kashrut from a previous Jewish employer. Fannie Kaplan recalled Maggie McEwen's horror when Kaplan once attempted to put Crisco into a "meat" skillet using a "milk" spoon. The mistake never happened again.

When observant Jewish peddlers traveled country roads outside cities such as Memphis, farm families did their best to provide foods they could eat. The best option was usually hard-boiled eggs, since even cooked vegetables were flavored with pork. How to respect Jewish dietary laws in a region that consumed not just barbecue, but bacon, ham, lard, head meat, chitterlings, pig feet, salt pork, fat back, side meat, white meat, pot likker, and pig ears was a challenge. Joe Gray Taylor noted that "so long as he had pork, the Southerner ate it every day and at nearly every meal."

A Jewish peddler in Perry County, Alabama, was invited to eat dinner with a farm family. He hungrily consumed the roast pork and black-eyed peas cooked with fatback and sopped up the remains of the pot likker with his lard-enriched biscuit. The farmer's wife watched in amazement and said to the peddler, "But, Mr. Schwarz, I thought that Moses forbid the children of Israel from eating anything from the pig!" "My dear madam," replied Mr. Schwarz, "if God had spoken to Moses in Perry County, Alabama, he would never have issued such an edict!"

Memphis Jews, like their Gentile neighbors, longed for the camaraderie that could only take place near a smoking barbecue pit or at a table laden with a "mess of ribs" and sides of coleslaw, baked beans, and potato salad. And even more tempting than community was the quest for that flavor of true Memphis barbecue. Seeking both taste and community in 1988, the Jews of Anshei Sphard-Beth El Emeth found it.

Melvin Katz has been interested in cooking on grills and smokers since the late 1950s, when he first discovered this method of cooking while in the army in El Paso, Texas. Katz brought this interest with him back to his native Memphis, where he and his Texas-born wife, Estaline, live today. Longtime members of Orthodox congregation Anshei Sphard-Beth El Emeth, they have grown increasingly observant and today maintain a kosher home. Melvin's religious beliefs somewhat complicated his interest in barbecuing. His original barrel smoker, constructed by his Texas father-in-law, did not satisfy the laws of kashrut. Today, Melvin's collection of barbecue equipment has expanded to include a fish grill, a fish smoker, a meat grill, a meat smoker, and a smoker exclusively for use at Passover.

After challenging the superiority of each others' smoked briskets for many years, Melvin Katz and his friend Ira Weinstein decided it was time for a kosher barbecue contest. In the late 1980s, they approached the officials at the Memphis in May Barbecue Cooking Contest about sponsoring a kosher event, but the idea was never approved. The congregants at Anshei Sphard-Beth El Emeth decided to go it on their own, and in 1988 the world's first kosher barbecue contest was launched. In a traditional barbecue contest contestants bring their own customized grills and smokers, secret sauces, spice mixes, and meat purchased from their suppliers. Not so in a kosher competition. Officers of the shul agreed to purchase barbecue pits for each team, and these pits remained the property of the shul for future contests. Each team pays the shul one hundred dollars, for which they receive a slab of kosher beef ribs, a kosher brisket, and a certified kosher grill to use for the contest. The team also receives other ingredients necessary for sauces, spice mixes, and marinades that are preapproved by the shul and then purchased by a volunteer at one of the local kosher food purveyors. Contestants are allowed to use the shul kitchen on the Thursday prior to the Sunday contest and are not allowed back in the kitchen until after Shabbos on Saturday evening.

Of course, each team has their own special recipe. Melvin Katz's recipe came from Rosie Niter, the African American wife of Robert Niter, a former employee for the Katz's auto business. Knowing her reputation as a wonderful cook, Katz asked Niter for help. "I need to know how to make a good barbecue sauce," said Katz. "That's no problem," said Niter. "I can show you." When Niter showed up with Katz at the synagogue on the Thursday night prior to the first contest, Katz's friends accused him of bringing in a "ringer." The Niter/Katz sauce is a sweet hot sauce, flavored with garlic, lemon, and sugar. He also makes up a spice rub of black pepper, garlic powder, cayenne, and white vinegar that he rubs on the meat and then uses as a basting sauce during the smoking process.

Today, the contest has grown from ten to thirty teams and, like the Memphis in May competition, has its own corporate sponsor and celebrity judges. Kroger's supermarket hosts the contest and supplies all the kosher ingredients, including the meat. Past judges have included Corky's Barry Pelts and Nick Vergos, son of Charlie Vergos, who founded the Rendezvous, a celebrated institution in Memphis barbecue history. Each team now receives two grills, one for ribs and one for brisket, which are the two main categories for the contest. Awards are also given for best team name. Memorable names include "The Holy Smokers," the "Alte Cookers" ("alta cocker" is Yiddish for old man), "Grillin n' Tefillin," the "Three Brisketeers," and "So Fine Bovine."

Barry Pelts says the most common question he is asked about his involvement in Corky's is, "What's a nice Jewish boy doing in the barbecue business?" "Everybody kids around," says Barry, "that you either have to be black or Jewish to work at Corky's." Following in the footsteps of his father, Don Pelts, who founded Corky's in 1984, Barry actively develops new products for the company. He recently developed a kosher barbecue sauce and is now selling kosher barbecued beef, brisket, chicken, and smoked turkeys by special order and for fund-raising events.

Corky's caters many events in the Jewish community, including Temple Israel's annual Chanukah party and its brotherhood dinners, which feature barbecued beef brisket and chicken. Providing a kosher product, however, is a much larger challenge. When the restaurant first opened, it was criticized by the Orthodox. "The rabbis talked about it in shul," said Pelts. The criticism ceased over time. Fourth-generation members at Temple Israel, the Pelts family contributes to Jewish causes throughout the city and donates Corky's non-pork mail-order barbecue for Jewish functions across the country.

When Orthodox leaders at Memphis Hebrew Academy called and asked Corky's to cater their annual kosher fund-raising dinner, Barry Pelts and his father Don agreed they would rise to the challenge. "Everybody that is Orthodox here in Memphis can't eat our food," said Barry, "but they hear about it." Catering the fund-raising dinner gave the Pelts family an opportunity to share Corky's flavor with the Orthodox community with the assurance that the meal was certified kosher. After three months of planning with Rabbi Nathan Greenblatt, who oversees the Memphis va'ad (a local organization of rabbis and mashgiachs, Orthodox Jews who inspect and makes sure all laws of kashrut are observed), Corky's team was ready. They purchased new utensils, scorched the ovens, and thoroughly cleaned the production kitchens to kasher them for the kosher barbecue. The rabbi met in Olive Branch, Mississippi, with Corky's suppliers to ensure that all the ingredients were kosher. "It was the talk of the town," said Barry. "It was the biggest fund-raiser they've ever had at Hebrew Academy. . . . The whole Orthodox community, they went nuts over it."

In the fall of 2002, Don and Barry Pelts again offered their services to the school, which by then had changed its name to the Margolin Hebrew Academy. Having just purchased a new cooker, the Pelts realized that before the equipment became tainted with pork would be an opportune time, as well as a mitzvah (a good deed), to prepare one more round of kosher barbecue for the school's fund-raiser. The exciting news was posted on the academy's website, proclaiming that kosher barbecue from Corky's was available "one time only . . . under strict supervision of Rabbi N. Greenblatt and the Vaad Ha-Kehiloth of Memphis, Tennessee." A postcard advertising the glatt kosher barbecue was mailed to the Memphis Jewish community. It stated, "First it was M & Ms, next it was Oreos . . . and now the WORLD FAMOUS Memphis' own #1 barbecue goes KOSHER!" Corky's famous logo of a pig in a chef's hat was temporarily replaced with a smiling cow. The card advertised various packages of kosher barbecue delicacies, like the "Ultimate Shabbos Special," which included barbecue beef brisket, hickory-smoked barbecue beef spare ribs, barbecue chicken "drummies," barbecue sauce, and barbecue beans. The chefs at Corky's also prepared kosher, hickory-smoked turkeys for Thanksgiving, advertising them as "turkeys with ta'am [Hebrew for flavor]."

Barry Pelts was raised in Memphis and frequently ate both his mother's beef brisket and pit barbecue from the restaurant Leonard's. Leonard Huebuerger is credited with inventing the Memphis pork-barbecue sandwich, which features pulled or chopped shoulder meat flavored with a tomato-based sauce, topped with coleslaw, and served on a bun. A frequent advertiser in the *Hebrew Watchman* (a Jewish newspaper published in Memphis that served the mid-South Jewish community), Leonard's promised "the best take-home sandwich pack in Dixie. Come in for a meal you'll really enjoy. . . . The Old Reliable with the Know-How." And Jewish customers came . . . after Sunday school at Temple Israel, on dates, and after the movies. Barbecue drew Jews to other popular Memphis drive-ins and restaurants in the 1940s and 1950s. "We'd never go home without going by the Pig and Whistle," said Jack Abraham of Memphis. "My parents knew I was going. They didn't know I was eating barbecue. I'd tell them I had an order of French-fried potatoes, [and] forget to mention the barbecue."

Jewish love of Memphis barbecue continues today and is particularly strong among Jews who have moved to other regions of the country. Just like the Southern Jews who buy Jewish "soul food" when they visit cities such as New York, Jews who moved away from the South fill their suitcases with Southern "soul food" when they come home to visit. "I never left Memphis to return to my home in Philadelphia or D.C. without a stop-over at Corky's window or Seessel's Grocery for ribs and shredded pork," said D. D. Eisenberg, a Memphian who now lives in Potomac, Maryland. Even Jews who live in Mississippi, a state famous for its own delicious barbecue, view Memphis as the "northern capital" of Mississippi and frequently visit the city for a taste of its "'que." During the summer of 2001, Macy Hart, a native of Winona, Mississippi, was honored in Jackson, Mississippi, for his thirty years of leadership in the Jewish South as director of the Henry S. Jacobs Camp. Three hundred guests attended the event and were, of course, served barbecue chicken and beef from Corky's.

In Blytheville, Arkansas, a small town seventy-five miles north of Memphis, congregants at Temple Israel come from towns located throughout northeastern Arkansas and southeastern Missouri. The temple was most active in the 1960s and 1970s, and members often made long drives home after services on Friday night and after religious school on Sundays. A popular stop before they headed back home was the Dixie Pig, Blytheville's renowned barbecue restaurant. Founded by the Halsell family in 1923, the Dixie Pig's specialty is hickory-smoked pork shoulder served chopped on a plate or on a bun with a side of coleslaw. Dixie Pig's chopped barbecue is so beloved that when Blytheville residents die, locals bring a tray of barbecue, sauce, and buns to the home of bereaved relatives and friends. Huddy Cohen, a member of Blytheville's Temple Israel adopted this custom and has delivered many a barbecue "shiva" (mourning) meal to her Protestant friends and neighbors.

Although Memphis is the center of barbecue culture for Jewish Southerners, the relationship between Jews and barbecue is not limited to this region. Examples abound throughout the South of Jewish cooks and kosher butchers melding "Jewish" dishes with the cooking methods of barbecue, and of Jewish customers devoted to their local barbecue restaurants. In practically every Southern state, Jewish cooks take pride in their regional version of barbecued brisket, a favorite dish for Shabbos dinners, synagogue potlucks, and other community functions.

In the early 1980s, Rachelle Saltzman collected oral histories for the Center for Southern Folklore's "Lox and Grits" documentary project on Jewish life in Memphis. Saltzman suggests that "Jews who live in Memphis consider themselves as Southern as their Gentile neighbors, but they also regard their community as being as Jewish as any in the Northeast." Her observation is confirmed time and again by individuals within the diverse congregations of the city. While the members of Temple Israel, Baron Hirsch, Beth Sholom, and Anshei Sphard-Beth El Emeth do not share the same styles of worship, food, or social events, they do share a common identity as Southerners and as Jews. Each congregation expresses their identity in ways that speak to the larger Gentile community about their expectations for social acceptance and their experiences of religious observance.

Perhaps one of the strongest symbols of Memphis food culture, barbecue also links the Jews of Memphis. Regardless of their level of observance, Memphis Jews have made peace with barbecue and found ways to embrace its distinctive regional taste. In the words of the old Halpern's Delicatessen motto, Southern Jews "say it with food." Some speak with barbecue, others with kosher brisket, but all share a common culture by bridging their Jewish and Southern heritage at the table.

By the Light of the Moon
The Hash Pot Runneth Over

SADDLER TAYLOR

Somewhere in the wistful nostalgia of years past, I can imagine writing an article on hash for newly transplanted South Carolinians. Residents from Iowa or Nebraska—one of the states that always looked really big and square on the wall map. Folks that needed an introduction to the enigmatic South Carolina dish called hash. Reality bemoans the fact that things have changed in South Carolina. I am painfully aware of this because my "Got Hash?" bumper sticker causes less Pavlovian lip licking than eyebrow raising. Even some in local law enforcement, known for their attraction to culinary lures, eye me with keen suspicion.

Dismaying as it is, many suffer from an unfamiliarity with hash that now runs several generations deep. Hash carries with it a significant amount of baggage and a sense of unsettling intrigue. Unlike Brunswick stew, the darling of two neighboring states, hash has the distinction of containing unrecognizable ingredients. Not being able to identify individual ingredients tends to be a cause for alarm. In the words of at least one North Carolinian, "It's pre-chewed, made for people with no teeth." While hash has come a long way, it is still synonymous with random hog parts—you know, all *that* stuff. Traveling through the state, I am frequently left with the impression that many look upon hash with the same sense of pity and puzzlement as they do the lone shoe spending its final hours on the shoulder of a highway. Where exactly is the other shoe? Are there really snouts in your pot of hash? Fortunately, this stew ignorance has led to a renewed sense of importance for many Carolina hash makers.

The South has no shortage of fine local barbecue houses. Not a soul with any amount of unforgiving girth in the waistline would argue. Most of these community-based gems operate without obese marketing budgets or brightly coiffured mascots. Despite the reality presented by restaurants poised like perky teenage flirts off exit ramps from Hardeeville to Dillon, the Palmetto State can still boast a dynamic hash tradition.

The stories surrounding these establishments are as colorful as they are varied. In spite of the wanton consumption of the collective petri dish of mass-produced food, most local barbecue joints have a firm grip on their agricultural roots. While many have phased out such traditional delicacies as souse, liver pudding, and hogshead hash, they maintain a clear vision of whence they came. Symbolism runs high—PawPaw's cast-iron kettle, Dad's heralded sauce recipe, Auntie's special coleslaw.

One commonality among regional food traditions—whether crawfish boils in Louisiana, clambakes in Massachusetts, or burgoo in western Kentucky—is an emphasis on individual variation. This surge of individualistic pride among hash makers is an anathema to the incessant standardization of corporate food. Variation in preparation (and consumption) involves relationships between numerous factors, one being the dynamic and powerful influence of folk belief. One of the most widely circulated folk beliefs associated with hash involves the most beneficial time to prepare the stew. Cooking by the light of the full moon is acknowledged by many to be the best scenario, though very few restrict their cooking to this particular time.

Mister Hawg's Bar-B-Q is one of the exceptions. Owners Marion and Davis Robinson produce hash and barbecue on a schedule dictated by traditional moon lore. Nestled deep in the heart of Fairfield County, the barbecue pit my wife now considers my second home proudly proclaims to have "Fairfield's finest butts and ribs." The area is dominated by pine forest that thrives in shallow, rolling pastureland. One hundred years ago it looked much the same.

Due largely to South Carolina's agrarian roots, many widely circulated folk beliefs, customs, and superstitions are directly related to early thoughts on farming practices and crop growth cycles, specifically those regarding the moon and its subsequent effects on harvesting. While most modern farmers rely on the nightly television weather report more than a well-worn copy of the *Farmer's Almanac*, these same agricultural folk beliefs have been adapted to apply to other aspects of South Carolina life, particularly the preparation of hash.

Mister Hawg's Bar-B-Q, like most South Carolina barbecue restaurants, grew out of a localized family tradition—the "shade tree" cooking of so many other recognized barbecue masters. With humble beginnings in the backyard of the family home place, brothers Marion and Davis helped their father and grandfather cook barbecue and hash for neighbors. From the backyard to the full service restaurant, the brothers experienced both the joys and the struggles. Early on in the restaurant business they decided to alter their cooking schedule. The decision was made to sell barbecue and hash one day a month—the last Saturday.

During one of my visits to the feed trough, I asked Marion why they picked this particular day. Bigger crowds? Work schedules? Financial considerations? Marion stared at me through piercing eyes, "You ever hear about digging post holes on the dark of the moon?" With a look so earnest and penetrating it left no doubt as to the seriousness of the question, he continued. "Why, if you dig a post hole on the dark of the moon, you aren't going to have enough dirt to fill that hole back in." Other men in the room grunted in agreement, and the stories began to flow. Cutting down trees for firewood, filling up baskets and buckets with harvested crops—all of these personal experiences dealt with the ability to maximize one's resources when the moon is full or "on the light side." Marion explained, "You see, the last Saturday of the month is always going to be on the light of the moon, and our hash pots will overflow if we aren't careful."

The common-sense solution was to cook only when the same amount of ingredients would produce more hash. This is not a strange blip on the traditional hash radar screen. Barbecue chefs, stew makers, and hash masters alike continue to speak quite earnestly about the powerful influence the moon has on food preparation. "By the light of the moon," "right side of the moon," and "waxing moon" are all phrases of deep importance, verbalized from back roads to the strip mall.

By its very nature, folk belief is extremely versatile and has the ability to adapt with a remarkable degree of fluidity. The commonly regarded belief that the moon has very real, measurable effects on agricultural activity might no longer dominate the talk around the checkerboard at the local co-op, but it is mentioned with regularity around the hash pot.

There was something of a cathartic moment when Marion divulged the reason for the Saturday hash preparation. On some level, he seemed a bit concerned about disclosing these stories and how it might affect my impression of him. In very short order, I learned three things about Marion. One, he cared very little about my impression of him and his reasons for when he cooked his hash. Their system works; they are proud of their hash and have no need to justify anything to me. Two, he had only a cursory interest in my reaction to all the "moon talk." Finally, and most important, the brothers make a darn good mustard-based hash.

Normally, after any lengthy interview or day in the field, I would pack up my gear, offer deep thanks for a day well spent, and be on my way. Not so with the Robinson brothers. I have yet to leave without being offered a glass of sweet tea, a comfortable chair, and a large plate of white rice smothered in the yellow, steamy concoction—straight from the iron kettle and always under the watch of a full moon. This is why the lure of the sultry teenager on the off-ramp will never draw me in to her culinary web. As for the rest of the societal caravan, the proverb rings true—more die of food than famine.

The Ribs Hit the Fan

MAX BRANTLEY

Yes, I love barbecue, even to the point of going to ridiculous lengths to try a new variety. But surely there are very few other zealots like me lurking around Arkansas.

That's what I thought before articles I wrote about my favorite barbecue spots appeared in these pages a few weeks ago.

Boy, was I wrong.

You think crime, pollution, bigotry, and official abuse of power are raging concerns of the day? Think again. Judging from the response to my articles, the next presidential candidate better have a barbecue plank in the platform.

I received eight letters, dozens of phone calls, and a disturbing late-night visit from an irate barbecue man. Little of the response was even partially complimentary, most of it consisting of scoldings for my neglecting a favored barbecue joint.

Now you may think that reporters for major metropolitan newspapers are swamped with letters and calls after every by-lined effort. You may even think that swooning teenagers line up outside the portals of the oldest paper west of the Mississippi to tear hunks of clothing from Arkie Wood-steins. If you think that, you are wrong.

Not long after I came to the *Gazette* in 1973, I wrote an article about raising turtles, the kind that dime stores paint yellow so kids can buy them for a dime and lose them under the house. The article was noteworthy, although it took me a while to realize it.

You see, I got a note from an interested reader the day after the turtle opus appeared. Two years would pass before I again got an indication from someone other than a friend or my mother that anyone out there was reading. (And then it was from a state political figure who called me at 7 A.M. to wonder why I was "crucifying" him for reporting about his drunken driving arrest.)

Take my word, the response to barbecue was astounding.

Here's a sample.

A woman from Malvern referred to McClard's at Hot Springs, my favorite, as a "greasy spoon." Moreover, she said, she planned to begin avoiding my "socialist paper" henceforth because my article failed to mention Stubby's at Hot Springs — "Oh those beans in the little clay pot."

Stubby's had the most vocal supporters. A Tulsa ad man took me to task in two lengthy letters for neglecting Stubby, although conceding that McClard's was plenty good, too. The omission of Stubby's was an oversight. It is good, and I had intended to mention it as the Avis to McClard's Hertz at Hot Springs, but space ran out.

One thing bothers me, though. Every Stubby's booster mentioned the wonderfulness of his baked potatoes. How do you ruin a baked potato?

The venerable Shack responded quickly and curtly to my assessment that their product wasn't as good as it used to be. The firm canceled its advertising, but only after I had a telephone conversation with the boss. He insisted that I tell him what I didn't like about the place; I did, and he was not amused. Nor was the one Shack supporter who also called to register his exceptions.

Some North Little Rock residents were offended that I would cover their hometown's offering with only a mention of Lindsey's. "You actually eat there?" one woman asked incredulously.

Richard's Hickory House and the Burger Basket north of the river had their fans. Cabot folks plumped for the Hickory Pit, whose owners were kind about my omission, certain that a meal there would put them at the top of the list.

One blowhard told me that the barbecue sandwich was invented in the Arkansas Delta; another pinned the spot down as Blytheville. Bowles' at Osceola got a particularly high report.

Some folks spent their own money to call long-distance with recommendations. Among them were supporters of the Little Pig at Hazen and Tommy's and the Triple-B at Pine Bluff. The most intriguing suggestion was for an unnamed black man's house at Arkadelphia where you knock on the door and receive a barbecue sandwich, presumably after the proper incantation.

Gratifying responses came from those whose establishments received good words, as well as many offers of freebies. To some of you callers, I repeat, every meal was paid for. (The closest anyone came to a free meal was when an unscrupulous reporter from a Tennessee paper tried to impersonate me at McClard's after the articles appeared. The ruse was uncovered and, lucky for him, the McClards were too nice to give him less than their normal heaping platter, albeit at the normal price.)

The most disturbing thing about the whole business was the reaction of Robert McIntosh, the major domo of Say McIntosh, a restaurant that some insist has the best barbecue and sweet potato pie going.

I'm not so enchanted by Say's barbecue — and said so. That was in the first article, and he phoned his disappointment the next day. But when the concluding article appeared, in which I dared to compare Ballard's pie to Say's, the ribs hit the fan.

McIntosh stormed into the *Gazette* newsroom about eleven P.M. the next day, toting a sack of 'tater pies. The point, which was missed in the hubbub, was that the pies were Ballard's and that McIntosh wouldn't serve such a lowly offering. By the time he had explained that to me, a crew of *Gazette* copy editors had demolished two pies. McIntosh did not laugh. Nor did his huge companion, who mostly uttered ominous sounding "that's rights" at pauses in McIntosh's machine-gun delivery.

McIntosh's main point seemed to be that I had never said my barbecue pronouncements were only my personal opinion. I would have thought that was obvious. But just in case:

Yes, Mr. McIntosh (and friend), it is only my opinion that Ballard's barbecue is better and that his sweet potato pie is just as good.

THE
CURRENT
SCENE

Cheer Up Mama

PETER KAMINSKY

Early November is a picture-postcard time to drive through North Carolina. The oak leaves are turning—not the flaming scarlets and golds of New England maples, but rather a dark red to dry brown. The air is cool, but there are still the remnants of summer warmth in the sea breeze. And since it was only a four-hour detour, which is nothing at all for a barbecue fancier, I drove from a fishing trip on the coast up to Mitchell's Barbecue in Wilson, just east of Raleigh.

The highways were numerous, well maintained, and fairly empty, a sign that it pays to have Jesse Helms as your senator: gazillions of dollars for magnificent thoroughfares that seem to go nowhere. On the feeder roads, one finds another sign of government largesse: at lunch hour, every barbecue stand has a full complement of highway maintenance trucks parked on the roadside, as their crews sit down to trencherman portions of cue. In that way, those millions of highway dollars, far from being wasted, are helping to support the small barbecue businesses of the Carolinas.

If the call for barbecue has not summoned Eddie Mitchell from his large and modern restaurant, you may see a fifty-three-foot semi parked outside Mitchell's on Highway 301. On the side panel Mitchell's smile beams through his salt-and-pepper beard. Mitchell is so energetic and outgoing that the thought occurs, upon meeting him, that there is easily enough vitality left over here to fill up another body or two.

Although the term "best" is a completely subjective matter when comparing things in the very top tier of any enterprise, one can say with confidence that Mitchell's is about as good as it gets for eastern North Carolina barbecue: that is, whole hog and a vinegar-based peppery sauce.

I followed the smell of wood smoke up the last half-mile or so of highway where Eddie, a man with the build of a fullback (actually he was both quarterback and running back at Fayetteville State), was in the process of muscling a couple of hogs off the grate. Not for the first time, the splayed pig brought to mind a human body about to be cooked. Maybe it is that similarity between naked pigs and naked people that caused Polynesian cannibals to refer to human meat as "long pig" (as reported by Robert Louis Stevenson in *Tales of The South Seas*). It might even have something to do with the Jews' and Arabs' pork taboo.

As Eddie and his crew pulled the meat from the bones, hot and steaming, the tantalizing smell of fat and flesh hung heavy as night air in August just before a cloudburst. Eddie piled the meat in front of him and pounded out a steady beat with two hatchets as he chopped the cooked pork.

I prefer bigger pieces of meat to the finer mince commonly served in the Piedmont region, and Eddie accommodates my request for bigger pieces, making sure to include moist and tender meat from deep within the pigs' flesh, mixing it with crispy skin and "outside brown" (the dark red meat completely permeated with smoke and fire). He serves it on a bun, drenched in piquant vinegar sauce and piled with cool, sweet coleslaw. It has an intense, almost overpowering taste, the spicy seasoned meat tempered by the coleslaw. The soggy bun—mooshy from the sauce and slaw—helps the barbecue slide down your gullet, as Howlin Wolf once said "like Baby Jesus in satin pants."

Mitchell's is among the biggest barbecue establishments I have seen, much bigger even than its large clientele would warrant. But Eddie Mitchell sees his place as a future school for barbecuers who want to preserve the old-time tradition.

That tradition is never far from Eddie's conversation. For that matter it is never far from the customer's view, as Mitchell has commissioned a mural in the American Primitive style that dominates the dining room with its depiction of an old-fashioned "pig-picking." Eddie told me that a young man in town who was "very artistic" (more on that later) had painted it. The scene, as Eddie told the story, is typical of what one would have come upon in the countryside at the end of the tobacco harvest. He added, "Once the last truck comes to the barn it's time for the pig-pickins."

Eddie's generation is probably the last to attend these farm-family feasts. His youth was the heyday of tobacco as the driving wheel of the North Carolina economy. The pictures in the mural trace the story, beginning with planting tobacco in the spring and concluding with slaughtering the pigs and rendering the fat, with the women making sausages, the men tending a barbecue pit, a huge table with seating for fifteen, and a gracious old Southern mansion in the background. In those years, I imagine, the tobacco plantation pig-picking was one of the few occasions when whole families of blacks and whites sat down to dinner at the same table. In addition to platters of meat, the table is laden with watermelon, fried chicken, sweet potato soufflé, ham, corn on the cob, iced tea, cakes, black-eyed peas, lemonade. "A real pig-out," Eddie said. "You put everything out for the pig-picking, so that is why, I think, you have the term 'pig-out.'"

Somewhat to my puzzlement Eddie recounted that it was a real challenge for him to work with the artist. "The thing with him is if I can just keep him focused it takes about a day to work with him to get it all doing and get it all working and so."

"Why is that?"

"Like I said, he's autistic."

"Oh, it's your accent," I explained. "I understood you to say 'He's artistic,' which I already knew from looking at the painting."

We laughed. In our era, when the stand-alone barbecue stands that sprung up after the Second World War (before which time eating out meant church dinners or a food put on by a campaigning politician) were starting to look, and taste, a bit run down, barely holding their own with franchise fast food, there is a dynamic air about the Mitchell place. Mitchell, with his attachment, both sentimental and financial, to old-fashioned barbecue, is a New South success story. A high school and college football star, he moved up North to work with the Ford Motor Company, first in Detroit and then as a regional manager in Waltham, Massachusetts. But when his father fell ill in the early seventies with what they thought were early symptoms of the lung cancer that finally killed him, Eddie moved back South to be near his mother, who ran a mom-and-pop grocery store (at that time increasingly more mom than pop). Eddie took a position as assistant director for the Employment Standards Division of the State Department of Labor.

The death of his father in 1990 threw his mother into despair. The family store, which had suffered declining business for some time, was in very bad shape. One night, in an effort to cheer her up, Eddie said to his mother, "Mom, I see you got some collard greens cooking, what else do you feel like eating?" And she said, "I have me a taste for some good old-fashioned barbecue." "That was my signal to go out to the local store and buy a little thirty-four pound pig and come back and put the guy on the barbecue," he said. "Later that day, someone came in to buy a hot dog or a hamburger, and he could smell the smoked meat.

"'Mrs. Mitchell, you got barbecue now?' he asked.

"I stuck my head out and answered for her, 'Yeah, we have barbecue, sell the man something.'... So she made the guy a couple of sandwiches, and I left to go back to work. When I returned about 7:30 to escort her home, she was all bubbly.

"I said, 'It's nice to see that you have a difference in personality.'

"And she said, 'You know I sold that barbecue, don't you—yes I did. I sold every bit of it!'

"As we got ready to go out the door, someone was trying to come in, and I'm thinking someone's trying to rob us. So I put a little bass in my voice, I say, 'Yeah, who is it?'

"'We want to know if you got anymore barbecue.'

"'No, we don't have anymore today, but we'll have some more tomorrow,' which we didn't have, but I just played along to get the guy from the door. For the next two weeks everyone kept asking my mom about barbecue. So she said to me, 'You know, folks still asking me about the barbecue and none of the other stuff is selling; the groceries are still on the shelves.'

"So I got her another pig, and when that sold out, I went and got a third one, on my own without her having to ask. And sure enough, that went too. At that point in time, it didn't take a rocket scientist to figure that out that something's going on here.

"Momma said, 'Son you'd be surprised, you go back cooking this stuff the old-fashioned way, like they did, you add some collard greens and mustard greens. You'd be surprised.'

"That's Momma talking and I'm a momma's boy, and I listened, but I didn't put a lot of starch in it. But time progressed, buying a pig, buying a pig, it became too much for me, the two jobs. I found myself coming from work in Raleigh, literally changing into my cooking clothes in the car. Finally I was in the full-time barbecue business. And that's how I found Mr. Kirby."

I noted he used the honorific "mister," observing the old-time tradition still kept alive among African Americans of a certain generation as a genteel way of showing respect for one's elders.

Like many kids in the South, Eddie remembers growing up with barbecuers. "I would always hang around when my dad and grandad and uncle were cooking. I got interested when I was eight or nine, and I cooked my first pig when I was about fourteen, and they realized I was good at it, so the next time, the older men let me cook the pig while they hit the moonshine. It kind of evolved into a job, and once it became a job, like most kids I wasn't interested any more.

"Still the cooking process was always present in my home. On the holidays we would cook our own barbecue; my family, most of which had migrated north, (largely to New Jersey) would come home at Christmas time and we would all barbecue.

"As time progressed the old guys died out, but the art itself had been somewhat passed on. I still knew how to cook a pig and so did my brothers. But there were certain things the old guys did that I hadn't paid attention to. When I decided to really get into this business my mother said to me, 'You go learning this barbecue the old-fashioned way, you'll be surprised.'

"So I asked my mom, 'who's still alive?' and I went to some of the older guys, but they weren't into getting back into it—the labor was so intense if you were serious about doing it. The last guy I went to was James Kirby."

Eddie began this tale as a prelude to a visit to Mr. Kirby, who lives in a neat little bungalow nearby. The day was fair, about seventy degrees or so; however inside Mr. Kirby's knotty-pine living room it was warm. I noted the thermometer read eighty-two, which, coincidentally was the age of the handsome gentleman who sat in a recliner, holding on to a cane and half rising to greet us while he hit the remote to turn down the volume on *General Hospital*.

"I just keep the TV on for company," he explained in a deep country accent, barely intelligible to my New York ears.

"They want to know how you got me into all this crap," Eddie said. And while Mr. Kirby nodded or interjected an occasional "Yes, that's so," Eddie told the story.

"Mr. Kirby and I used to play poker together. When I first approached him about learning barbecue from him he said, no, he really wasn't interested. But as it turned out, that night at the poker game his luck was down, and he ended up going broke. Now James was an older guy than most of us around the table, and he could get very ornery."

Mr. Kirby gave the huff of an old lion, half skeptical and gruff.

"So he sat there with no chips, no money, and the guys who were waiting to get into the game were afraid to ask him to get up because they didn't want to face his orneriness. So he just sat there as the deal went around.

"Now, my luck was pretty good, so I just reached in my pocket and gave him fifty dollars. He didn't pick it up. He just looked at me. Honestly, I didn't know if he was going to take it or not. I just did it out of a gesture. The deal went around once. He didn't throw in any money that time. The deal came around again, and he picked up ten dollars and anted up. I had won all I wanted to win so I got up so that another guy could sit down at the table. I stood around having a drink or two while Mr. Kirby's luck caught on and he won a few hands. After a while I was ready to go, and he said, 'Wait up. I want to talk to you.' So I waited.

"He said, 'Do you still want to learn about barbecue?'

"And I said, 'Yeah.'

"He said, 'I'll show ya. I'll be by your place tomorrow.'

"Now I had been searching around before Mr. Kirby came forward, and I had heard about Mr. Herbert Woodard, who is a gentleman who was noted back then for cooking barbecue, and he used to own a hotel/motel. For whatever reason he changed the old tradition. He bought a cooker (an electric smoker) and stopped cooking in the ground. When I got into the business, I wanted to do something to speed up the process, and I thought about buying that cooker. I told Mr. Woodard I would be out at his place to look at it. So when Mr. Kirby came by that next day I asked him come on and look at this electric cooker with me."

At this point Mr. Kirby, a woodsmoke traditionalist, affirmed, "Yes, that's right," and at the same time gave a shiver of disapproval, as one might do in recalling a meal that made you sick to your stomach.

Eddie picked up the tale. "So we go out there. Mr. Woodard had the cooker out to show how it works. Mr. Kirby is standing there. He never says a word. So I cut a deal for $200 for the cooker. I began to reach in my pocket to get my wallet to pay for it. And every time I did that Mr. Kirby, who was standing behind me, would tug on my arm. So I would start to hesitate and carry on a meaningless conversation trying to figure if there was something about the cooker that Mr. Kirby saw that he didn't like but also didn't want to come out and say. You see, Mr. Woodard and Mr. Kirby and all the old-timers grew up together and were real competitive barbecue cookers, real pit masters. So the bottom line was Mr. Kirby didn't want to say anything in front of Herbert because Herbert was his friend. So the last time I tried to pay Mr. Herbert, Mr. James started to tug on my arm again. I said, 'Excuse me a minute, I'll be right back.' And I told James, 'Come with me outside. I can't seem to find my money or something.' And he came on out, and I said, 'What is it? What is it?'

"And he looked at me, and he said like he had after the poker game, 'Do you really want to get into the barbecue business?'

"I said, 'Yeah.'

"So he said it again, 'Do you really want to get into the barbecue business?'

"And I said, 'Yeah, man, I really want to get into the barbecue business.'

"He said, 'Well if you really want to get into the barbecue business I will put you in the water, but it will be up to you to learn how to swim.'

"And I said to him, very boastfully, 'You put me in the water, and don't you worry about me learning to swim.'

"He said, 'Well, you tell Herb that you'll be back and c'mon let's go.' So I went back to tell Mr. Woodard I didn't have all my funds and that I'd be back later.

"As we went back to my car Mr. James said, 'I don't want to waste my time with you if you don't really want to do this.'

"I did not fully understand what he was talking about, but I came to see what he meant was people think they want to cook barbecue this way, but when they are standing over the hot pits it makes you have a different trend of thought. If barbecuing is in your heart—cutting the wood, shoveling, turning the hog—then all that is something you need to have a burning desire for. Although I didn't know all of that at the time, what I did understand him to be saying was, 'If you want to be a true pit master you have to be ready to go the whole way.' And if I wanted to go the whole way he would teach me.

"At that time we had an old storage shed out back where my Mom keep crates and stuff. Mr. Kirby said, 'What you doing with all this here?' So we started to clear out the shed, and when we had cleaned everything he got down on his knees and drew out the pit. Then we got a mason come in and line the pit with cement blocks, and then we filled it with sand for the 'incubating period.'" Eddie was referring to his trick for slow-cooking by lining the pit with sand, which holds heat remarkably using relatively little fuel and requiring less fuss.

"Then we went around and got two old oil drums. We went to the welding shop and had them cut those barrels in half. Then Mr. James set the barrels down into the sand. Once we got the thing completed it was a 'real orthodox work of art!'" Eddie said with a good deal of nostalgic pride.

"After we got the pigs, we left them to soak in salt water and vinegar. This is one of those steps, prepping the pig, getting him ready, that people don't do anymore. But a pig is supposed to go through a twelve-hour soaking period of vinegar and seasonings, which cuts the fresh taste.

"So the very first night we were going to try it out I was all excited. From what I knew about barbecuing I was thinking we had to prepare to be there all night. I went home and told my wife I was going to be up all night cooking pigs. So I made a couple of sandwiches, made me some coffee, took my flashlight. Mr. James was supposed to be there at six o'clock and we were supposed to put on the pig. Well I was there at six o'clock, and no James."

At this point in Eddie's tale Mr. Kirby laughed as if he were recalling a delicious practical joke. Eddie responded with the kind of smile that one reserves for a favorite uncle or grandparent.

"About seven or eight he comes up. We split some oak and some hickory and left them to soak in a tub of water. We put two twenty-pound bags of charcoal in each cooker. When the coals got good and hot, he raked the coals to the side, and then he put the grate on top. He took the pigs and washed them and then he salted them down the back so that the skin would paunch up. Then we put the pigs on and shut the drafts.

"Next thing I knew Mr. James reached over and grabbed his jacket and slung it over his shoulder. He put his hat on his head and began walking out the door, and he leaves me sitting there. I said, 'Where you going? You gonna leave me here?'

"He said, 'Oh hell, you can sit there and watch the pig if you want to, but I'm going home and going to bed.'

"Having no knowledge of the old school, I thought we had to sit there all night and tend the pig. Anyway I couldn't wait til morning. I was like a kid on Christmas. I got back about four in the morning, and I took a peek and there was the prettiest golden brown pig! Mr. James came in about 5:30, and we flipped the pig and started basting. That, to me, was one of the most memorable times since I started. That was my first experience of the technique called banking."

At the mention of banking Mr. Kirby and Eddie both shared a mutual scoundrel's grin, like they had just let me in on a big and funny secret, that secret being that you didn't have to stand watch over a roasting pig like a sentry in a war zone (or for that matter, like all the other pit masters).

I bit.

"Eddie, what is banking?"

"In this part of the country, we used to have wood heaters or coal heaters. When I was growing up, we would put coal or wood inside of the heater and shut off all the drafts. That technique is called banking, in other words, it shuts the drafts off so the fire won't burn fast, and you have a slow-burning process all night long which will radiate all over your house (back then we didn't have central heating). That was a mechanism that the old-timers used to keep the house warm, but Mr. Kirby, he implemented that particular technique in cooking the pig. Most people say you have to sit out there all night. Mr. Kirby, as far as I'm concerned, invented this technique." Eddie brought the story to a close (along about the time that Mr. Kirby appeared to be settling into a light doze). "Every thing I learned I learned from him. This is how the term pit master came about: 99 percent of the time you find an old black guy sitting there all night long, nursing a fire (or in Mr. Kirby's case not nursing the fire). However you do it, my thing is if you really want to get back to the original, somebody needs to preserve that and pass it on."

Mr. Kirby stirred, "Yeah, that's right. That's right."

Artrageous Cookers, Jackson, Tennessee

Amy Evans, who heads the Oral History Initiative for the
Southern Foodways Alliance, shot the photographs in this section. To
view more of her work for the SFA, log onto ‹www.southernfoodways.com›.
Originally from Houston, Texas, she received a B.F.A. from the Maryland
Institute College of Art and an M.A. in Southern studies from the University
of Mississippi. Amy is also an exhibiting artist, freelance photographer,
art educator, and cofounder of PieceWorks, a nonprofit community
arts and outreach organization based in Oxford, Mississippi.
(Photographs used by permission of the photographer)

Helen's Bar-B-Q, Brownsville, Texas

Helen's Bar-B-Q, Brownsville, Texas

Marlowe's Ribs & Restaurant, Memphis, Tennessee

My Three Son's Bar-B-Q, Henderson, Tennessee

Papa KayJoe's Bar-B-Que, Centerville, Tennessee

Papa KayJoe's Bar-B-Que, Centerville, Tennessee

Sam's Bar-B-Q, Humboldt, Tennessee

When Pigs Fly West

LOLIS ERIC ELIE

When I told friends that I was setting out in search of California barbecue, they reacted as if I had said I was starting a unicorn collection. "There is no such thing as California barbecue," they insisted.

If you assume that the slight, light, barely cooked aesthetic of California cuisine defines the cooking of the whole state and not just the style of some of its most celebrated restaurants, it's easy to understand why the thought of California barbecue would seem like an oxymoron. Who ever heard of free-range ribs? Who ever bothered to put organic micro greens in coleslaw?

"Barbecue is Southern," my doubters told me, forgetting that both Kansas City and Chicago are barbecue capitals and that neither of them is in the South. "Immigrant food in California comes from Mexico, China, Indonesia, not America," they said, forgetting that while emigrants from Mississippi and Tennessee brought barbecue to the Midwest, their counterparts in Louisiana, Texas, and Oklahoma often headed west to the Golden State.

Besides all that, I have been to the places you're supposed to go for great barbecue. In 1994, I traveled much of the country with Frank Stewart, a wise-cracking photographer who prefers his ambrosia smoked. We were writing *Smokestack Lightning: Adventures in the Heart of Barbecue Country*, a book about American culture as expressed through barbecue. We learned quickly that barbecue authorities are a dime a dozen, and their opinions often are worth even less.

Oh, for a while we did listen to them. We calculated the number of flies the restaurants attracted, the girth of the proprietors, even the ratio of rich patrons to poor ones. We soon learned you are just as likely to find bad food at fly-infested restaurants with fat chefs and diverse clientele as you are to find it anywhere else.

I also knew that, even when people brag about how great the barbecue is in their town, they really mean that there are one or two favorite restaurants they frequent. I went to dozens of restaurants in barbecue-crazed Memphis, but there are only a handful I wish to go back to. And even though barbecue is a sacrament in Kansas City, with the passing of Otis P. Boyd and the closing of his restaurant a few years ago, my recent visits to Kansas City have left me feeling that the church has lost its steeple.

So I didn't expect to find a million great places in California. But I figured that its combination of black immigrants, hard wood, international influences, and great barbecue weather, the state had the ingredients I needed to prove the doubters wrong.

My conviction that I would find good barbecue in California was not entirely fantastic. For years, I'd been hearing the names of two legendary Bay Area barbecue restaurants, Flint's and Everett and Jones. My friend Walter Gomes grew up in Los Angeles, but his barbecue loyalties lie up North. "If you don't go to Flint's on Telegraph in Berkeley, you have not lived," he told me. "If you don't like it, you must be dead."

Walter's challenge frightened me. It's scary enough to get tested at your doctor's office and learn that you have some dreaded disease. But to bite a piece of barbecue and realize that you're already dead is even worse. So I asked Nancy Freeman and Tim Patterson, two friends and Berkeley residents, to join me in sampling the fare in the East Bay. That way, if I didn't like the barbecue at Flint's, I'd at least have someone around to notify the next of kin.

Flint's epitomizes the look of the urban barbecue joint. It's a shallow, white, cinder-block building. The counter is but a step or two from the entrance, and the pit is but a step on the other side of the counter. I was rudely informed that you can't order sauce on the side at Flint's. I naturally assumed that the sauce was so good, the proprietors feared their formula would be stolen. My interest peaked.

After leaving Flint's, we ordered take-out a bunch of other places in the Oakland-Berkeley-Emeryville area. Then we spread the offerings out on the kitchen counter and dug in.

Biting a pork rib from Flint's, I saw my life pass before my eyes.

What I first tasted was the pleasing flavor of spices and smoke, but the only moisture emanating from the rib was a small trickle of grease. Then things got worse. The links were dry; the beef ribs were impossibly tough. Though the brisket wasn't bad, it wasn't good. Flint's sauce, which I got on the beef ribs, was very thick, very sweet, and very dark, as if it had been infused with grape jelly.

Everett and Jones, the other stalwart of East Bay barbecue, has several locations, but they vary in quality. The sausage at the three location we tried was good. Unlike many of the sausage links you get in California, the meat was ground, not emulsified like the meat in hot dogs. The brisket was bland at each of the outposts and had almost no smoke flavor at the location on Telegraph. The best offering from any Everett and Jones location was the pork ribs on Telegraph Avenue, which had a wonderful garlic flavor.

So much for the assumed superiority of Bay Area barbecue.

My impressions about Los Angeles barbecue were formed in 1996 when a friend and I drove along Central Avenue, the heart of South Central Los Angeles. Though the area is better known for riots than ribs, it seemed to me I saw nearly a dozen barbecue places then, though I didn't eat at any of them.

Central Avenue is to Los Angeles what Beale Street is to Memphis, the commercial and cultural heart of the African American community. As early as the 1920s, Central Avenue was being referred to as the "Harlem of the West." In part because racial segregation relegated black musicians to playing on Central Avenue or in Watts, a vibrant music community developed there During World War II, as migrants came west to build military machinery, the African American population grew. But as early as the 1950s, as black Angelenos started moving to other parts of the city, Central Avenue was already in decline.

I started my search on that street, but I found little sign of the restaurants I had passed even a few years before. I found one old place near 92nd Street. It had the look of a good barbecue joint and the smoke to match, but the food was not memorable. Because of the large number of barbecue places on Slausson Avenue, I was tempted to conclude that I had found my new barbecue boulevard. But after tasting the food at the first two places I saw, I feared the avenue was mostly show. Then I stopped at Woody's Bar-B-Que, a take out place with a gray-and-white bulldog painted on the outer wall urging passersby to stop. The menu at Woody's included the usual assortment of barbecue meats: pork ribs, sliced beef, chicken, as well as chicken links, an unusual addition. I ordered a combination plate and braced myself for more disappointment.

But first, I digress: The tasting of barbecue is a precise affair involving an assessment not merely of quality but also of authenticity. While it is possible to enjoy tender, well-seasoned meat bathed in barbecue sauce, I make a distinction between good food and good barbecue. Good barbecue must be smoked over hardwood or charcoal, and the flavor of that fuel must penetrate the meat. Since red meat is emblematic of barbecue, I always get an assortment of whatever beef, pork, and sausage are available. But after eating the amazing barbecued Cornish game hens at Cozy Corner in Memphis, I've learned to bend this rule whenever I see something unusual on the menu.

Most restaurants simply slather sauce on their meat after you order it. Since I can slather as well as they can, I always get my barbecue with the sauce on the side to better taste the meat itself.

And barbecue should be tender. Merely placed in close proximity to a fork, brisket and pork shoulder should yield with little additional effort. Ribs should separate from the bone without excessive pulling and tugging. The difficulty is cooking the meat long enough to attain this degree of tenderness and smokiness without drying it out. Some of the best pit masters cook indirectly. They separate the meat from the wood or charcoal so that the smoke flavor gets through, but the grease from the meat doesn't cause the fire to flare and the meat to char. Other cooks, no less skilled, insist that barbecue gets its flavor in part from the seasoned smoke that rises when the grease from the meat hits the coals. I have had great barbecue cooked with both methods.

In the matter of sauces, I have one overriding prejudice, and it concerns the particularly silly brand of chauvinism that demands that men prove their masculinity by ingesting the most fiery sauces available. Even the dullest of palates and dimmest of wits can understand that the more pepper you put in a sauce, the more difficult it is to taste any other ingredient. Why should a chef even bother to fine-tune the balance of his seasonings if the final ingredient will be a truckload of crushed habanero peppers?

In the parking lot, I unwrapped my Woody's assortment, and immediately my rental car smelled like a barbecue joint. Like all good barbecue, the meat at Woody's has a smoke ring, a pink layer just below the surface that meat gets when it is smoked. My tongue made the acquaintance of the seasonings on the outside of the pork ribs and sliced beef and met the rich smoke flavor as my teeth plunged deeper. I am suspicious of any sausage made from the meat of a two-footed animal. But I dismissed my misgivings when I tasted these chicken links. They were lighter in color and heft than their beef counterparts, but they had a surprising peppery kick. The beef ribs were tender and richly marbled like the top of a rib-eye steak.

California barbecue sauces, even the hot varieties at most restaurants, tend to be fairly tame. The essential balance that cooks there strive for seems to be between sweet and sour, not hot and mild. Almost invariably, in California, sweet wins. But at the two locations of Phillips Barbecue, which is owned by Woody's cousin, Foster Phillips, the competition between these opposites is especially acute. The ketchup-based sauce is a jarring combination of very sweet and very tangy. But the meat has a rich blackened crust of smoke-seared dry seasonings that contains its own hint of sugar.

Both Woody and Foster hail from Keatchie, Louisiana, a small town about twenty-three miles southwest of Shreveport. Woody says he developed his barbecue conception after arriving in California, "I had to leave Keatchie to come to California and make some barbecue," he says, having arrived here in 1960 and opened his business in 1975. Foster's barbecue inspiration came from Drew Lover, a barbecue restaurateur in Keatchie who inspired Foster to go into business for himself. Though their inspiration comes from different places, their barbecue is quite similar. Phillips's barbecue is a little spicier, both in terms of the vinegar in the sauce and the salt and pepper in the dry seasonings. But they are similar enough to share a space at the top of the Los Angeles barbecue rankings.

Both Woody's and Phillips's include greens on their menus as a side dish, exemplifying a curious mixing and mingling of traditional barbecue side dishes with pot-food menu items more typical of soul food restaurants that don't specialize in barbecue. By the same token, many soul food restaurants I found in California offer real barbecue on their menus, as opposed to the oven-baked, sauce-smothered meats typical in black, Southern-style restaurants in other parts of the country. It's as if these restaurants were one-stop repositories of black Southern culinary traditions, while similar restaurants in the Southeast are more specialized.

In the Pacific Bell Yellow pages, there is a small listing for "barbecue stands." There's no listing at all for barbecue restaurants. It's as if all the barbecue places are located in alleys between pawn shops and filling stations. It would be impossible to imagine barbecue getting such a slight in a place such as Memphis or Kansas City, where the whole identity of the cities is wrapped up in their reputation for smoked meat. But the idea of "barbecue stands" conjures up the image of little, out-of-the-way places awaiting discovery. At least since Jan and Michael Stern began finding good food in such places, Americans have been fascinated with the possibility that they will luck upon some unsung culinary genius hidden in plain view. So one Saturday, I abandoned the various guidebooks and recommendations I had collected and took out for deepest, darkest South Central Los Angeles. I figured that somewhere in that famed suburban ghetto there had to exist a great barbecue restaurant that the food experts had missed simply because, despite their lust for great food, their passion for self-preservation and their fear of urban violence had limited their culinary explorations to safer neighborhoods. So I traveled through Inglewood, Crenshaw, Baldwin Hills, Baldwin Village, and View Park. At first I found little of note. Then I found religion.

I would like to say it was divine inspiration that led me to Prayer Assembly Church of God in Christ on East El Segundo Boulevard that Saturday afternoon, but the truth is that Roderick Phillips, Woody's thirty-two-year-old son, led me there and then secured from me a promise to bring him back some barbecued turkey necks. But it was divine inspiration that led the Rev. Clevester Williams Sr. to add a barbecue stand to the reception hall, commercial kitchen, offices, and two sanctuaries that comprise his stucco-and-stained-glass edifice. The reverend's office, which itself has a kitchenette and complete bathroom attached, is testimony in part to the success of the barbecue business. "I started forty years ago because I had built a church downstairs, and I needed $10,000 to buy some pews," Rev. Williams told me. "I went to bed that night and asked the Lord how I could get the money. And the Lord revealed to me the barbecue, the spices, and the wood."

The reverend's barbecue vision had its doubters at first, but they have been supplanted by the people who line up every Saturday at the take-out trailer beside the church. As I took my place among them, I looked across the parking lot and saw two smoke-oozing pits tended by a man wearing a gas mask. The mask, a practical accouterment, is neither attractive nor common. But if the gas mask was in some small way responsible for the fine barbecue that was packed on to my styrofoam take-out plate, then all pit masters should wear them. In the case of the ribs, which had a wonderful smoky sweetness, the simple seasonings had become one with the meat. That flavor didn't permeate the sliced beef as thoroughly, however. The turkey necks were fall-off-the-bone tender, but they lacked a deep smoke flavor, as if they had been partially boiled or baked. The sauce, which was among the best in Los Angeles, was neither too thick nor too sweet. It was well spiced with chili powder and flecks of red pepper.

For all the charms of Prayer Assembly barbecue, the pleasures of lining up in the church parking lot on the hottest part of a Saturday afternoon are not for everyone. A very different aesthetic awaits diners at The Pig, a yearling restaurant that combines down-home inspiration and upscale sophistication. Though Daly Thompson grew up eating barbecue in Memphis, he and his wife Liz learned their trade at white-tablecloth places before opening up their Los Angeles restaurant. He was a chef, she a pastry chef. The decor at The Pig is 1950s diner chic, and the menu ranges from New Orleans chicken-wing appetizers to Memphis-style pulled pork to a South Carolina–style mustard barbecue sauce. "I wanted to bring some true Memphis-style barbecue here, but also bring some other influences," Thompson said. His collage of inspirations shows up in some unexpected ways. For example, though beef brisket is most famous as a Texas staple, Thompson smokes his beef with apple wood rather than oak, mesquite, or hickory, as would be done in Texas. And he dresses it with the mustard barbecue sauce rather than a traditional tomato-based sauce. The combinations and juxtapositions are neither jarring nor inappropriate, except perhaps to people for whom the regional purity of barbecue is sacred. I'm not that much of a purist, though the pecan pie was my favorite item on the menu.

Far from the hip crowds on South La Brea, Gadberry's is an island of barbecue on South Broadway. The old neighborhood had been primarily African American, but the residents these days are mostly Spanish-speaking immigrants whose appetite for barbecue is not so large. "I guess my best years are behind me," said John Gadberry, whose father opened the business in 1953. The elder Gadberry came to the barbecue business by way of the brickmason's trade. Figuring that cooking barbecue would be easier on his aging body, he built himself a pit and opened a restaurant. Although the Gadberrys hail from Yazoo City, Mississippi, John Gadberry grew up in Los Angeles. "I don't know if the barbecue is Mississippi style, but my father came up with his recipes and his whole style by himself. He grew up in Mississippi, but I don't know if his food is typical or not."

The typical California barbecue menu mirrors that of Louisiana and eastern Texas: baked beans, potato salad, coleslaw, pork ribs, chicken and sliced beef, and a sweet, tomato-based sauce. Californian menus are distinct in only a few obvious ways. Almost invariably, they include beef ribs. And, with few exceptions, they don't include the pork shoulder that is the staple of Memphis and the Southeast. Despite the obvious ways in which barbecue could not possibly be classified as health food, California restaurants make an ostensible concession to health concerns by offering patrons the option of substituting sliced, bland wheat bread for the usual sliced, bland white bread.

While most barbecue regions differentiate themselves based on their sauces, there is no distinct California barbecue sauce. With relatively little variation, the sauces in the typical barbecue restaurants in Los Angeles and the Bay Area taste like versions of the thick, tomato-based sauces that are marketed commercially in supermarkets.

As barbecue has become more popular across the nation, sophisticated restaurateurs are studying barbecue and creating menus designed not just for homesick Texans and Tennesseans but rather for people whose loyalty is to good food, not regional accuracy. The best such student I met in my California explorations was Bob Kantor, a New Yorker who opened Memphis Minnie's in San Francisco. It may well be the finest barbecue restaurant in the state. The restaurant is named not for the late blues singer but for Kantor's mother, who grew up in Memphis before moving to New York. Though Jewish, she loved pork. Her concession to dietary orthodoxy was that she tried not to fry any bacon when she knew the rabbi would be visiting.

While Kantor may not be a religious zealot, he preaches his philosophy of barbecue with all the fury of a new convert. The first rule is that Kantor does not serve sauce on his barbecue. Sauce is available on the tables if you want it. "I'm just trying to get people to look at barbecue as something other than sauce," he explains. "If barbecue is nothing but sauce, why do I spend sixteen hours working on my brisket?"

While Kantor may not slather sauce on his finished product, part of his technique includes putting his mustard-based sauce on the raw meat before adding the dry seasonings. His brisket was without doubt the best I tasted in the state. Like the pork shoulders, the brisket was fall-apart tender, crusted on the outside with spices and slightly charred meat, and richly seasoned the rest of the way through. Kantor accomplishes this in large part with longer cooking times than most California pit masters employ. He cooks his briskets and shoulders at 190 degrees for about sixteen hours. His pork ribs cook four or five hours.

Across the bay from Memphis Minnie's, the real standout was the pork ribs from KC's Bar-B-Q. They were succulent, densely smoked, and mildly sweet. KC's is also impressive for the collection of antique furniture and fixtures that give its dining room a feel somewhere between a restaurant and a secondhand shop. The "KC" in the name refers to the home town of the original owner. But in 1968, after two years in business, he decided to move back to Kansas City and sell the restaurant to the father of the current owner, Patrick Davis. "The Bay Area has quite a few different barbecue places," he tells me. "But the style is all based out of the South."

Maintaining the taste of the South was a conscious effort on the part of transplanted black Southerners, argues historian Shirley Ann Wilson Moore, author of *To Place Our Deeds*, a history of the African Americans in the East Bay. "They brought with them their expectations of advancement and a freer life than in the Jim Crow South, but they didn't want to leave their cultural traditions behind," she told me in an interview. I confessed to Moore that I had been disappointed that there were so few good barbecue restaurants in California.

I got the impression from our conversation that, just as the black exodus from the South was linked to the politics of Jim Crow, the decline of Southern culture in California can be linked to the emergence of more militant black politics in the 1960s and 1970s. Younger people, born in California, no longer felt a connection to the barbecued meats and blues music of their Southern-born parents. As they created a culture more reflective of their own experiences, the remnants of Southern culture that flourished in California in the 1940s and 50s lost much of their potency.

There are still plenty of places to get barbecue in the state but, just as the South no longer holds the depth of cultural significance it once held, the meaning of the food and the people that serve it has been chipped away by time and circumstance. What we are left with are not the vestiges of Southern barbecue, but the vestiges of the vestiges.

Whole Hog

JEFF DANIEL MARION

Who knows where a quest begins—or ends? Perhaps life is a series of overlapping beginnings, launching out, seeking, turning back, circling, maybe once in a while arriving. So perhaps this all began with the birth of my son, Stephen, when we traveled on a cold February evening in 1964 from Rogersville to Knoxville, only to be told by the doctor that we should find a place to stay that night, "This baby isn't ready to arrive yet. Maybe tomorrow." Time then for a late snack at Bill's Drive-In on Kingston Pike of what I believed to be the finest barbecue I had so far tasted, rivaled only by the fiery homemade concoction served up at the Dixie Queen back in Rogersville.

Whatever magic existed in that long-ago sandwich on the eve of my son's birth has surely haunted us down through the years, has marked our relationship, joined us in the common bond of barbecue brotherhood. As a boy Stephen grew up on Buddy's Barbeque, back in the days when Buddy's was take-out only, and you stood cramped in that tiny space on Kingston Pike waiting for Buddy or Lamuriel to dish out the unmistakable savor of hickory smoke. And from there to the days of Buddy's Pickin' and Grinnin' Friday and Saturday shows, bluegrass and barbecue served up with a mix that suited an array of tastes. Those lazy summer days we floated on Price's Pond, casting plastic worms for bass, drifting in the little aluminum boat Stephen has christened *Satisfied Mind*, daydreaming of the ultimate feast of the gods. Heather, our Shetland sheepdog, settled in the belly of the boat, lulled by the cool waters, was soon fast asleep.

We branched from Buddy's to discover other East Tennessee possibilities—Johnson City, we found, had Firehouse Barbeque, a North Carolina vinegary sauce much to our liking, and not far away, outside Bluff City, was Ridgewood, an East Tennessee tradition—if not the finest barbecue around then certainly the best baked beans anywhere. Period. And judging from the girth of those serving such fare, this was substantial food, the kind that would, according to my Uncle Dennie, put meat on your bones and lead in your pencil.

But it was in 1986 when I accepted a summer teaching appointment at the Governor's School for the Humanities in Martin, Tennessee, that the real quest began. We had long heard of Memphis barbecue, the true Tennessee Mecca for all those seeking the most succulent pork this side of paradise. So now I would be within a couple of hours of the city—plans could be made for the two of us to make the journey. But true to the nature of the quest, this was no straight line, Point A to Point B progression, for as I approached McKenzie, Tennessee, on my way to Martin, I caught a whiff of an unmistakable aroma, the one that whets the appetite and twangs the old taste buds in a salivating frenzy of anticipation—yes, hickory smoke! And there perched on a hillside along Highway 22 was a sign mounted on a twelve-foot metal pole proclaiming, "od to go." In passing I caught a glimpse of what appeared to be a shack, although shack is far too grand a word for that contraption of a building I saw. I made a mental note to return after I was settled in Martin for a month-long stay at Governor's School.

And return I did after a few days in Martin sampling Damron's Barbecue and finding it very good, for still I hankered for that deep-down, soul satisfying, ultimate barbecue, the wellsprings where I would bring my son for communion. I was beginning to understand the hunger of those Indians from the days of Hernando de Soto and his exploits into this territory, bringing to the new country the first hogs, introducing the natives along the way to hog meat slow-cooked over a pit of smoking embers. Now I had some notion of why those natives, once having had a taste of such meat, would risk having a hand chopped off for stealing de Soto's pigs, sneaking into the dark forests to fulfill the hunger that led them to such risks on their quests.

I entered what I came to know as Wood's Barbeque, a pine-slab, unpainted structure with a rough, slanting concrete floor, a single smoke-filled room with slab benches beside homemade tables, a potato chip rack with bags in disarray, a thin patina of ashes coating them all, a counter up front with a variety of items, including a small tin that read "Road-Kill Possum," a calendar on the back wall with the month's centerfold prominently displayed, a scantily clad shoat in a provocative pose. Soon a black face emerged from the even smokier pit room in back of the counter and said, "What for you?

"How's your barbecue?" I replied.

"It's pulled, man."

No "chopped," "chipped," "shredded," or "sliced," no: for years I've considered this answer to my question and now know what mysteries and truths are embedded within it. He did not say "Great," "Good," or "the Best." He said simply the last step of a long journey. For here the journey is the destination, heat culminating in mouth-watering succulence, a transformation by fire little short of miraculous, flesh to flesh and finally flesh to spirit. So this is the ritual: slow cooked over a pit, the hickory coals kept from reaching a flame, the meat pulled by hand.

He passed the jumbo sandwich across the counter to my waiting hands. On first bite I knew in a delicious shiver—this is the mark against which all others will be judged, great chunks of pork, tender, with no hint of greasiness, succulent, with both the flavor and aroma of hickory, some bits of brown, crusty outer skin meat mixed in with the white. And the sauce was vinegary, just enough tomato to flavor, enough pepper to give it real zest.

Here in a room that would defy any carpenter's level, cause the floating bubble to go astray and even disappear, here I had found the shrine to the pig. When Stephen visited with me a couple of weeks later, my deep pleasure was doubled in watching him experience what I had earlier known. From that day forward we knew the best—not that we would cease our search, but that we had "home base" from which to measure, a kingdom from which to judge. Now the test was to find an equal and, who knows, just maybe one that would surprise us and actually surpass Wood's.

And a time or two over the summers we came close. Traveling to Shiloh from Martin one year, we came upon a newly opened small barbecue stand in the middle of farm country. The owner invited us back to the pit, showed us the shoulders slowly soaking up that hickory flavor, let us linger and ask questions and savor the sandwiches. We never knew his name, only remember his kindness, his delight in explaining the art and process of real barbecue. And our trips to Memphis from Martin became standard parts of the visit: we sampled Topps and found it good; relished the visits to Rendezvous, but knew the pursuit of barbecue ribs was another quest altogether, found their complimentary red beans and rice a favorite; were disappointed by Gridley's. So far nothing surpassed Wood's, and it was here that we brought friends and colleagues, made barbecue dinner runs between classes and plenary sessions at Governor's School, hauled carloads of Yankees in the hope of converting them, trying to show them at least one solid reason for not crossing the Mason-Dixon Line in a northerly direction. At one point, Danny, the pit man at Wood's, after seeing how many folks we had brought to sample their wares, exclaimed, "You boys sho do like barbecue." Many, many others shared our taste in Wood's, for it grew from the primitive shack to a huge barn-like structure complete with banquet room. And, to our amazement and delight, the quality of the barbecue remained the same.

Year after year, from 1986 to 1994, we made our trek to Wood's, a month in

JEFF DANIEL MARION

summer and two days in February. Mid-February was time to read applications for Governor's School, and I was a lucky one, chosen as a reader. One February, Stephen, Ernest Lee, and I made our way to Martin following an ice storm, dodging trees fallen across Interstate 40, arriving at Wood's to find the lights out, the pig weather vane on the roof frozen in a sheet of ice. But Colonel Wood himself was there, served us the last barbecue sandwiches before closing due to weather. We have photographs of us sitting in the car chowing down on those last barbecue sandwiches. Arriving home from that trip I decided to write my friend and Governor's School colleague Keith Daniel in Yankee Massachusetts about those last sandwiches. I had saved one of the wrappers, even smeared a bit of sauce on it, and thought I would tease his taste buds. I began the letter, but what evolved was the following poem:

Song for Wood's Barbeque Shack in McKenzie, Tennessee

Here in mid-winter let us begin
To lift our voices in the pine woods:
O sing praise to the pig
Who in the season of first frost
Gives his tender hams and succulent shoulders
To our appetite:

Praise to the hickory embers
For the sweetest smoke
A man is ever to smell,
Its incense a savor
Of time bone deep:

Praise for Colonel Wood and all his workers
In the dark hours who keep watch
In this turning of flesh
To the delight of our taste:

Praise to the sauce—vinegar, pepper, tomato—
Sprinkled for the tang of second fire:

Praise we say now for mudwallow, hot grunt and pit squeal,
Snorkel snout ringing bubbles of swill in the trough,
Each slurp a sloppy vowel of hunger,
Jowl and hock, fatback and sowbelly, root dirt and pure
Piggishness of sow, boar, and barrow.

Those mid-winter sandwiches proved apocryphal, for a year later in the summer when we arrived at Wood's parking lot we noticed with a sinking feeling that the place looked abandoned, weeds growing wildly everywhere. Only later were we to learn of the colonel's death, the closing of his business, no one in the family to continue the tradition. We were forced then, to try a spot just down the road from Wood's, a little nondescript block building that announced simply Mayo's. We sat inside and talked to Mr. Mayo, then an elderly man who told us of Wood's death. Mayo's barbecue was nearly as good as Wood's, but within a year, Mayo too was gone, his business dying with him.

So on we traveled, following tips of special places in Memphis, discovering Interstate Barbeque and finding it mighty fine, but Memory is an unforgiving mistress, and will allow few if any contenders. In a moment of great sadness at the loss of Wood's and simultaneously a moment of sheer delight in remembering the place and its food, I asked our friend John Egerton, food writer and critic, if he had ever eaten at Wood's. When he said, "no," I went on to describe the barbecue to him.

"You need to go to Bozo's," he said. "And here's how you get there . . ." So it was on another trip to Memphis that we found Mason, Tennessee, a wide space in the road that boats both Bozo's Barbeque and Gus's World Famous Fried Chicken. Yes, Bozos is as good as Wood's, but the sauce at Wood's still seems better, just the right edge of pepper and vinegar (begrudging Memory again!). On our annual southern pilgrimage this May, Stephen and I stopped again at Bozo's, declared the barbecue sandwiches as good as ever. As we were about to leave, I asked the waitress about a particularly delicious-looking chocolate pie behind her. "Oh, that's German chocolate pie," she said. "It's so good it'll make you want to slap somebody." Whereupon another customer standing in line said, "I always heard it's so good that it make you want to slap your mama." We laughed and agreed that wouldn't be advisable, but we both knew the joy of finding something so good it's almost inexpressible, so powerfully fine you are set into motion, so moved to speak in the most elemental gestures. And so with quests: something stirs deeply within, occasioned by season or weather, and we're off; as Geoffrey Chaucer long ago noted, "folks long to go on pilgrimages." Whatever. Come spring, expect to see Stephen and me on the road southward, still searching, loving every step of the journey.

JEFF DANIEL MARION

Kicking Butt

MATT MCMILLEN

Inside the machine shop, the smoker begins to take shape. A hulking, 275-gallon residential oil tank, stretched out on a support frame, has been cut in half. A fifty-gallon drum, which will serve as the firebox, has been grafted onto one end, not exactly with surgical precision.

"It'll work," says Andrew Stoddard, thirty-seven, from behind a welder's mask, "but it's the ugliest welding job I've ever done."

Leaning against a wooden counter littered with tools, a rusted-out smokestack waits its turn in the operating room while Stoddard points out where the tuning plates will go. As he draws a chalk line inside the tank to mark the spots he will solder through next, he explains: "Tuning plates will run the length of the interior to hold movable slats. These aid in the distribution of heat."

That heat, which Stoddard will maintain at 230 degrees Fahrenheit, will cook six twenty-pound pork shoulders at Safeway's National Capital Barbecue Battle Saturday and Sunday in downtown Washington. "It's the money," he says. "That's why I'm building it myself. To buy the best smoker at the size I'd need, I would have to spend at least $5,000."

Stoddard, who's been working on the hardware since April, got the tank from a scrap dealer, the brother of a coworker. The wheels were snatched off a junked golf-course mower at the country club where he is chief engineer. The smokestack was plucked from a friend's back yard. Total expenses so far (not counting the meat): fifty dollars.

That's a frugal turn from Stoddard's early days. Seven years ago, inspired by a chapter on authentic barbecue in Chris Schlesinger and John Willoughby's *The Thrill of the Grill*, Stoddard, a Bethesda native, bought his first smoker. "At the time we were tight," says Stoddard, speaking of his and his wife's finances, "and it was totally inappropriate to spend $300 [on a smoker]. That didn't go over well. But the [resulting] barbecue smoothed things over."

Now he's hoping that his smoked pork will have an equally salutary effect on the judges of this year's competition. The Barbecue Battle, which attracted tens of thousands of people last year, is fought over two days, and, while Stoddard will be competing with smoked lamb on Saturday, it is Sunday that most excites him. That is the all-pork day, judged by Memphis in May–sanctioned judges. (Memphis in May, one of the biggest barbecue competitions in the nation, requires its judges to attend several hours of seminars on how to rate smoked pork and instructs them on the complex scoring it uses to determine a winner.) At the D.C. competition, three judges visit each of the sites of the more than forty teams of competitors at twenty-minute intervals during the course of an assigned hour, while four others judge blindly. (Most competitors are teams, but Stoddard will be accompanied by his wife, Jeanie, working as the pit boss handling all the details and leaving Stoddard to focus on the cooking.)

"It's all fun, and everyone is having a great time," says Doug Halo, competition coordinator and two-time Barbecue Battle champion, "but when the judging starts, it becomes dead serious."

No surprise there: The grand champion walks away with $1,500 and paid entry in the 2003 Memphis in May contest, where he or she will compete for the World Championship Pork Barbecue Title.

At 1:00 A.M. on a chilly May night, when Jeanie has long since gone to bed, Stoddard stands watch over forty pounds of pork shoulder. The night is unseasonably cold, so he leans against the now completed, freshly painted smoker to stay warm. A table, set up under a tent on the front lawn of his Bethesda home, is stacked on one end with plates, forks, and napkins. On the other side, a portable stove keeps last week's defrosted practice pork warm. "I smoked seventy pounds last weekend," Stoddard says. "I told the Montgomery County Police that I'd be serving it from 3:30 P.M. Saturday until 3:30 P.M. Sunday. I'll be cooking the whole time."

So far, though, only two of Stoddard's friends have shown up. One is a vegetarian.

Stoddard's specialty is the pulled pork sandwich. He cooks in the Memphis style, using indirect heat. The pork is given a dry rub—a complex, and secret, combination of spices—and left to render its fat and absorb the flavorful hickory and oak smoke. After about twenty hours, the pork is astonishingly tender and pulls away from the bone like strands of cotton candy. A pink smoke ring penetrates half an inch into the meat, deepening the flavor.

Though Stoddard turns the pork shoulders only once during cooking, the day-long vigil is anything but idle. "I set my alarm for an hour," Stoddard says, referring to his sleep schedule. "You just have to catch an hour when you can."

His eyes can't stray for long from the two thermometers he has embedded in opposite sides of the upper half of his smoker. Part of his practice routine is getting to know the idiosyncrasies of his homemade cooker. The transfer of heat, the setting of the dampers, the position of the tuning plates, the amount of wood used at a given time: everything has to be precise and in its place. As the clock passes 2:00 A.M., one of the thermometers shoots up to 300 degrees, far above the target temperature of 230. The firebox glows too brightly— there's too much wood. Stoddard throws open the top of the smoker to let the heat out, takes a quick look at the shrinking shoulders (each shoulder will lose approximately half its weight while cooking) and shrugs. "They're fine," he says without conviction.

Three weeks, 100 hours of cooking, and more than 160 pounds of pork later, Stoddard has the smoker under control. One side is twenty degrees hotter than the other, but he can live with that. "I'm not sure it will ever get tuned perfectly," Stoddard admits. He might not get the heat adjusted just right, but he won't risk overcooking the shoulder. A metal probe, inserted in the pork and connected to a digital thermometer via three feet of wire, measures the internal temperature. When it reaches 195 degrees, Stoddard's pager will sound, and he'll pull the shoulder off the grill.

In the meantime, he sips his beer and stands by calmly. He's relaxed, in control, and under few illusions about his chances. "Zero. Honestly, zero," he says without hesitation. "If I finish better than dead last, I'll be happy." He pauses, rethinks, smiles. "I think I have a chance—my pork's pretty good."

Real Barbecue Revisited

VINCE STATEN

I eased my car into the parking lot of the new Border's bookstore in Louisville and was readying to go inside for a book signing when I noticed a giant new structure hulking over the Border's parking lot. "Smokey Bones BBQ Sports Bar," read the sign, the first time I'd ever seen "BBQ" and "Sports Bar" in the same sentence. The sign wasn't crooked. There were no misspellings. There wasn't even a wood pile to be seen anywhere. For all the world this looked like the outside of an Outback or a Ryan's Steakhouse. But it said "BBQ" on the sign.

They're at it again, I thought. The franchisers.

It's been fifteen years since Greg Johnson and I published *Real Barbecue*, our ode to the slowest of the slow foods, in which we had the audacity to try and pick the top 100 barbecue joints in America. At that time there were hundreds of handbooks for those seeking out the great French restaurants of America but no glove-box guide to great barbecue.

There was a reason for that, a couple of reasons as a matter of fact. One was that barbecue was still referred to in the pages of the *New York Times* and other influential journals as "Southern barbecue," as if it were a regional delicacy found only in that eccentric part of the country below Baltimore on the map. And the other was that no one thought there was a market for such a guide. On the later point they were right. *Real Barbecue* was a poor seller, despite flattering reviews. Even *Vogue* lifted a delicate pinky and called it the most delightful food book of the year.

Our publisher, Harper & Row, gave the book every shot. They printed up 20,000 copies, a healthy first printing (and, as it turned out, last printing). Ten books later I still can't read a royalty statement, so I don't know how many copies *Real Barbecue* ended up selling. My guess is fewer than 8,000 went out the door. No major remaindering company stepped forward to snap up the unsold copies so Harper & Row pulped them and dumped them into the river. I bought 300 copies at a buck apiece.

A year after its 1988 publication *Real Barbecue* was history. I moved on to write *Unauthorized America: A Travel Guide to the Places the Chamber of Commerce Won't Tell You About*, a book that landed me a guest spot on David Letterman's old NBC show. Greg returned to his normal life as features editor of the *Louisville Courier Journal*. He's still there. I'm still writing books.

Every couple of years I'll get a frantic phone call from a book editor somewhere who has just heard about this "wonderful barbecue guide" and is interested in publishing an update. I ship off one of my remainder copies and never hear from the excited editor again. I think it may just be a ruse to get a free copy, since the book has acquired something of a cult status among serious chowhounds.

The ruse is over. My box of 300 is now down to two. The next editor is going to pay market price, which is $125 in the used book stores.

When I contemplate an update—and I contemplate it often—I think about how much has changed in the barbecue world in the last fifteen years, but how much remains the same. The Smokey Bones's and Famous Dave's and Red, Hot and Blues continue to try and tame barbecue, homogenize a food that prospers because of its many peculiarities and regional differences. Shiny advances in technology, like the Trager cookers that burn wood pellets, tempt those who'd like to dream that barbecue could be set-it-and-forget-it.

But the future of the un-fast food will remain in the hands of the rugged individualists who hand-letter their signs and spot-solder their homemade pits. It's still the people's food. There's more talk about barbecue today than there was fifteen years ago. I think that fully 10 percent of the population now knows that barbecue and Sloppy Joes are not one and the same. But I don't think consumption is up. I see too many shuttered BBQ joints to think that barbecue is flourishing. It's still a specialized taste, an acquired taste, although it is acquired very easily if you live in the neighborhood of a first-class joint.

That's where the action was, is, and will continue to be: in the joints. And for whatever else they want to be, Smokey Bones and company don't want to be known as a joint. Can't take grandma and the kids to a joint. And that's not good for the bottom line.

In Louisville, where Greg and I both reside, there has been a barbecue restaurant explosion in the last fifteen years. There was only one good place in town when we wrote *Real Barbecue*. Now there are a half-dozen, all of them owned and operated by guys who do it for the love of 'cue. None of them is driving a Mercedes.

Now these 'cue stalwarts have been joined by a couple of well-financed franchise boys, Smokey Bones and Famous Dave's. Red, Hot and Blue was well-financed too, and it's gone from Louisville after a short run. Even a town with no real barbecue tradition, like Louisville, can tell the difference between a barbecue restaurant and a barbecue-themed restaurant. Even McDonald's has tried to muscle in on the barbecue action with something called a McRib, which rears its ugly head every spring at selected Micky D's. God forbid your Mickey D's is selected. I remember the first time I ate one of these preformed meat-like products. I bought a second and took it to Greg. He examined it, took a bite, rolled it around on his palate, then passed judgment. "If pork is the 'other white meat,' then this is another white meat."

Still, despite their earnest efforts, it's a safe bet that barbecue won't ever be left to the multinationals like McDonald's. It's too much of an individualist's cuisine, fueled by hard work and seasoned with the hope that keeps bubbling up like all those secret sauces.

There was a funeral this fall in Kentucky; "Pappy" Bosley passed away in Owensboro. Back in 1963, Pappy and his wife had sold their own home to buy a little thirty-seat barbecue joint that specialized in serving mutton. Forty years later, at the time of his death, they'd managed to turn that tender, musky mutton into $5 million in annual sales at the Moonlite Bar-B-Que Inn.

The same quirky vision of success lives on in smoke-stained pits across the country. With the right sauce and a little luck, the sky's always the limit.

Greg sometimes takes a Sunday drive in Indiana on a little country road that runs along the Ohio River just north of Louisville—at least it used to be a little country road. Now it's also the main thoroughfare to the huge Caesars riverboat casino that bobs offshore about seven miles away. A few weeks ago, at the point where eager gamblers head out of New Albany onto Ind. 111, a new sign appeared: Back Porch BBQ. The owners had opened up in a building that used to be something else. They were excited, even fawning, as a seasoned customer bit into a bun stuffed with sizzling pulled pork.

It brought back memories of the nationwide quest for 'cue that had been at the core of *Real Barbecue*. Was this sandwich "the best we've ever had"? No, not really. Was this BBQ joint a bigger gamble than the tourists were taking at the casino? Yeah, probably. But when a few pieces of pork tumbled out of the bun and landed on the plastic cafeteria tray, they had that smoky red richness that only comes from a hand-tended fire and a pit man with patience. Picked up and dipped in a little sauce, it was still as true as ever: this is what the American Dream tastes like.

To the Unconverted

JAKE ADAM YORK

This is the meal equally set.
— Walt Whitman

Mud Creek, Dreamland, Twix-n-Tween,
the joints rise through smoke
and glow like roadhouses on Heaven's way.
Or so the local gospels raise them,
every tongue ready to map the ramshackle
of shacks and houses, secret windows
and business-sector hip in some new
geography of truth. If the meek shall,
then a rib-mobile may shame the fixed pit
in a reading from the book of skill,
the grill-less one cook himself to legend
rib by rib. The great chains' links
are live and hermetic as bone
and where cue burns hotter than politics,
every mouth's the forge of change,
all scholars temporary and self-proclaimed
One says he half-sublimes each time he eats
a rib and expects to go in a puff of smoke
when he finds the perfect pig:
he wanders like a ghost, his eyes trying everything, a genuine R&D,
and once a day he proclaims the latest find,
a homegrown Moses canting
a vernacular Talmud changeable as wind.
A word could crumple him, some backyard-
master slapping mustard on a country rib
to turn the state of things entire.

So every word reverberates and mystery's
sown again. Rib or rump, dry-rub or ketchup,
the eternal terms turn and barbecue's rooted
or pulled anew. Theories proliferate
like flies after rain, but that's the usual business.

JAKE ADAM YORK

THE PEOPLE

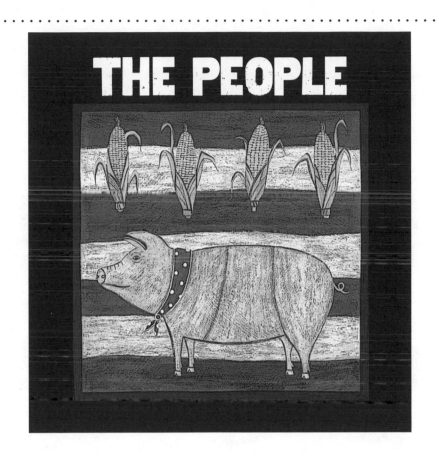

In the Kitchen

LINDA PARSONS MARION

Always uncertain at first, slowly we circle,
nosing out our places at the counter.
You take up sharp instruments, find
the rhythm of root and rind. I gather
the wood of our meal, sesame oil for tinder,
sherry for fire. I've never had a man
in my kitchen, a man with his own recipes
and a yen for dark vinegar. I've always had
plenty of elbow room, the plates to fill
as best I could—meat & three, come rain
or shine. After all that pork loin, all those pies,
I've let you into my den. You bring me groceries
like a prospector who struck the mother lode
and wants to spread the wealth—shiny colander,
Beaujolais, expensive Kalamata olives.
My table opens its leaves, the smells begin
their swirl, we season the cutting board
like old hands. You pepper the air,
I'll sweeten it with ham, and we'll let
the crumbs fall where they may.

Willodene

JULIANA GRAY

There are several items, tools and tricks of the trade, without which any Southern kitchen is incomplete. A good paring knife. Mason jars and fresh canning lids. A big iced tea pitcher. Bacon fat. And, perhaps most essential, a cast-iron skillet. As any Southern grandmother will tell you, this last item is an absolute must. The solid metal distributes heat evenly over the cooking surface, ensuring perfect fried green tomatoes and pork chops. A well-seasoned pan will be practically nonstick, so that cornbread and pineapple upside-down cakes slide out effortlessly. With proper care—and they do require extra attention, even obsession—an iron skillet can last over a century, longer than the grandmother singing its praises, possibly longer than the child receiving the lecture.

My own iron skillet once belonged to my grandmother, Willodene. It is pure black, glossy as fresh tar, weighs three pounds, and has a number 8 stamped into the bottom. This 8 is a mystery. I thought it was a measurement until my trusty ruler showed the skillet to be nine inches wide at the bottom, over ten at the top. I could almost pretend the 8, turned on its side, is the symbol for infinity, but even the most lovingly cared for iron skillets won't last that long.

This skillet was one of a few items Willodene gave to my parents when they married in 1967. She didn't have much money for lavish gifts, but neither did my parents, and they were glad to receive it. How long she owned it before then is uncertain; my father was a boy when it was new, still dull gray and rough, unseasoned. As she went through the seasoning process of heating, greasing, reheating, regreasing, and so on, she sent my young father into the yard to polish the skillet with sand. That must have been in the late forties. For twenty years or so she used it, baking and frying innumerable suppers, dinners, breakfasts.

My mother, working girl that she was, used it less often. She preferred pots and pans with cheap nonstick lining; they weren't as good, but they were less trouble to clean and care for, not as hefty, less likely to burn her hand if she unthinkingly grasped the handle. I can only remember her using the skillet to bake biscuits, following the recipe Willodene had taught her. So exclusively was this method used that it wasn't until after I went to college and married that I realized that most people baked biscuits on cookie sheets and used those prissy little biscuit cutters to make each one the same shape and size.

Willodene's skillet passed to me when I went away to the University of Alabama in 1990. I remember the sobriety with which my mother settled it in the bottom of a cardboard box labeled "JULIANA — KITCHEN." As she crumpled newspaper and arranged lesser pots and pans around it, Mom eyed me warily. I was eighteen, gangly and unsure, just starting to learn about the world and, more importantly, cooking. Clearly, I needed instruction.

"Always wash it right after you use it," she said sternly. "Never leave it wet. Always heat it on the stove eye until it's completely dry, and then oil it while it's still warm. Don't cook tomato sauce or anything acidic like that in it." I was on the verge of telling her that if she was so worried about me ruining it that she could keep the damn thing, when my father spoke up.

"Take good care of it," he said, his voice quiet. "It belonged to my mother."

Willodene was a pretty woman, though my memories of her as a grandmother are less flattering: dyed brown hair, slightly rounded shoulders, cat-eye glasses on a beaded chain around her neck. In old photos, she is lovely, slender, smiling. The droplet of Creek Indian heritage shows in her high cheekbones, which my father says I have inherited. In one picture taken in the early forties, she leans against a car, laughing at something, maybe a joke the photographer made. Her hair blows carelessly around her face, and her lips are full and dark, as if she's just been kissed.

It didn't last. Her marriage to my grandfather was unhappy, and after thirty years — not long after my birth — they divorced. A few years later she remarried, to a man who owned chicken houses in South Alabama. His name is never mentioned in my house, but then I called him Granddaddy. It was during this period that I knew her. My parents would send me down to her house for weeks at a time. They enjoyed the break from child-rearing, and I loved being pampered. She catered to my finicky eating habits, keeping a cabinet stocked with Campbell's soups for me to slurp while she cooked peas, squash, country-fried steak, banana pudding, lemon squares. In her iron skillet she fried okra and chicken and baked the heavy biscuits she had taught my mother to make, as Mom would teach me. These are not the typical fluffy biscuits the size of a fifty-cent piece that most grandmas make. These are formidable biscuits, fist-sized, with bottoms made crunchy by the meeting of cool dough and the hot, oiled pan. Add a slice of fried ham or a spoonful of home-made fig preserves and bliss will follow.

Her house was full of wonders: a butter churn whose paddle I inexpertly banged around, a swivel chair in which I spun until made to stop, a coffee table vase of what appeared to be roses but were actually pink-tinted seashells attached to wire stems. I was given free rein of the house and sometimes even accompanied my stepgrandfather to his chicken house, where I was allowed to take eggs off the conveyor belts and proudly line them up in cardboard flats. The new grandfather didn't talk much. At the chicken house, he'd leave me to my work for a few hours and give me a pocketful of change when he returned. At home, he mostly lay in his recliner and slept, his shallow snores rumbling like distant thunder beneath our kitchen laughter.

Parents are the original masters of misinformation. When Willodene came to stay with us, she came alone, and I was told she was just paying a grand-motherly visit. Sometimes she stayed a few days, sometimes weeks. On one of these longer visits, when I was about ten years old, her house burned down. No official cause was ever named; possibly something was left on in the kitchen, possibly the wiring shorted out. Her husband was not at home at the time. Luckily, he'd gone into town to eat dinner. Even luckier, some of his fa-vorite possessions were in his truck, others being repaired in town, others loaned to friends. Willodene lost everything but the rings on her fingers and the few things she had packed for her visit with us. She had to go home.

The next time we saw her, she and her husband had erected a double-wide trailer over the old house's charred foundation. She hated it, hated living in this box that pretended to be a house, hated the tiny, prefab kitchen, hated the slightly raised seam that ran down the center of her cramped new living room, joining the two sections. I thought she was unhappy over losing her things, so I sorted through the ash piles under the trailer, looking for lost jewelry or other valuables. I pried up a few scraps of blackened linoleum that had once been her kitchen floor and hid them away. I still have them, little chips of yellow patterned with lacy brown like butterfly wings, sooty and crumbling around the edges.

About a year later she paid another visit, and it was clear from the suitcases and boxes piled in her car that she intended to stay. Dad turned the downstairs study into a bedroom, reinforcing the sagging daybed mattress with a sheet of plywood and adding an old chest of drawers, a lamp, a space heater. Mom seemed relieved when Willodene took over the kitchen. She gently brushed aside Mom's concerns about sugar and kept a big pitcher of cherry Kool-Aid in the refrigerator for my sister and me, and brewed iced tea for the adults. She worked in our garden, keeping us in tomatoes, zucchini, and hot peppers, and baked cookies and fruit breads and pies. I do not remember her using the old cast-iron skillet, but I know she must have. She must have been pleased to see it, to feel its heft, to know her gift had saved it from the fire. Once a bouquet of bright flowers was delivered for her, but I was not allowed to read the card, and the flowers ended up in the trash.

Hindsight has a way of recasting a series of events, of simple choices and movements, into fate. My father says now that when his mother left to bring the rest of her things from her not-house, he had a deep, certain feeling he would never see her again. My mother claims to have had a "bad feeling" about her departure. As for me, I remember her taking me aside, kissing me, and telling me something a grandparent should never tell an already pampered child. "You're my favorite," she whispered, her glasses chain dangling over my shoulder. "You remember that."

Whatever our premonitions, real or imagined, what happened was neither mystical nor fantastic. While she was staying with a neighboring couple, waiting for a time when the house would be safely empty, her husband walked in and shot all three of them. He shot Willodene repeatedly in the face and body, killing her. He killed the neighbor woman and wounded her husband, then turned himself in to the police.

This, too, was largely concealed from my sister and me, little girls still struggling with long division, not yet ready to comprehend death, much less murder. We were told the bare bones of the story but did not attend the closed-coffin funeral. Newspapers were hidden as soon as they were delivered, but a friend clipped the articles and obituary for me. They sketched Willodene as a victim of a possessive, abusive husband who was enraged by the divorce proceedings she had instigated, and I suppose this must be true. But it is hard to reconcile this with the memory of a man who, when I was present, mostly slept in his recliner, though he occasionally kicked his dog a little too hard and seemed, perhaps, to enjoy throwing the dead hens from the chicken house into a neighbor's pen of devouring hogs.

I am a pack rat by nature; compounded with sorrow, this urge to save things turns compulsive. Before my parents could gather her belongings, I slipped into Willodene's room and took a few small things—a hair net, an emery board, a small circle-shaped pin—and added them to the box containing my newspaper clippings and the charred bits of her kitchen floor. Mom gave me her sewing kit, contained within a Danish butter cookie tin, which I still have.

But saving those things felt like stealing. The cast-iron skillet is a gift.

The problem with writing about our Southern grandmothers is that so many have already addressed the topic. Southern grannies are practically a genre unto themselves, along with the innumerable anecdotes of their toughness, their strength and endurance, their kindness, their love. The problem is, really, that we all think our grandmothers and their stories are special. And they are. Mine was.

Willodene has been dead for over sixteen years, buried in a small churchyard outside Clanton, Alabama. The church there still tends to her grave, placing wreaths and Easter lilies on it as they do the Confederate graves at the cemetery's heart. I have not been there since shortly after her funeral, and my father says he does not remember the name of the cemetery. But this may, again, be mere misinformation, intended to protect old wounds.

The cast-iron skillet Willodene bought, seasoned, cooked with for years, and passed on to her only child is still in my care. But, times—and owners—having changed, the skillet is as likely now to hold tofu Marsala and vegetarian chiles rellenos as fried green tomatoes. I don't know what Willodene would make of these new-fangled dishes; she enjoyed pork brains and eggs at breakfast, so maybe I should give her credit for having an open mind. I hope she would not object to the strange stuff that sautées, braises, and sizzles in her skillet. I hope she would be patient with innovations like the golden flecks of wheat germ that speckle my biscuits—her biscuits. I hope she would not mind what I have written about her, a little of the only truth I know.

Creole Contretemps

BRETT ANDERSON

In 1949, Kenneth Holditch traveled with his father from Mississippi to New Orleans for what would turn out to be a life-changing meal of trout amandine at Galatoire's. He remembers the meal vividly, particularly what he calls "the elegance and skill of the waiters." Fifteen years after that first visit, Holditch left his job in Memphis and joined the faculty at the University of New Orleans so he could "live in this unique city and dine at Galatoire's whenever I wished," as he explained it in a recent letter to the restaurant's nine-member board of directors. And dine he has, often at a twice-weekly pace and, for the past twenty years or so, usually as the customer of his favorite waiter, Gilberto Eyzaguirre.

Eyzaguirre, "Gilbert" to his legion of customers, was fired from Galatoire's after a female employee filed a sexual harassment complaint against him. It was the second such complaint filed against the waiter by an employee in less than two months. If this were a story about anywhere else but New Orleans, or perhaps anyplace else but Galatoire's, that would be the end of it. Instead, it was only the beginning.

Galatoire's general manager Melvin Rodrigue declined to comment on the particulars of Eyzaguirre's dismissal. "Even if Gilberto's not with us anymore, we have an obligation to him and the rest of our employees to keep that information confidential," he said.

Galatoire's files may be confidential, but Eyzaguirre's dismissal is hardly a secret. And his popularity among customers is enduring. The firing is what occasioned Holditch's letter, which was not a fan's note but an impassioned protest. The treatise was written on May 20, 2002, a month after the firing. A few days later, it was delivered in a bound volume along with 123 others to the Galatoire's board.

The letters, many of which were written by prominent New Orleans doctors, lawyers, judges, and business people, have been posted on ‹www.welovegilberto.com›, a website devoted to the cause of persuading Galatoire's

151

management to rehire Eyzaguirre. The list of letter writers is impressive; Pulitzer Prize–winning author Richard Ford and noted Louisiana State University historian David Culbert are among them.

"The purpose of this letter is to request that the members of the Board of Management of Galatoire's find a means to bring Gilbert back into the fold," former U.S. attorney Harry Rosenberg wrote.

Many of the writers express displeasure with what the volume's opening page calls the "peremptory firing." But to read the letters as a whole is to realize that Eyzaguirre's supporters are concerned about much more than their favorite waiter's job status. In his letter, Holditch echoes the concerns of many when he bemoans the changes that have occurred at Galatoire's since Rodrigue became the first non-Galatoire family member to be named general manager and chief operating officer of the restaurant in 1997, at the age of twenty-five. The most seismic of those changes was the controversial renovation that was completed in 1999. With the renovation came new dining rooms upstairs and the opportunity to reserve tables, a first in Galatoire's nearly century-old history.

"I felt almost the same way when they opened upstairs," Robert Barnwell, a letter writer who first dined at Galatoire's fifty years ago, said of Eyzaguirre's firing. "It was like when Brooks Brothers opened forty stores all over the United States. I liked it when there was only just one."

When viewed through the prism of Galatoire's overall makeover, Holditch writes, Eyzaguirre's firing "has made many of us 'old-timers' aware of the fact that something drastic is afoot, a renovation not only of the physical features of the classic old Creole eatery, but a renovation of its very soul."

There's no such thing as a subtle change at Galatoire's, at least not in the eyes of its most ardent customers. The restaurant's food is a testament to the virtues of trend resistance, and the kitchen's renderings of classic French-Creole dishes are hard to surpass. It's tempting to imagine the best of them—trout amandine, soufflé potatoes, stuffed eggplant, shrimp remoulade, oysters Rockefeller—tasting exactly as they did in 1905, the year Frenchman Jean Galatoire bought Victor's Restaurant on Bourbon Street and gave it his family's name.

Galatoire's is remarkably well preserved, though it actually has the feel of being older than it is. Its majestic atmosphere is derived not just from the tiled floors, nineteenth-century chandeliers, polished brass, and tuxedoed servers, but from the sense that those things extend from traditions rooted deep in New Orleans's exotic past. It's a restaurant one can envision existing nowhere else so easily as Paris, the world's capital of sophistication, and many of the people who are upset about Eyzaguirre's firing are equally upset that Galatoire's management would allow this elegant luster to be tarnished by, among other things, relaxing the dress code.

"The last time I was in there—I've only been there once since Gilberto left, which is unusual for me—there were people sitting at the table next to us who looked as though they should have been dining at the counter at Woolworth's," said Holditch. "I don't mean to sound elitist. But on the other hand, when you go to a nice restaurant, I think you ought to treat it as the kind of temple of food that it is."

Galatoire's has been subject to some culinary tinkering over the years. The restaurant only recently unveiled its first printed wine list. Portobello mushrooms are now a vegetable offering. These are the type of changes that would not warrant mention at another restaurant. But nothing goes unnoticed at Galatoire's, which is not so much a restaurant as an institution, complete with a board of directors—eight Galatoire family members and one non–family member—charged with overseeing the restaurant's operations. Constancy is part of the allure, and the regulars, many of whom were introduced to Galatoire's by their parents and grandparents and who are now taking their own children and grandchildren, find comfort in the familiar details.

In his letter to the Galatoire's board, Thomas Uskali recalled a meal he ate at the restaurant in 1994 with chef Louis Arbot and Dr. Brobson Lutz. "Gilberto served Chef Arbot 'the best Sazerac in memory,' and saw to it that our table ate exceedingly well, with inspired choices both on and off the menu," Uskali recalled.

Rosenberg, another Eyzaguirre customer, first started eating at Galatoire's in the early 1950s with his parents. "I still walk in and have that sort of visceral gastronomic sensation," he said.

It's a restaurant where management has agonized over whether or not to buy a toaster for fear that it would change the quality of the bread served with the oysters en brochette. In 1992, the decision to start accepting credit cards caused an uproar. Holditch recently noticed that the stuffed eggplant started to arrive without the eggplant skin. "It's still just as good, but I miss that eggplant skin," he said.

Nashville businessman Gary Smith was one of many people who protested the restaurant's decision in the mid-1990s to switch from hand-chopped ice to the machine-made variety. "I used to love watching the waiters chop that ice," he said.

Smith has been traveling to New Orleans with his wife, Cathy, every six weeks since 1968. "I call them eating trips," he said. These trips always include two or three meals at Galatoire's. For the past eighteen years, the Smiths were served exclusively by Eyzaguirre. In fact, for the Smiths, each of whom wrote a letter supporting Eyzaguirre, finding out that their waiter isn't going to be in town for one of their visits is enough to make them change their plans. "He's that important," Smith said, and by way of explanation asked: "You know how you feel when you're halfway through your second martini? That's how I'd feel when I'd enter Galatoire's and I'd see Gilbert."

Many of the people who wrote in support of Eyzaguirre liken eating at Galatoire's to being part of a "club." Prerequisites for membership would include longtime regular patronage; a steadfast devotion to Galatoire's rituals (i.e., eating lunch every Friday, or early evening dinner on Sundays); and, the ultimate status signifier, having a special relationship with a waiter.

For years, ordinary citizens have complained that privileged insiders have been allowed to circumvent the line in front of Galatoire's to gain easy access to its downstairs dining room. That may well be, but legend has it that Galatoire's old first-come, first-served policy was so unbending that Charles de Gaulle's request to have a table reserved was denied.

Club membership, if you want to call it that, is supposed to be accompanied by certain privileges, which is part of what is driving the discord sparked by Eyzaguirre's firing. Many regulars simply can't believe that action was taken without their consent. "We're all terribly upset, all of his customers," Marda Burton said shortly after the firing. A longtime regular, Burton is collaborating with Holditch on a book about Galatoire's history.

"The loss of your waiter after twenty-two years, it's just kind of a shock," Burton said. "And I think the customers should have some kind of say in this."

Galatoire's service staff has a relatively large concentration of career waiters who bring to the table requisite amounts of expertise, arrogance, and savoir faire. They've traditionally been granted a wide berth in Galatoire's dining room. Over the years, waiters have been known to actually cook off-the-menu specials for valued customers. And before the restaurant switched to full-time bartenders in 1999, they mixed drinks — usually with a heavy hand.

"I walked out of there once so soused I got into an argument with a hitching post," recalled riverboat pilot Captain Clarke "Doc" Hawley, who ate his first dinner at Galatoire's in 1959 with *Dinner at Antoine's* author Frances Parkinson Keyes.

By all accounts, Eyzaguirre, fifty-six, was a deft waiter who knew how to win the favor of customers.

"I think he saw waitering as a profession," Uskali said. "I had been with Gilbert for fourteen years, and that included almost four years in Florida, coming back every few months or so, and he still remembered odd little bits.

"I brought my mother a couple of times, and he remembered her name. He was a throwback to how we assume things used to be."

"Gilbert always remembered your name and your family's name and your children," Holditch said. "When I've needed somebody to drive me to the hospital or something, he's done it."

"I can think of no other server who could surpass him," Barnwell wrote of Eyzaguirre in his letter, "unless it is the Canadian VIA Rail's Chaleur dining car steward, Cyril Landry."

But in the spring of 2002, Eyzaguirre ran into difficulties. On March 3, he received a written notice from Galatoire's management for "purposely patting a waitress on her back which also had the effect of her dropping several beers on the floor." The notice went on to say that "sexual harassment is not permitted by law" and that any further sexual harassment complaints filed against Eyzaguirre would result in his termination. Soon after came the second complaint, and his dismissal.

While many avoided the issue, a sizable handful of Eyzaguirre's letter-writing supporters chose to address the reason for his firing. While none could claim to have better than secondhand knowledge of the particulars surrounding the dismissal, the waiter's dazzling performance on the dining room floor was often enough for them to cast doubt on the legitimacy of the sexual harassment allegations.

For much of the twentieth century, the Galatoire's dining room has been a place run by men, filled with men, and catering largely to men. It is only in the last decade that women were hired to work on the waitstaff, and it is one of the many examples cited by the restaurant's old guard as a change for the worse.

It was in this environment that Eyzaguirre honed his craft and rose to the level of a near-legend among the regulars. Some of those regulars even praised the qualities that may not have served Eyzaguirre well in the new Galatoire's. "Gilbert's Latino, he's gorgeous," said Burton, who has a hard time believing her waiter would be capable of doing anything untoward. "He's flirtatious with his customers, and we all love it."

Burton's letter was fairly typical of many written by the regulars, whose views on sexual harassment, far from reflecting a twenty-first century ethic, often seem to emanate from the same Old World sentiments that inform their love of the restaurant and its anachronistic ways.

"Having been in the academic world, I know what a really slippery slope this business of sexual harassment is," said Holditch, who likened Galatoire's male-dominated, banter-filled waiter culture to that of a sports locker room.

"If you go into a situation like that, I think you need to sort of be prepared for what's going to happen," he continued. "Even if they are hiring waitresses, this is basically a man's world, that waiter situation. And I must say that generally I prefer waiters."

Holditch said the letter writers are "asking for a hearing and they're suggesting, and I think this is true, that there was a rush to judgment." And Richard J. Tyler wrote: "Obviously, we are not privy to the events that led to his termination. I can tell you, however, that the word on the street is that his discharge was for insubstantial conduct that has been blown out of proportion."

For his part, Eyzaguirre has helped advance conspiracy speculation. He denies any wrongdoing and characterizes the circumstances surrounding his dismissal as a set-up devised to get rid of him. He claims that Rodrigue resents his popularity among Galatoire's customers. "The waiters make the restaurant, not the managers," he said. "Some people feel that the waiters have too much power."

Eyzaguirre said the complaint that got him fired stemmed from nothing more than his touching the hand of a female bartender in order to get past her in the restaurant's kitchen.

"My bottom line is I didn't become a sexual harasser in two months," he said. "What about the other twenty-three years?"

Rodrigue would not respond directly to Eyzaguirre's characterizations.

"What he chooses to tell his loyal following is up to him," Rodrigue said. "We're in an unfortunate position because we can't disclose what we have."

But a lawyer for one of the victims of Eyzaguirre's alleged advances begs to differ with the waiter's account. While none of the sexual harassment complainants has sought the spotlight, the person who filed the second written complaint, the one that lead to Eyzaguirre's dismissal, responded to requests for comment through Anthony Glorioso, her family's lawyer.

"Would Galatoire's fire him if it wasn't significant?" he said. "It's not like Gilberto did something and she ran off crying and filed [a sexual harassment complaint] right away. He wouldn't stop. She even asked him to. He wouldn't stop, so she gave in. She said, 'I've got to tell somebody. I want to work here.'"

Glorioso, who said his client is a college student, added, "I think that Galatoire's is very fortunate in this situation. It could have been a lot worse for them."

Chris Ansel agrees with the dismissal. His grandfather was a Galatoire, and he worked at the restaurant for seven years. Today, he sits on the Galatoire's board.

Ansel has listened to customers worry over the restaurant's mystique for years, particularly when change was afoot. He appreciates the interest of the regulars, but he said there was nothing vague about Eyzaguirre's situation. "There are rules and regulations on the books, and we have to follow them," he said. "I remember years ago when desegregation came in. A lot of customers asked my grandfather, 'What are you going to do?' He said, 'We're going to obey the law.'"

When Rodrigue took over management of Galatoire's, he was effectively appointed head of the club without being offered membership into it. A brief history printed on the menu lists Galatoire family members David Gooch, Justin Frey, and Michele Galatoire as the restaurant's managers, with no mention of Rodrigue.

He was hired with a mandate to increase revenues for a growing number of family shareholders, and even some of his detractors will admit that he has been successful in this mission. But the changes that have transpired under his watch have not always endeared him to the old-line regulars.

"I knew when I interviewed that [Galatoire's] needed a whole lot of help. The wiring in the walls looked like spaghetti," Rodrigue said. "People always say, 'Don't fix what's not broke.' Well, how do you know what's broke?"

In many ways, Rodrigue's mandate was bound to bump up against Galatoire's waiter-driven culture. If all of your oldest customers like everything the same—including their waiters—the agent of change isn't going to be the most popular person in the room.

Thus in many of the letters, it doesn't take long for the subject of Eyzaguirre's firing to give way to conspiracy theories about a power struggle between Rodrigue and the waiters. There is no question that the waiters at Galatoire's have power. Even after being fired, the years of accumulated goodwill left Eyzaguirre in what his supporters seemed to believe was a position of influence. One prominent local lawyer even asked to go off the record before admitting that he occasionally used waiters other than Eyzaguirre when he visited Galatoire's. More than one lawyer refused to comment on the matter due to the fact that they had been giving Eyzaguirre legal advice. Brobson Lutz, a physician, letter-writer, and fierce Eyzaguirre advocate, paints the waiter's firing as merely the endgame of a Rodrigue power play. "This was an opportunity for [Galatoire's] to get rid of somebody who was perhaps more popular than the restaurant itself," Lutz said. "I think Gilberto is a masterful artist, and I don't think Melvin had the management ability to handle him. Gilberto probably made more money than Melvin."

In a rageful, exclamation point–laden three-page letter, Galatoire's fixture Mickey Easterling takes exception with, among many other things, what she calls the management's "overt effort to get rid of all (one by one) the long-term dedicated wait staff by assigning them" to work in the upstairs dining room, a move Easterling claims serves the dual purpose of chasing off the "old-timers" who insist on eating in the original dining room downstairs.

It's a common complaint among Eyzaguirre supporters. Some feel that Rodrigue would rather fill tables with quick-eating tourists than with long-standing regulars who have the habit of lingering for hours on end. Eyzaguirre's firing is simply an extreme manifestation of a larger strategic plan at Galatoire's, their thinking goes.

But for these conspiracy theorists to be correct, Galatoire's had to decide that firing its most experienced waiters is the key to its financial future — certainly an unorthodox business strategy.

Rodrigue himself dismisses the theory as a claim too absurd to dignify.

"It's what this restaurant has been built around, the relationship forged between the waiter and the customer," he said. "We want that to go away like we want a hole in our head. It's what we are."

Captain Hawley was among many regulars to send his letter directly to Galatoire's management immediately after Eyzaguirre's dismissal. In response, Hawley received a note signed by Rodrigue and John B. Gooch, the chairman of Galatoire's board.

"Based on your letter and others received from interested customers, the Board and management have conducted a complete review of the situation with Gilberto Eyzaguirre," the response letter read. "We do not believe that any further action is warranted."

But even as Galatoire's management stood firmly by its decision to fire Eyzaguirre, the protest letters continued to pour in to the restaurant and to Holditch, who had taken responsibility for compiling the letters in a bound volume.

From the outset, the organizers proved adept at marshaling support for their cause. Holditch said artist George Dureau even offered to design signs for a protest that was discussed but never took place. Everyone involved waited anxiously for Galatoire's board to meet to discuss, among other things, the letter-writers' concerns. Rodrigue, who is not a member of the board but attends its meetings, said the board voted unanimously to support his decision.

When asked how he felt about the news, Lutz responded, "I don't know.

I'm still in healing mode. You go through stages with any sort of tragedy in your life."

Lutz, like many of Eyzaguirre's supporters, wouldn't commit to boycotting the restaurant.

"I fully intend to go back—if they'll let me," he said, "but I don't know what it's going to be in a month or a year. You hope that things change for the better. When they change for the worse, they don't usually last."

Holditch mentions the song "The Night They Drove Old Dixie Down" to illustrate what he feels is happening to Galatoire's. He's still committed to finishing the book he's writing with Burton, but he can't bring himself to return to the restaurant he loves as much as New Orleans itself.

"And I miss it," he said.

Epilogue: Eyzaguirre has worked at several New Orleans restaurants since his dismissal from Galatoire's. At the time of the book's printing, he was waiting tables at both the Bombay Club and Tommy's Cuisine. The uproar over his firing spawned a theatrical production, "The Galatoire's Monologues," which ran sporadically for over a year at Le Chat Noir. All the performances sold out. Eyzaguirre also filed a lawsuit against his former employer, which in turn filed a counter suit. The matters are still pending.

The Viking Invasion

MOLLY O'NEILL

A hundred years ago, Greenwood, Mississippi, in the heart of the Delta, was the cotton capital of the world. Now many of the squat brick buildings downtown are vacant, and Greenwood seems stuck in an era when shoe repair, sewing notions, and feed stores were big business. Fewer than twenty thousand people live within the city limits, although when the households of the surrounding county are added, the area has a population of about thirty-seven thousand. It is, as residents say, one of the poorest places in the poorest part of the country.

Nevertheless, in some respects, Greenwood recalls a way of life that many Americans feel they have lost. The outskirts of town are fringed by cotton, corn, and soybean fields, and acre after acre of the square, watery pens where catfish are farmed. Blues performances are advertised on hand-painted signs stuck to telephone poles, and people sell their folk art—paintings, bottle-cap constructions, primitive whirligigs—from their homes. In the early morning, the sounds of duck calls and shotguns ting against the hydrangea-blue sky. Hickory smoke hangs in the evening air as hints of pork, cumin, and ketchup mix with the smells of fried chicken, catfish, baked ham, and redeye gravy. Instead of restaurants and takeout places, there are oil drums rigged for barbecue in people's backyards.

Most people drive around Greenwood in pickup trucks with gun racks or in small, late-model American cars, but shiny new s u v s, Subarus, and Volvos are usually parked in front of the old opera house on the banks of the Yazoo River, where Viking Range Corporation installed its headquarters fifteen years ago. Formerly divided into storefronts, the renovated Victorian building is a curious amalgam of past and present: the exterior has retained its New Orleans–style porch and curlicue ironwork, but through the front door one can glimpse a spare white industrial interior that looks like a loft in SoHo. Just to the left of the entrance, one last storefront remains: a tiny establishment with the words "Buford Cotton" on its awning. This enterprise appears to be moribund, but the proprietor, Bubbe Buford—who spends much of his day shoo-ing the cars of Viking visitors out of the single parking space in front of his store—won't sell.

Just inside the Viking headquarters is a 90-C Special Deluxe Model Chambers Range—an Ozzie-and-Harriet vintage white enamel gas stove with six burners, two ovens, and big chrome knobs. Manufactured in 1948, and weighing in at 545 pounds, the Chambers, which is displayed in an elevated niche, is the honored ancestor of all Viking ranges. Fred Carl, the company's fifty-four-year-old founder, told me that the stove originally belonged to his grandmother-in-law.

"When I could finally afford to build my wife a decent kitchen, she wanted a range just like her grandmama's, but they didn't make them like that anymore," Carl said as we sat in his office on the second floor of the opera house. And so he set out to design one, and ended up creating a new category of—and price range for—kitchen stoves. I was already familiar with this story; it is the standard introduction to the Viking legend, quoted by every person who works for the company and included in most of its publicity materials. But Carl's soft Delta drawl was tinged with his wonder, and I scribbled down his words as if I'd never heard them before.

Carl is a short, thick, partly bald man with a neatly trimmed white beard. He wears short-sleeved cotton shirts—plaids or prints, mostly—and khaki trousers. He is perpetually flushed and morbidly shy. When he was young, he was kind of a geek; now his physical restlessness and the darting motion of his blue eyes behind his wire-rimmed glasses suggest a man with unlimited physical and creative energy. This quality, coupled with an obsessive persistence, has earned him acceptance in the kitchen-appliance industry—a close and deeply conservative society that tends to shun newcomers.

Carl's father was a building contractor in Greenwood, as was his grandfather; Carl never questioned that he, too, would be in the building business, but he wanted to be a designer or an architect. When he was a young boy, he tried to design a better dump truck and moved on to make sketches for a gravel-washing plant, a boarding school, and a military academy. Carl even wanted to build a better Disneyland. But his enduring passion was Greenwood. "I'd look at the old, ugly buildings and wonder how I could make it pretty and right," he said. "I wanted to make the perfect Main Street, U.S.A."

After his sophomore year of college, he joined the navy and served two years in Iceland before returning to Mississippi to finish his business degree, at Delta State University. Carl had hoped to go on to study architecture; then his father, a brilliant builder but a terrible businessman, lost everything. "I'd signed some loans for him," Carl said, "so there I was, twenty-three years old, married, my parents broken and needing my help, and I'm bankrupt, feeling like this little boy, this little piece of dirt."

For ten years, Carl worked in construction and sold Herman Miller office furniture to hospitals to pay off the family's business debts. To escape the tedium of these jobs, he stayed up late, immersed in what he called his "side projects," studying architecture newsletters and books like *Eames Design* and *High Tech*. Gradually, he became the leading contractor in Greenwood, specializing in contemporary houses complete with the industrial-style kitchens he'd seen in postmodern design books. To lure customers, Carl set up a showroom where he displayed cabinetry by Rutt, as well as appliances by Thermador, KitchenAid, Sub-Zero, and Jenn-Air. The showroom barely broke even.

In the early eighties, when Carl's wife, Margaret, requested a sturdy, old-fashioned stove, he began to consider designing something that was both more powerful and more stylish than the typical General Electric. Suddenly, cooking and lifestyle magazines were full of restaurant stoves, and his customers wanted to buy them. "They'd be putting in a $50,000 kitchen and they'd ask me to put in a commercial range, and I'd have to tell them it was too dangerous," said Carl. "It says so right on the label on the back of those ranges: 'Not for Household Use.'" The stoves made exclusively for restaurants can pose a fire hazard in private homes, because they are not well insulated; they depend on the fire walls, insulation, and venting systems that are customary in restaurant kitchens. But Carl also thought that industrial ranges were energy hogs and impractical for home cooks because they have no broiler. He began doodling—in his truck while waiting for deliveries at construction sites, at his desk while talking to suppliers on the phone. He worked on specifications for insulation, pilot lights, and broilers. Soon he was thinking about his stoves all day long and trying to run his construction business at night. After eighteen months, he'd come up with a design.

For the next two years, Carl met with most of the major commercial stove manufacturers in the United States and tried to persuade them to buy his design; they were not impressed. Failing to sell his idea, he paid the U.S. Range Corporation, in Gardena, California, to manufacture his stove. "I was convinced that if I built something beautiful and powerful and safe, there were people out there who'd buy it," Carl said. He waved his hand toward the Yazoo River outside his office window, as if to direct my eye past the river to the world beyond the Delta.

In 1986, Patricia King was renovating her kitchen on Waverly Place, in New York City. King, who works with her husband in his mailing-list brokerage business, is an avid cook. She wanted a restaurant stove, and she was dismayed when her architect showed her the ductwork and insulation that local ordinances required. "I would have lost six square feet," she said. King wasn't willing to sacrifice that much of her kitchen.

Then, after months of research, her architect produced a photocopy of a flyer describing the Viking range—one of the several thousand flyers that Carl, despairing of finding a national distributor, had mailed to kitchen designers around the country. It was a massive restaurant stove look-alike, and although Viking later became known for its stainless-steel ranges, the first model was black enamel. It had a big oven and a powerful gas broiler, and it was well insulated—King could use all six burners at once without setting her house on fire. The price of that first Viking was $3000, approximately three times as much as a conventional range. When King put down a hundred-dollar deposit, she had no idea that the Viking Range corporation had yet to build a single stove and that it had precisely two (unpaid) employees: Carl and his assistant, Tawana Thompson. Carl framed King's check, but even before he shipped her range—nine months later and six months behind schedule—he was forced to cash it.

King's new range was a disaster. The electric pilots didn't work properly, and gas leaked into the kitchen. The oven doors would not stay open; once, as she was putting a pumpkin pie in the oven the door slammed, burning her hand. As each problem arose, King called Viking headquarters; Carl had recruited several friends, including an engineer, to help him part time, and Viking's entire staff, now numbering four, would get on the line. Sometimes, Viking sent in a local appliance repairman, and Carl talked him through the job over the phone. Once, the company even flew in engineers. "They must have rebuilt that stove about four times," King said. "I began to suspect they'd sold me a prototype, but they were so nice and they cared so much I couldn't get mad." In early 1988, her range was finally working well, and the company sent King a basket shaped like the state of Mississippi filled with gourmet food from the Delta. The card was addressed, "To the director of the Viking Range Corporation New York Test Kitchen."

By then, Carl had gathered a group of ten partners—including his doctor, the local Chevron distributor, an insurance agent, and several farmers, each of whom invested an average of $12,600—and rented a small abandoned factory in Greenwood. In 1989, he began building his own stoves.

For serious cooks, the appeal of the Viking stove lies in its size and power. Its burners, unlike those of most domestic ranges, are powerful enough to sear ingredients, caramelizing their exterior and sealing in the moisture. (Food sautéed on a conventional range often dries out before it browns.) The size of the range also allows an ambitious cook to prepare simultaneously all the components of a fashionably layered dish, such as Chilean sea bass with pan-roasted wild mushrooms, herbed polenta, wilted greens, and a preserved-lemon sauce. The broiler is powerful enough to crisp sugar over a crème brûlée in an instant, and its oven is large enough to bake a Thanksgiving meal for twenty.

Carl couldn't afford to advertise extensively, so he offered to lend his ranges to chefs, food writers, cooking-school teachers, and television cooks. Soon, chefs and food writers were calling the Viking "the Mercedes-Benz of stoves." When I was building a test kitchen for a web-based food-media company I had cofounded, a public-relations firm representing Viking called me and offered to outfit it. The strategy worked: like thousands of other food professionals, I was impressed by the appliance's look, power, and easy maintenance.

Word of the luxury range—and its growing market—eventually reached Stephens Inc., the investment bank, based in Little Rock, Arkansas, that had taken Wal-Mart public. In 1992, when several of Carl's investors became impatient and threatened to take over his company, Stephens stepped in, assigned the Viking Range Corporation a value of $10 million, formed a partnership with management to buy the company, and appointed Carl the CEO.

Stephens's investment allowed Carl to attract experienced executives to Greenwood, double the size of the company's factory space, and increase its advertising budget. That year, as the company's annual Christmas party approached, Dale Persons, its vice president of public affairs, begged Patricia King to find her canceled hundred-dollar check, which Carl had always regretted cashing. After rummaging around, she found the check and sent it back to Greenwood. Not long afterward, Carl shipped King a new stainless-steel range.

Doug Martin, who oversees the Stephens partnership with the Viking Range Corporation, knew nothing about stoves, but he knew that the Viking range could appeal to more than a few hundred thousand cooking-obsessed Americans. "We saw this whole demographic of baby boomers moving into the time of their life when they have disposable income, saw them spending on their homes, especially their kitchens. They wanted solid, ultra premium, they wanted stainless steel. It didn't matter what it was, as long as it was stainless steel."

Months after Stephens invested in the company, its advertising firm, the Ramsey Agency, of Jackson, began creating an ambitious print and television campaign that placed the thoroughly modern range alongside potent icons of the past: in one ad, the industrial-looking stove gleamed in an amber-hued kitchen of vintage linens, heirloom silver, and an old farmhouse table. The campaign proved so successful that Viking reportedly had twenty million dollars' worth of orders backlogged for twenty-two weeks. In 1994, Carl instituted the Toyota Production System, making each range to order and shipping it within a month. It takes twenty-three people three hours to turn out a range; to shape the 18-gauge sheet metal, bake on its porcelain coating, and assemble the parts.

Meanwhile, in New York, King received a letter from Fred Carl, telling her that she was now one of many celebrities—including Bill Cosby, Madonna, and Alexander Haig—who owned a Viking. At her dinner parties, the guests were talking less about her cooking and more about her stove. "The Viking had become the darling of the entire swanky deluxe style in the United States," she said. "It's not just a stove—it's a trophy."

Stoves have always been status symbols in America. In the Colonial era, even fireplaces were signs of conspicuous consumption: built without angling walls to slow the draft or help radiate the heat, they burned fuel swiftly, displaying the owner's access to the rich timber resources of the New World. As the Colonial population grew, however, the wood supply dwindled, and stoves—which burned fuel more efficiently and provided steadier heat—became more popular. By 1820, stoves were outfitted with cooking tops and began to compete with the fireplace in meal preparation as well.

The storage area of the Albany Institute of History and Art, in New York State, contains a collection of about fifty American stoves made between the early nineteenth and the early twentieth century. Tammis Grott, the chief curator at the institute and one of the country's leading cast-iron-stove scholars, recently gave me a tour. "From the beginning," she said, "stoves were a very accurate reflection of aesthetic taste and what people cared about."

The earliest American stoves are small and squat, decorated with Gothic-style bas-reliefs of biblical scenes. With the birth of the new republic, Moses' tablets and Noah's ark gave way to eagles and stars-and-stripes. By the mid-nineteenth century, when the art of casting iron reached its height, stoves had become pieces of sculpture, advertising their owners' wealth. In the institute's collection, there are stoves cast as miniature Federalist-style houses, stoves with twin columns molded into dolphin shapes, stoves whose walls feature intricate pastoral scenes of flowers and birds.

As the century progressed, however, the hearth became a focal point for a number of social anxieties, from industrialization to immigration and urban growth. "Whenever the culture gets scared, it runs home, and there is no more powerful symbol of home and family than the stove," Priscilla Brewer, a historian and the author of *From Fireplace to Cookstove*, said. But the stove's symbolic value cut both ways: some nineteenth-century social critics blamed stoves for the breakdown of the American home, just as twentieth-century observers would mourn the demise of home cooking. In an 1843 essay, "Fire Worship," Nathaniel Hawthorne bemoaned "the invaluable moral influence which we have lost by our desertion of the open fireplace," even as he installed stylish stoves throughout his house.

There were also misgivings about the hygiene and culinary superiority of stoves. Catharine E. Beecher and her sister Harriet Beecher Stowe argued that food had tasted better when it was cooked over the fire or in the chimney. "We cannot but regret, for the sake of bread, that our old stead brick ovens have been almost universally superseded by those of ranges and cooking stoves," they wrote in their book, *The American Woman's Home* (1869). The authors were part of the growing Cult of Domesticity, a nineteenth-century movement that glorified the quotidian, the traditional, the handmade. In response, stove manufacturers published cookbooks and sponsored cooking schools, adroitly positioning themselves as indispensable to the return to a simple life while simultaneously encouraging the notion that everything, including the hearth, could be improved upon.

By the 1870s, the stove industry had moved from New York to the Midwest, fleeing the violent labor uprisings among the ironworkers in the Albany-Troy area. In Michigan, Illinois, and Ohio, cast-iron cookstoves evolved into ranges constructed of sheet metal. And as wood fuel gave way to coal, and then to oil, gas, and electricity, the art of cooking came to seem more like a science, a by-product of technological innovation. The 1907 Acorn cookstove in the Albany collection—a shapely black cast-iron box with six burners, a single oven, short church-lady legs, and shiny nickel-plated decorations—looks like a grandmother of the modern range. And although many wealthy Americans are still seduced by the promises of industrial-strength stoves like the Viking, others have become more enamored of their predecessors. "At the beginning of the twentieth century, people were nostalgic for fireplaces," Groft said. "Today, everybody's nostalgic for stoves like the Acorn."

Edward Semmelroth, the thirty-four-year-old founder of ‹Antique-Stoves. com›, can't restore old stoves fast enough to satisfy his customers. Semmelroth is tall, lumbering, and bespectacled, and he lives in Tekonsha, Michigan. One of about fifty antique stove dealers in the United States he chose his occupation for sentimental reasons. "I wanted to be born before planned obsolescence," he explained. "You know, when Dad worked and Mom stayed at home, and every town had a diner and chrome was king—the kind of stuff that gives you a warm and fuzzy feeling." For years he lived a life of quiet tinkering, not unlike that of an appliance repairman in the 1950s. Then suddenly in the early nineties, he started getting twenty to thirty calls a day—"the Hollywood types, big corporate types, techie types, the super rich."

Like Fred Carl, Semmelroth reads food magazines, but he isn't looking at the pictures; he's looking for recipes. And the more articles he reads about the demise of home cooking in America the more his telephone rings. Semmelroth calls this "the great compensation." Not surprisingly, stoves like the Magic Chef and the Chambers—the white enamel ranges from the twenties and thirties, the green-and-cream models from the thirties and forties, and the rare bright blue, red, and yellow models of the fifties—are now the most sought-after. "They have that retro chic, the beginnings of an industrial look," he said. "They are big enough to be restaurant stoves and outfitted for much more ambitious cooking."

Semmelroth has about fifty antique stoves in his own collection, and another two hundred or so that are being restored. Behind the nineteenth-century farmhouse where he lives with his mother, there are three barns full of stoves and two additional acres covered with the stoves that he keeps for parts. He won't touch a stove made after 1955. "They're all hunks of junk," he said. "Don't get me wrong, these new industrial ones are almost an exception. They are a step back in the right direction, if you know what I mean. But all that electric gadgetry—the electric pilots, the convection function—isn't going to hold up. I bet you that nobody's going to be cooking on a Viking or a Wolf a hundred years from now."

The choicest pieces on Semmelroth's collection are on display about half a mile from his home, in his storefront showroom in downtown Tekonsha. Visiting his store is not unlike touring the storage area at the Albany Institute. Semmelroth is particularly proud of his Magic Chef 63, which was built in 1930. An austere, no-nonsense range, it weights 745 pounds and has eight burners. Below the burners is a large, all-purpose oven, and stacked to its right are a bread-warming oven, a baking oven, and two broiling ovens. The range was built in Lorraine, Ohio, and originally cost $600. "At that time, you could get a brand-new Chevy for $1600," Semmelroth said. Like the grand custom-cast stoves of the nineteenth century, the deluxe models of the early twentieth century were owned by wealthy people who kept household staffs and entertained frequently. Semmelroth, who found this particular stove in a former diplomat's home in Yonkers, spent several hundred hours restoring it and plans to sell it for just over $20,000.

It can take weeks of trial and error, Semmelroth says, to learn which burners on a vintage range run hot enough to sauté and which will burn the Teflon off a nonstick skillet. Nevertheless, he cooks regularly on his stoves—for his mother, for the two friends who work part time for him, and for anyone who happens into his shop. He simmers soups from the baby vegetables that a farmer friend sets aside for him, roasts the free-range chickens that another friend delivers, pan-fries fish from Lake Michigan, and makes fresh bread and pastry. "I'm like, you know, retro nerd meets gourmet snot," he says. "I'm almost cool."

Semmelroth knows, however, that forty-nine out of fifty of his customers are merely buying a design element; that's why he's finding it hard to part with his Magic Chef. He has a waiting list of ten potential purchasers, but so far none meet his standards. "I want this baby to go to a cooking home," he said. And that's the problem. The people who can afford to buy vintage stoves cook even less than the average American. In fact, like the people who buy industrial ranges, they hardly cook at all.

Five years ago, Fred Carl gave a Viking range to Tawana Thompson, the employee who has been with him the longest. She never uses it. "I live alone, I get home late, I microwave something to eat," Thompson said. "But I love looking at my Viking. Sometimes I turn it on just to feel its power." The salespeople who distribute and sell Viking ranges estimate that the vast majority of their customers are "look, don't cook" people, who prepare elaborate meals only on holidays or special occasions. Most Viking owners are happily anticipating a time when they can start cooking seriously—whether or not that time will ever come. Trophy stoves are the culinary equivalent of a retirement plan; as some save for a world tour or a Florida condo, others now invest in a showcase kitchen. The Viking range symbolizes its owner's intention to have, one day, the family life that is supposed to go along with it.

The Carls live in a modest Creole-style house in Northeast Greenwood where, at least once a week, a small crowd assembles for dinner. The night that I joined them, there were about a dozen adults gathered in the kitchen—relatives, friends, and those Carl calls "members of the Viking family"—and several children playing in the adjoining room. But there were no vials of 200-year-old balsamico in the kitchen, no imported cheeses warming on the sideboard, and neither Fred nor Margaret did any cooking. The two matriarchs, JoJo Leflore and Lorraine Carl, made dinner. As Lorraine Carl later told me, "You don't need fancy food if you have family to eat with, and Freddy always understood that."

The mothers had put an eggplant casserole in one of the two ovens of the

Carls' Viking range before I arrived. They conferred on the seasoning for what they called gravy—a red Bolognese-style sauce made with a shoulder roast, tomato paste, onions, garlic, basil, oregano, sugar, salt, and a heap of black pepper—which was simmering on the stove. Fred Carl offered drinks; Margaret Carl sat at the table and chatted. While JoJo Leflore put on the water for pasta shells, we dug into smoked pork ribs.

People served themselves, heaping their plates from the platters that were arranged on the counter. As they moved into the dining room, Fred Carl said, "most people don't have this. They feel like something's missing—something that works, something that lasts." It is precisely this sense of deprivation that Carl has so adeptly exploited. Analysts estimate that in the year 2000 the Viking Range Corporation generated $200 million in sales. Carl intends to more than double this figure over the next five years.

Viking's success has spawned many competitors; small companies like Dacor and Wolf and appliance giants like Thermador, Frigidaire, and General Electric began introducing commercial-style ranges for the home. The knock-offs may not all be as durable or as powerful as a Viking, but they usually cost less and tend to be more widely available and easier to service. Viking's service has not kept up with the company's expansion, and the formerly unimpeachable range has begun to garner occasional criticism.

Viking's luxury status is also being challenged. Upscale shelter magazines have moved on to other stoves, like La Cornue, AGA, and Diva de Provence. An elaborate, French-made, country-style range, La Cornue costs between $11,000 and $28,000, and is now sold by Williams-Sonoma. In part, the range's chic is based on scarcity. Tiny companies like La Cornue make several hundred stoves a year; Viking produces that many in a week.

In response, Carl is diversifying furiously. He has expanded his line to include wall ovens and cooktops, refrigerators, dishwashers, trash compactors, pots and pans, and cutlery. He has bought Rutt and St. Charles, another cabinet company he admires— "St. Charles cabinets! Fallingwater has St. Charles cabinets!"—and he plans to introduce small electrical appliances, such as mixers, blenders, and microwave ovens, over the next few years. An increasing number of developers are installing complete Viking kitchens in luxury homes and apartments.

Viking is now Greenwood's second-largest employer, after the local medical center, and Carl has been buying up as much real estate in town as he can. He is spending several million dollars on renovating the long-vacant Hotel Irving and reclaiming many other buildings downtown, and his new project is occupying more and more of his workday. "Things are starting to move in this old Delta," he said. Pushing aside the two books on his desk—*Taking Charge* and *The Disney Way*—he drew a map of the area on a yellow legal pad, tracing a triangle that began in Greenwood and spread west toward Cleveland and Clarksdale.

"The blues triangle!" he cried. "We're starting right here with the Hotel Irving and building a blues-tourism industry—restaurants, hotels, folk life. A blues hall of fame! We're pulling together the people and the money. It could save this old state. Anyway, I don't think we've begun to tap the market for super-premium ranges. At least, I hope we haven't," he added, laughing.

"I was reading in a magazine about the Land Rover Company and how they set up these places where people could learn how to drive the car on all sorts of terrain," he went on. "Don't you think people should be able to test-drive a Viking range, too?" To that end, Carl plans to spend more than $30 million to open several dozen Viking Culinary Arts Centers across the country over the next five years. He has already opened two, one in Memphis and the other in Nashville. The centers include retail stores, where steel shelves are stocked with gourmet groceries, copper bowls, and porcelain molds. They have amphitheaters for cooking demonstrations. And, of course, they have sprawling kitchens for classes where potential customers can pay to try out every appliance that the Viking Range Corporation sells.

The centers won't sell Viking stoves, however; anyone who feels like ordering one will have to go to a distributor. As Fred Carl knows, the supply of customers willing to pay for trophy stoves just to look at them is finite, so he's resorting to extreme measures: "We're going to teach people how to cook."

Never Give a Child an Artichoke

JENINE HOLMES

Never give a child an artichoke to eat.
Never.
In their limited time on earth
they can never know what lies
within its folds.

Never give a child an artichoke to dine on.
They do not look upon the new with intrigue—
but fear.
The prickly bits designed to keep them out
do.

Never give a child an artichoke to feast upon.
They'll never get past the choke.
Its frightful, slender, funny bits
will scare them for sure.

But if they are brave
they quickly learn it all falls away.
So easy.
Here the softest
sweetest bits
wait for the man who
takes mouth tender flesh over tongue
teeth
rolling sweet warm butter
only
to call out for more.
And that man is the luckiest bastard in the land.

The Power of Memory
and Presence

· ·

RANDY FERTEL

There's been lots written over the years about my mother, trying to explain her incredible success. She bought a little restaurant, Chris Steak House, and succeeded, the story goes, because of her hard work and incredible intelligence and spirit and charisma in creating an international empire called Ruth's Chris Steak House. But to some extent that describes rather than explains. The more interesting question is how to explain that intelligence and spirit and charisma. What made it all work, what motivated it, what was the mainspring that made that clock tick?

I want to try to begin to answer those questions by talking about a paradox, the paradox of memory, which in its nature is about absence, but also about the attempt to bring what is absent into presence, into the here and now. Food always tries to have it both ways. It is always about the past, and it is always about presence, at least when we're doing what we're supposed to be doing when we eat, that is, enjoying ourselves, using our senses and our spirit, as Molly O'Neill would say. But if food is about presence, food and its traditions are also about memory. What meal can we cook that is not an attempt either to recreate or to avoid recreating our mother's table? Presence and absence are inextricable, a woven braid. Memory is about absence, things no longer in our lives, and the effort to bring them into presence. Presence is about the here and now, ignoring, or seeming to ignore, past and future. My mother managed to combine these two.

For me here to invoke my mother's presence, surely I must begin with her guts, of which she had a large measure. Or her zeppolahs, those round donuts Italians serve at street fairs, as her longtime friend and fellow restaurateur Joe Segretta put it. "She had 'em big as zeppolahs," Joe announced one Friday over lunch at Peristyle. Big brass ones.

And surely the best story about her brass and guts is the one about the time she beat Carlos Marcello's nephew at gin. Yes, Carlos Marcello, the head of the New Orleans mafia and, in the minds of many, the man behind the Kennedy assassination. Mom was a great storyteller, but often you had to pull the tales out of her. This was one I got her to tell every time we drove to Mosca's, the wonderful Italian restaurant out in the country known for its, shall I say, colorful past. Mama Mosca had come from Sicily via Al Capone's kitchen to be Carlos Marcello's cook, till he gave her permission to cook her chicken grande for the larger world. So I'm driving her to Mosca's with my kids, and I say, "Mom, tell Matt and Owen about the gin rummy game with Carlos Marcello's nephew."

"Yeah," she said, "he brought his nephew in and said he wanted me to play him one sheet of gin for $15,000. I said, I don't play for those kinda stakes. But he insisted, so we played, and though a sheet usually takes half an hour, I had him skunked in ten minutes. Then Carlos insisted I give him a chance to get his money back. 'But you said one sheet,' I said. But he insisted, so we played again. And ten minutes later, it was $30,000."

"So, Mom," I asked, dragging it out of her, "what happened?"

"Well, he was slow to pay."

"So what did you do?"

"Well, I called Carlos, and he sent my money over."

That's my mom. Brass ones, big and shiny enough to dun Carlos Marcello. I wonder if she insisted on the vig. I never thought to ask. And, by the way, would you have had the phone number—let alone the balls—to call Carlos Marcello?

Mom did not mince words. I was about eighteen when I heard my mother say on one end of a telephone conversation about some business deal that had gone awry that she thought she was getting "screwed," and, "at least I like to get kissed when I'm screwed." It was then that I knew for a certainty that my mom was cool in ways that moms weren't ordinarily cool.

Brassy, salty, cool. No doubt about any of them—and each of them in spades. But, mainly, to understand my mother's presence I must talk about another of her qualities that was at once brassy, salty, cool, and pure velvet. For at the heart of her presence was her presentness, how she was there, here, now, with you, not somewhere else calculating where she wanted to get or what she wanted from you, nor stuck in some past elsewhere working a grudge rather than experiencing the moment. She was present tense all the way. Here. Now.

This made her a great businesswoman and a great traveling companion, always there, riding the edge of the present moment, open to what comes, fearless. When she came back a couple years ago from a fancy cruise in the Mediterranean I asked her how the food was, expecting to hear raves about the cruise ship. "Awful," she said, but added, "One time we got off the boat somewhere in Greece, and I had the best tomato salad of my life." And there they were: the juicy tomatoes and the feta and olive oil and salt right there before you, and the light of the Greek islands flooding the moment. That was the essence of my mother, the lady from Happy Jack, Louisiana. A tomato salad eaten not in the first-class dining salon but in some marketplace in some nameless, podunk Greek town. In my family we argue about the proper way to cut a Creole tomato, those wonderful fruits of the dark alluvial soil of her native Plaquemines Parish. For Mom everything—here, now—mattered. God is in the details. All of the details. And now she's gone, having missed the Creole tomato season that started as she lay dying.

Another way she was present was that, whoever you were, she made no effort to stand above you. Be you grand or not so grand she assumed you were on equal footing with her and she with you. She didn't pull rank. I can't tell you how many times as I traveled from steak house to steak house around the country, how many servers and kitchen workers approached me and said, "You know, I have to tell you: the first time I saw your mother at this restaurant's opening, she was peeling shrimp." They'd say, "There she was, the Empress of Steaks, and everyone was in the weeds, and she saw the need to peel shrimp, and she jumped right in." From that they knew they were in the right place.

Somehow Mom transferred her gift of presence to the people who worked for her and the dishes she served and the tables she set and the restaurants she created around the country. This was part of the magic of Ruth's Chris. Maybe it's the sizzle that does it, but, anyway, in another sense this presence, this presentness, was the sizzle, the essence of the sizzle, the presence that sizzle helps create and that the sizzle expresses. In this world of cookie-cutter dining and generic interstates everywhere, with Ruth's Chris you are somewhere when you get there. Even on North Broad Street at the very center of New Orleans's oh-so-elegant Mid-City, where Mom not only founded her empire but had her home, right behind the restaurant. You don't need to be somewhere else. This is the place, this is where the magic is. Don't look over your shoulder, because it's happening right here. Right now. That's what Mom created. It was an expression of the magic of her presentness.

I know the magic worked not just because of the incredible numbers: eighty-five restaurants, the largest upscale restaurant family in the world. I know it also or all the more so because of what people tell me they experience at Ruth's Chris. When I managed the flagship on Broad Street, I can't tell you how many people came up and offered the same litany: "When I was a kid, Chris Steak House was my favorite restaurant; when I dated my wife, we ate here, and when I asked her to marry me it was here; when she announced our first child was in the oven, it was here, and all our daughter's birthday parties are here. Now it's her favorite restaurant." Woven into the fabric of our lives, Ruth's Chris is about personal histories like that which are now part of the magic and keep it alive and are part of her legacy; and they exist because of the magic she created with her very special presence.

New Orleanians, when they dine—which is what they mostly do—have a habit of discussing other great meals they've enjoyed at other great restaurants. I suspect when they dine at my mother's table they are more likely to talk about past Ruth's Chris meals or the next one. Why let your mind wander anywhere else? That was part of her gift to us. Presence. A model of how to live life, to the hilt, in the present moment, burning always with a hard, gemlike flame. That was my mother.

"There is not a road ahead," writes Nellie Morton. "We make the road as we go. Maybe the journey is not so much a journey ahead but into presence." My mother certainly never articulated this wisdom to herself or anyone, and yet she lived it. It helps explain one of the paradoxes of her incredible business career. She had no plan. The empire was built by accident, always in reaction to the present moment. I once heard Francis Ford Coppola answer the question, why did he do all those different things, why not just make films? He said, "The thing that makes me a good filmmaker is the same thing that makes me open restaurants in San Francisco and resorts in Belize and make wines in Napa Valley: you must be open to what presents itself." My mother had the same brilliance, a brilliance that is diminished by planning. Plan, and you aren't open to what presents itself. A fire closes her first restaurant? Well, I'll open in my catering hall four blocks away. Which she did, in one week. A good customer gets tired of having to drive in from Baton Rouge for a good steak and proposes she allow him to open his own franchise in Prairieville, Louisiana (in the midst of the chemical patch near the capital), and the next thing you know the franchises outnumber her own stores. And, of course, the most impressive shortsightedness of all: buy a seventeen-table restaurant for $18,000 and have to be convinced by the banker to borrow $22,000, "because you may need some working capital," and the next thing you know she is selling her company for upwards of nine figures. My mother didn't have foresight. She didn't have a business plan. She had presence.

Presence. Presentness. But to some extent that describes her success rather than explains it. The prior question is, what made it all work, what motivated it, what was the mainspring that made that clock tick?

Which brings me back to memory and to my mother's roots in the marshy terrain at the mouth of the Mississippi River, deep in the lower Delta, at Happy Jack, Louisiana. For the more I look at my mother's story, and the more my researches take me into my mother's family of origin, then the more I become convinced that Mom's success was in a crucial way an act of memory, her attempt to recreate in spirit the cornucopian table of her great-grandmother. So my new, adjusted view is that my mother's success is best explained by this tension between memory and presence.

Happy Jack, where Mom was born, has its foothold on a little sliver of land surrounded by river on one side and bayou and marsh on the other. The marsh they call prairie, from the French *pré*, as in Grand Pré, the town in Nova Scotia where the Acadiens' troubles first began in 1755. But the Frenchmen of the lower delta were probably mostly not from that grand dérangement but from the littler troubles (especially the threat of German conscription) that plagued Alsace at about the same time. They fled first to the "German Coast" (la Côte des Allemands) up river above New Orleans and then slowly found their way to the fecund soils and waters of the lower delta. In their minds they were "French-French," not Cajuns.

The lower delta brims with a great diversity of foodstuffs, and these Alsatians knew what to do with it as much as the Cajuns did: redfish and trout and shrimp and crab and oyster, duck and geese and dove and quail, deer and rabbit and alligator. And oranges, the best oranges in America, a little-known fact, and from which at least three generations of our family made orange wine that was fermented dry and that packed a wallop: 18 percent alcohol and up. Mom's mother's family, being Alsatian on both sides, brought to the table a cooking tradition that's just about unbeatable. The great cook in the family, according to family lore, was Mom's great-grandmother, who lived in the next town downriver, Home Place (you've got to love these names), and who raised Mom's mother, and who every Thanksgiving and Christmas laid a table that started with gumbo and ran through daube and crown pork roast and piqued duck and rabbit, fried sweet and Idaho potatoes, broccoli and cauliflower au gratin. The stuffed turkey was almost an afterthought, a token gesture made to merely local tradition. The pièce de resistance was oyster dressing made, as my mother's first cousin Audrey Cascio writes in her memoir, "in a giant washtub with seventeen sacks of oysters that had been fished by the men in the family from the bottom of the bayou and then shucked." It ended with half a dozen pies and cakes. All this was cooked in a house with neither electricity nor gas, on a wood burning stove and in an oven, my cousin exclaims, "with no thermostat!" Sometimes thirty-five people attended these affairs.

I know it was good because I grew up going down to my Uncle Sig's in Happy Jack, where his wife Helen and my mother did what they could to recreate that feast every holiday. Sig was in charge of getting the duck and rabbit, in or out of season. Helen and Sig ran a restaurant there, Sig's Antique Restaurant — in fact the first restaurant in the family. We had the run of it for the feasts. The table laden with food from which we served ourselves was often longer than the table at which we were seated.

Let me pause and share with you an assumption I'm working from here. We may not all subscribe to William Blake's recommendation that "the road of excess leads to the palace of wisdom," but I'm fairly certain we can mostly all agree that those huge slabs of red meat at Ruth's Chris are a celebration of excess. Is it an accident that her business, a gauntlet thrown down before the anti–red meat forces, nonetheless doubled and trebled during the economic and cultural excesses of the 80s and 90s? And what I'm arguing here is that that celebration of excess came out of my mother's experience of her great-grandmother's table. That table represents in my mind an utterly Pickwickian scenario, and just as Dickensian is the effort of memory that lay behind it, with all memory's vagaries and illusions and idealizations. Dickensian, too, was the role of trauma as a motivating force, the spring of action, for this recreation. What happened is this. Mom's grandmother, Angeline, died in her twenties when Mom's mother, Josephine, was almost eight. Her brother, three years younger, records their mother's horrible death by anthrax. He, or perhaps they, was taken by open skiff fourteen miles downriver to their mother's deathbed at grandmother's house in Home Place. "I remember vividly," he wrote, "when we got there, that she was dying. Her face was swollen to the breaking point, and when she saw me she tried to smile, and then she announced that she was to die at a certain hour, which she did at exactly the hour she predicted. I was then about four years old, too young to understand the agony she had gone through."

Nichole, their father, remarried, and in doing so redoubled the family trauma, for my mother's great-grandmother, also named Josephine, announced that if he, Nichole, thought he was taking his kids with him down the highway to live with his new wife, well then he would do so over her dead body. Those kids were staying right here, and she would raise them. My guess, then, is that my mother's mother was traumatized not only by the early loss of her mother, but by what must have felt to an eight-year-old like desertion by her father. Nichole, the dad, moved just a few miles down the highway and raised a new family of eight, half brothers and sisters to my grandmother. They were not allowed to speak. My cousin Audrey describes the families passing one another at mass on Sundays in silence but with longing looks. Pure Dickens.

I imagine that my mother's great-grandmother's grandiose feasts were her way of keeping the family together and that consuming those mountainous meals—seventeen sacks of oysters for the dressing!—were a way the family soothed themselves from the trauma of separation and loss that was carried down through the generations and which my mother was heir to. But this effort of memory, motivated by loss and the need for comfort, only goes so far to explain my mother's success in creating a table where a cornucopia of comfort food was king. For if memory lay behind it, what lay ahead was not the past but simply the present moment. Somehow, my mother managed unconsciously to weave the two, past and present, together in a way that totally effaced the past. Josephine and her daughter Angeline, lost at too early an age, have no role in the corporate story. The name Mom grew up with in Happy Jack, Ruth Ann, short for her birth name, Ruth Angeline, after her lost grandmother, was long forgotten in the move to New Orleans. So too the bounty of Mom's great-grandmother Josephine's table, which was transformed into the bounty of Ruth's holiday table and, I believe, into Ruth's Chris's table. But key vestiges remain. Ruth's Chris's famous creamed spinach is in reality the exact recipe that in our family is called Uncle Martin's creamed spinach. This Martin is the brother of Angeline, who died of anthrax. It was he who took Josephine and Nichole downriver by skiff in the dead of night to see their mother on her deathbed.

Mircea Eliade, the great University of Chicago mythographer, explains that the sacred is invoked by creating a special time and place, in a word, a special presence, or what he calls a "heirophany," a temporal revelation of the sacred. What plagues the modern world is that we are always somewhere else, in the past, in the future, daydreaming of some better place, trying to escape from where we really are. The priest or shaman or artist, through ritual and through art, makes this moment and this place holy. The success of Ruth's Chris is largely due to this rite. Somehow my mother created a holy place. Was it the sizzle, the commitment to quality, the downhome broads, many of whom, like her, were single mothers and who welcomed you like family and asked if you wanted "yer regular rib eye medium rare, extra cracked pepper." Was it her own special presence, sitting at her desk with cigarette, coffee, adding machine, and playing cards always at hand? Or was it all these things?

Or, biggest mystery of all, was it the absence/presence of Josephine, invisibly overseeing the whole show, keeping our families together as she did hers, by stuffing us with huge helpings of incomparable comfort food?

I kept to myself this philosophy of the restaurant business that I slowly developed as I worked the floor of the flagship on Broad Street. But it became clearer and clearer to me that Ruth's Chris (and the great restaurants like it) had taken on an almost spiritual role in the modern world. With all our institutional sources of value challenged—church, state, family—where are the holy places left to us but where we break bread? Breaking bread has always been a sacred act, but now more than ever our profane world needs a place where the heart can open to matters beyond the workaday world, whether it is family or friendship or some kind of unnamed spirit, to what Joseph Campbell calls "invisible means of support." Let me not cast too rosy a glow over this story of the inception of Ruth's Chris. Let me connect all the dots: if I am right that behind my mother's incredible success lies this equally incredible family trauma, perhaps trauma helps to explain her success. The obsession with comfort food, the indulgence of excess, the use of food to self-medicate, all these are ways to deal with trauma. Not very healthy ways, I might add, but also characteristic of the excesses of America's eighties and nineties, the very decades when Ruth's Chris attained its national success. The excesses of those decades cannot be explained by one cause. But surely the trauma of our war-torn century must be considered an important factor. So perhaps the Ruth's Chris success story fed on and fed, was a response to and responsive to, not just the personal family traumas but the traumas of our age. Like most empire builders, my mother stood on the shoulders of giants. They were among her invisible means of support. As my good friend Lolis Elie said in his tribute to my mother, "The food even of great chefs starts in the home, cooked by women, and the idea that this woman, this single parent, started this restaurant, mortgaged her future on it and made it work, and became such an important institution around the world, is just because it puts it back squarely where it should be, in the hands of women. And so in a certain sense her success is a tribute to all those women who labored over pots everywhere."

So, in view of this long culinary history I'd like to salute not just the presence of my mother, Ruth Fertel, but also the women that lay behind her skills and dedication, her fortitude and persistence: Josephine Abadie Hingle, the matriarch of matriarchs; her daughter Angeline Hingle Jacomine, my mother's namesake, who died too young; and Josephine Jacomine Udstad, my mother's mother, who by all accounts was the sweetest woman in the parish. And last but not least, for she just couldn't manage to get a granddaughter out of my brother and me, Ruth Angeline Udstad Fertel.

I guess we might sneak one of the family's men in, so, thank you, Uncle Nick, for your divine creamed spinach!

The Hamburger King

WILLIAM PRICE FOX

Out under the red and green and yellow fast-food neon that circles Columbia like Mexican ball fringe, Doug Broome was always famous. As an eight-year-old curb-hop, he carried a pair of pliers in his back pocket for turning down the corners of license plates on the nontipping cars; he was already planning ahead. He grew up during the depression in the kerosene-lit bottom, one block from the cotton mill and two from the state penitentiary. And, as the tale goes, when he was nine, his father went out for a loaf of bread and, in storybook fashion, came home eighteen years later. Doug left school in the fourth grade and worked his way up from curb boy at the Pig Trail Inn out on the Broad River Road, to Baker's on Main Street, and finally to a string of his own restaurants all over town.

Doug had energy, incredible energy. It may be the kind you see in skinny kids playing tag in a rainstorm or the stuff that comes with Holy Roller madness. He had black, curly hair and bright blue eyes, wore outrageous clothes, and every year had the first strawberry Cadillac convertible in town. He won most of the Jitterbug contests at the Township, taking shots at everything Gene Kelly was doing in the movies. He was wild with clothes. With cars. With women. Some of his checks may still be bouncing.

Sometimes he would sit down and list the problems he was having with his help. Someone was getting married before they were divorced, or divorced without benefit of attorney. Some couples would leave for a Stone Mountain honeymoon with the back seat stacked to the window level with Doug's beer and the trunk loaded down with Virginia Hams and cigarettes. Someone was always running off with a friend's wife or husband, getting drunk, wrecking the wrong car, and getting locked up. And a few of the more spectacular cases managed to do everything at once. But Doug would just grin and say, "We're just one great big old family out here, mashing out hamburgers and making friends." He never took them off the payroll. They stole a little, but Doug knew with some sixth sense about how much and made them work longer hours. It was a good relationship, and when the union came around to organize, they would just laugh and say they were already organized.

What I remember him best for happened one crazy night on Harden Street. It was July. It was hot. Oral Roberts was in town. Oral Roberts was always in town. He was still lean and hungry and doing Pentecostal tent shows. "No! I'm not going to heal you. Jesus is! Jesus Christ is going to heal you. So I want all y'all to place your hands on your television set, place your hands on your radio. And if you ain't got a radio, any electrical appliance will do."

At the air-conditioned eight-thousand-seat tent, it had been standing room only, and every soaring soul had descended on Doug's for hamburgers, barbecue, fried chicken, and onion rings. Doug and I were on the big grill, the broilers, the Fryolaters. Lonnie was on the fountain. Betty Jean, under a foot-high, silver-tinted beehive, was on the counter and cash register. The parking lot was jammed, and another string of cars was cruising in an Apache circle looking for a slot. In the kitchen the grease was so thick we had to salt down the duckboards to keep from slipping. The heat was 120 and rising. The grill was full. The broilers were full. There was no more room. There was no more time. We had lost track of what was going out and what was coming in. Horns were blowing. Lights were flashing. The curb girls and Betty Jean were pounding on the swinging doors, screaming for hamburgers, barbecue, steak sandwiches, anything. And then suddenly there was another problem. A bigger problem. The revivalists were tipping with religious tracts and pewter coins stamped with scriptural quotations. The girls were furious. "One of them gave me a goddamn apple! Look! Look at it!"

And what did Doug Broome do? I'll tell you what he did. He stripped off his apron and pulled Betty Jean out from behind the counter. Then he triggered "Rock Around the Clock" on the juke. No one could believe it! He and Betty Jean were dancing and doing red-hot solo kicks on their big breaks.

When the song ended, he announced that everyone was getting a $25 bonus for working the Pentecostals, who had scriptural support for their stand on no tipping. Then he flipped on the public address and sang out over the cars and the neon and the night. "Ladies and gentlemen and boys and girls, I'd like to take this opportunity to remind you that you are now eating at one of the most famous drive-ins in the great Southeast. Our specialties are hamburgers, steak sandwiches, and our famous fried chicken, which is served with lettuce and tomato, carrot curls, pickle chips, and a side of fries, all for the price of one dollar and forty-nine cents. And when you get home tonight and are telling your friends about our fine food and fast service, please remember to tell them that we have been internationally recognized by none other than Mister Duncan Hines himself. I thank you."

Then tying up his apron and angling his cap, he came back to the grill, and with some newer, faster, wilder speed I'd never seen caught the crest and broke it.

Well, Doug's gone now, and with him goes that high-pitched voice on the P.A. and the nights and the music and the great curb girls out on Harden who got us all in trouble. He's gone, and with him go those irreplaceable primary parts of Columbia that shimmered out there under the cartoon-colored neon. There will be no interstate cut-offs named for him, nor will there be a chandeliered Doug Broome Room at the Summit Club. But some nights out on North Main or Harden or Rosewood, when the moon's right and the neon's right and the juke box is thumping out some seventies jump or Fats Domino is up on Blueberry Hill, it will be impossible not to see him sliding double burgers and Sunday beers in milkshake cups down the counter. And if you're as lucky as a lot of us who knew him, you'll probably see him pinch the curb girl at the pick-up window and flash her that big smile and say, "Baby Doll, remember, there's no such thing as a small Coke."

While I was merrily failing everything at Wardlaw Junior High, Doug Broome hired me at his first spot on the 1200 block of Lady. He taught me everything: how to stay on the duckboards to keep from getting shin splints, how to salt the duckboards to keep from slipping, how to keep track of incoming and outgoing orders, and a dozen things that made life easier behind the counter. I copied his freewheeling moves with the spatulas and the French knife, his chopping technique on onions, and his big showboat take-away when he sliced a grilled cheese or buttered toast. It was a great way to begin a career and see the world, and I probably learned more from him than any teacher on down the road.

One day, years later, I interviewed him for a magazine, and it went like this: "Billy, I swear to God, these chain operations are ruining the hamburger. Ruining it. Most of them come from up North to begin with, so what in the hell do they know about any kind of cooking? Any fool right off the street will tell you the minute you freeze hamburger and defrost it you ain't got nothing. God Almighty, you slide one of those three ouncers out of a bun and throw it across the room, and it will sail. I ain't lying, that's how thin that thing is." He was eating his own Doug Broome Doubleburger and holding it out with true respect and admiration. "Now you take this half-pound baby right here. I don't care what you think you could do to it, there ain't no way in the world you can make it any better. No way. I use the finest ground meat there is, the finest lettuce, the finest tomatoes and onions, and Billy, I fry this piece of meat in the finest grease money can buy. Every one of these chains are getting their meat out of Mexico. Ain't no telling what's in it. Hell, I read that in a magazine put out by the United States Government."

He rolled on about how he had single-handedly gunned down the Big Boy franchise when it came to Columbia.

> Everybody in town knows I've always called my hamburger "Big Boy." Anyhow, they'd already steamrolled across everything west of the goddamn Mississippi. And here they come heading across Tennessee. Then across Alabama. Then across Georgia. But when they hit that South Carolina line, I got out in the road and said, "Whoa now! You ain't franchising no Big Boy in here because I am already the 'Big Boy.' Gentlemen, you and me are going to the courts."
>
> And that's what we did. They brought in a wheelbarrow full of money and eight or nine Harvard Jew lawyers, and all I had going for me was my good name and my good friends. And Billy, we beat them to death. I mean to death. They had to pay me sixty thousand dollars and every penny of the court costs.

He paused and sipped his Coke. "Well, you know the kind of guy I am, and you know I never like to kick a man when he's down. Those boys had all that money tied up on promos and 'Big Boy' neon, so I say, 'Okay, y'all give me another ten thousand and I'll change my "Big Boy" to "Big Joy."'" I knew a few of the facts, and I said, "Come on, Doug."

"Boy, why would I tell a lie about something like that? I'm telling you that's exactly what happened."

Part of the story was true. Outside on North Main, the sign on the old "Big Boy" read "Big Joy." But the eight or nine lawyers turned out to be one old retainer out of Camden. The sixty thousand dollars was right, but it went the other way; Doug had to pay them. The ten thousand dollars never existed. Doug was like that. Like all great storytellers, he was a consummate liar. A great straight tale would be transformed into a richer, wilder mixture, and the final version, while sometime spellbinding and always entertaining, would have absolutely nothing to do with the truth.

Doug had charisma and Doug had style, but it wasn't until later that I realized what a profound effect it had on me. I was on a New York talk show hustling a novel. The host had led me down the garden path in the warm-up, promising we'd discuss pole beans and the best season for collards. But when the camera light came on, his voice dipped into low and meaningful. We discussed the Mythic South, the Gothic South, Faulkner's South, and the relevance of the agrarian metaphor. I was a complete disaster. And then he asked me how I would define style. It was a high pitch right across the letters, and I dug in and took a full cut. I told him about one day during a rush at Doug's on Harden Street. There were a dozen customers on the horseshoe counter, and a man came in and ordered a cheese omelet. I'd never made one before, but I'd watched Doug do it. I chopped the cheese, broke three eggs into a shake can, added milk, and hung it on the mixer. Then I poured it out on the big grill. I'd used too much milk, and it shot out to all four corners, where it began to burn. I almost panicked. Then I remembered Doug's long, smooth moves with the spatulas and pulled them out of the rack as if they were Smith and Wesson .44s. I began rounding it up. As I worked I flexed my elbows and dipped my knees and did his little two-beat rhythm behind my teeth. I kept clicking and kept moving and just at the critical moment I folded it over, tucked it in and slid it onto the plate. Then with parsley bouquets on the ends and toast points down the sides, I served it with one of Doug's long flourishes and stepped back.

The man forked up an end cut. He chewed it slowly and closed his eyes in concentration to pick up the echo taste. Then he laid his fork down and, with both hands on the counter, he looked me in the eye, "Young man, that's the finest omelet I've ever put in my mouth."

I wound up telling the stunned interviewer that that was style, and all you can do is point at it when you see it winging by and maybe listen for the ricochet. I don't think he understood, but I knew I did. I knew that style wasn't an exclusive property in the aristocracy of the arts. A jockey, a shortstop, a used-car salesman, or a mechanic grinding valves can have it, and the feather-trimmed hookers selling their wares out on the Two Notch Road are not without it. And Doug Broome had it, and he knew he had it, and he staged it with wild clothes and great music and strawberry-colored Cadillacs and backlighted it all with red and yellow and purple flashing lights. There will never be another like him.

End of the Lines?

PABLEAUX JOHNSON

It's early in a Friday lunch shift at Uglesich's, and already owner Anthony Uglesich (pronounced "YU-gul-sitch") is fielding calls about "the transition." Tethered to the restaurant's front wall by a metal pay-phone cable, he reassures the caller with equal parts authority and ambiguity.

"Yes, ma'am," he says, "We're still open. No, ma'am, we haven't decided."

A group of dressy conventioneers—name tags partially concealed under winter overcoats—presses through the narrow doorway, letting in a blast of cold, wet wind. The party searches the tiny room for an open table or a maitre d'. They find neither. Instead, Uglesich leans over to welcome the new arrivals. Caught between his caller and his customers, he taps his pen on his ever-present ordering pad.

"No, ma'am," he says into the phone. "We don't know how long. I might be here half a year, might be another year and a half."

Workaday sounds from the adjoining kitchen—the clank of saute pans against burners, the burble of deep fryers—punctuate the conversation. He motions the group to a stack of laminated single-sheet menus. "Well, thank you, but it's a lot of hard work, and my wheels ain't what they used to be. But we're around for now. Yes, ma'am. Monday through Friday. We're open 'til four. Thank you. G'bye."

Uglesich rests the phone in its cradle. From his perch behind the stainless steel bar he now turns his full attention to the newcomers.

"C'mon in," he says with a serious smile. "What can I getcha today?"

In the past few years, Uglesich has fielded many similar calls from customers concerned with the future of his Central City restaurant. Despite its shabby exterior and less-than-prime location, Uglesich's eponymous eatery has become a culinary landmark for locals and a pilgrimage site for food-crazy travelers.

From its humble beginnings as a 1920s-era neighborhood bar and oyster house, Uglesich's remains a ramshackle, ten-table eatery—but now one with a fan base that includes high-profile restaurateurs Emeril Lagasse, Susan Spicer, and Frank Brigtsen. It's also one of the local establishments most recommended by the national food press. Here, visitors can continually rediscover a prototypical diamond in the rough, even if their simple lunch comes with a bottle of Belgian Trappist ale and sets them back thirty to forty dollars a person.

"There's always one iconic restaurant that exemplifies what New Orleans food is about, and for a lot of reasons, Uglesich's is that now," says Jonathan Gold, national restaurant reviewer for *Gourmet*. "There's an amazing amount of thought put into the food. It's rooted in traditional Louisiana cooking, but it's not hopelessly old-fashioned. If you get off the plane and go to Uglesich's, you get the feeling there's no other place in the world you can be."

Uglesich and his wife/cooking partner, Gail, have perfected a menu that balances deep-fried New Orleans classics with their own innovations: succulent shrimp stuffed with herbed lump crabmeat, delicate sautéed oyster "shooters" drenched in a cane syrup/sun-dried tomato vinaigrette, peerless grilled speckled trout, or the spicy-tart shrimp Uggie, tinted red with three different chiles.

"They do the classics better than anybody," says Susan Spicer, the culinary mind behind Bayona, Herbsaint, and Cobalt. "But he can also come up with something that's totally surprising. It's ALL moan and groan good. They're always on this eternal quest, open to exotic flavors while staying deeply rooted in the local ingredients."

In almost every way, Uglesich and his restaurant are at the top of their game. But regulars and friends watch anxiously as the restaurant seems to slide toward inevitable extinction. In December of 2003, Anthony turned sixty-five, traditional retirement age. He has no logical successor in the kitchen, no suitable business partner waiting in the wings, and neither of his two children are interested in carrying on the family business. Each year, fans fear he may close for his annual summer vacation and never reopen. Even under the best of circumstances, the restaurant's remaining life span will most likely be measured in months rather than years.

Talk of "the transition"—a sale, a change of heart, or another miraculous event that would keep the restaurant open—has become an annual tradition for Uggie watchers. They acknowledge that after fifty hard years in the restaurant business, the couple has earned a rest. But they also dread the day when Uglesich's shuts its doors forever.

"I've heard them talk about it over the years," says Frank Brigtsen, chef/owner of Brigtsen's Restaurant and longtime regular. "A few years back he told me it'd be another three years, maybe five on the outside. Then there was talk about finding somebody to take Gail's place. You never know. We had quite a panic last summer. When it looked like they weren't going to open, we couldn't believe it. We thought we'd missed our chance for one last meal."

The lunch shift at Uglesich's lasts for six hours, but preparation for that single service is a round-the-clock routine.

It's 8:30 A.M., and Uglesich already has been busy for nearly four hours. He's up every weekday at five talking to his seafood suppliers, then he works in his home kitchen for a couple of hours. By the time he pulls into the restaurant's parking lot, the back of his truck is filled with a jumble of mismatched Tupperware marked with names lifted straight from the menu. A bright red oil-based sauce sloshes in a tall container marked "Uggie" next to a two-quart plastic casserole packed with seasoned lump crabmeat. Other containers hold soups, sauces, and mixes that Gail and Anthony whip up during their predawn prep sessions.

"We bring some of the ingredients home so we can do our early work in the morning," he says. "You gotta get a head start."

The January cold cuts to the bone, and Uglesich, dressed in a denim shirt, fleece vest, and hooded sweatshirt, unlocks the back door. He picks his way past six oversized white coolers—fresh shrimp delivered the previous evening—and surveys the room where he's spent nearly fifty years of his working life.

Inside, Uglesich's is pretty much the same as it's always been—a twenty-by-twenty box with concrete floors and a low drop ceiling. Stainless industrial refrigerators and utilitarian plastic shelving units line the walls. Cases of Barq's long-necks, bottled spring water, and various beers support the six-foot wood-paneled divider between the small dining area and the even smaller ten-by-ten kitchen. Fifteen beige-flecked Formica tables (ten for indoor dining, five more for warm-weather sidewalk seating) clutter the main floor. A stainless-steel bar runs from the front door to the kitchen, with a six-foot extension—the famed oyster bar—jutting off at a right angle.

The room is still dank when the seven-person crew arrives to start prep work. There's not much talk; everyone still seems to be gathering momentum for the long day ahead. John Rea, the restaurant's only waiter, gets Anthony's keys and unbolts the outside doors. Line cook Zina Cooper greets her kitchen compatriots, Cynthia Mack and Michelle Rogers. Michelle's uncles—thirty-year oyster shucker Michael Rogers and dishwasher Anthony—arrange chairs to make room for trays, colanders, and other morning prep essentials. The group sizes up the mountain of ice chests.

"I'm glad we got this shrimp yesterday, because there ain't gonna be *nothin'* today," Uglesich says. "We need to deal with these shrimp and bag 'em. They're mixed, so separate them out by size. John, help me unload the truck."

Like his restaurant, Uglesich's accent is classic New Orleans—his waiter's name come out as "JAW-wuhn." The second-generation restaurateur is the son of a Croatian immigrant father and Italian/French mother from rural St. James Parish. His father, Sam Uglesich, came to New Orleans from Dugi Otok, Croatia, in 1924 after an unsuccessful attempt to jump ship in New York harbor three years earlier. The elder Uglesich originally founded a restaurant on South Rampart Street—a neighborhood establishment with a straightforward seafood menu to accompany its bar business. Anthony lists the old menu: "Raw oysters. Fried shrimp, soft-shelled crab, oysters, or trout. Sandwiches or plate."

In 1927, Sam moved the operation to Baronne Street in Central City, then a burgeoning neighborhood for New Orleans's flourishing Jewish merchant class. "Back then," Anthony says, motioning across the street to Brown's Velvet Dairy, "milk from the dairy was still delivered by mule."

Eleven years later, in December 1938, Anthony was born into the business that bears his family name. "I started working in the restaurant when I was about fifteen. Back then it was all family, my daddy ran it with my Uncle Tony and me, maybe a nephew. I'd open oysters, clean fish, work the kitchen— whatever they told me to do. But I can tell you, when I first started working there, and I found out how much work it was, I was *not* impressed. We'd be open from six in the morning until ten at night. That's just too much work, but people didn't know any better then."

In the early 1960s, Anthony met and eventually wed Gail Flettrich, a Marerro-born school teacher. The two started their own family, and Gail started working in the restaurant. In 1969, Sam began a five-year bout with cancer, and Anthony gradually took over the business, with Gail working in the kitchen.

The Sam Uglesich era was summed up neatly in the 1973 edition of the *New Orleans Underground Gourmet*. Author Richard Collins listed Uglesich's under the heading "workingmen's restaurants" with the following description: "This restaurant has been in operation since 1849. Across from Brown's Velvet Dairy, it offers good freshly shucked oysters, poor boys, and fried seafood with cold draft beer. Prices are inexpensive."

After his father passed away in 1974, Anthony inherited the restaurant, and the second era of its history began. Anthony and Gail built on the joint's mostly fried menu, expanding it with more creative seafood dishes. "We saw that people didn't want so much fried food, so we started changing," Uglesich says. "We put on more grilled items with our own seasoning, our own formula.

"My daddy was Yugoslavian, and his tastes influenced a lot of how we cook—lots of garlic, lots of olive oil, lot of oysters. We wanted to make our own barbecued shrimp recipe based on olive oil instead of butter, then we tried oysters instead of shrimp. It's been real popular."

The more diverse menu also allowed Anthony and Gail to accommodate their expanding family, which now included their two children, John and Donna. "When we first got married, I used to work in the back," says Gail. "But when we started changing the menu, I stayed at home and experimented. First with the gumbo, because we never had that. Then we added appetizers and the grilled seafood."

Many initial ideas were inspired by their favorite local chefs. Anthony says his first appetizer was based on the fried green tomatoes at Joanne Clevenger's Upperline. "But we wanted to do our own version of the sauce—something with good flavor, but no mayonnaise."

The home kitchen soon became a development laboratory to feed ideas to their production line—the restaurant kitchen. "When I first met him, I didn't cook much—I was a school teacher," Gail says. "Anthony was my taster. When we would work on a dish, we were each other's tasters. I would make, he would try. He would make, I would try."

This work ritual they started in the 1970s continues today. Gail begins her day well before sunup to prepare the day's sauces, soups, gumbos, and dressings. "I'm up at 4:30 doing my work in the kitchen, and by the time Anthony's up, I'm about done. Then he does his work."

Both are quick to describe themselves as "cooks" rather than "chefs," a recognition of their self-taught roots. "Gail and I are different kinds of cooks," Anthony says. "She's very precise in her measurements, but that's not the way I work. We'll help each other out in the kitchen."

Emeril Lagasse, local empire-building chef and Food Network personality, has admired their collaboration for years. "Their teamwork is about 75 percent of their success," he says. "Gail is just there for Anthony, wherever he needs her. Working the front, on the side, in the back. When you get a partner like that, it's a beautiful thing."

As the restaurant's 10:30 A.M. opening approaches, the kitchen crew races to finish its prerush prep work. Flashing knives mince onions, quarter new potatoes, and reduce bunches of fresh parsley to fine, fragrant powder. Cooper readies her station—six industrial-grade gas burners, a steel flattop griddle, and a double-basket deep fryer—for the first orders of the day. Mack and Michelle Rogers arrange piles of sliced tomatoes, mounds of shredded lettuce, and bins of lemon wedges on the top of a "lowboy" cooler. With the griddle fired up and burners heating two ancient pots filled with fresh frying oil, the morning chill is all but gone.

A few feet away in the dining area, Anthony carefully wraps shrimp in half-pieces of defatted bacon ("Something new I want to try today"). At the bar, Michael Rogers shucks well-iced oysters. With a blunt oyster knife in one hand and a heavy-gauge rubber glove on the other, he scoops up a jagged shellfish and slams it onto a curved soft metal anvil. Deftly finding the vulnerable spot near the oyster's hinge, he pries the rocky shell open, zips the knife through the strong twin adductor muscles, and plops the very surprised bivalve into a waiting bowl. For now, Rogers works quietly and quickly—when the rush starts, he'll be quick to chat up the waiting customers while performing his duties.

The practice of fresh-shucking "cooking oysters" is fairly rare in modern restaurants, since most kitchens rely on preshucked shellfish for fried or sauteed dishes. But old-school attention to freshness is a trademark of Uglesich's and its owner. "If the quality's not there, I'm not gonna sell it," he says. "I'd rather be honest with people. It kills your sales, but I'd rather tell people in advance.

"I love my Louisiana seafood, it's just got superior quality. The imported seafood puts a hit on the local producers, and it doesn't taste as good. I got people coming in here every day trying to sell me frozen, imported seafood for cheaper, but the flavor isn't there. I tell them, 'I like des Allemandes catfish—I don't care how cheap you can get me something else.' I like what I like."

"That's a big lesson I learned from Anthony," says Frank Brigtsen, "that you need to nurture relationships with your suppliers. Anthony doesn't nickel and dime his purveyors and builds a good relationship from both sides. Not all fish are the same, so if you want the best, you have to earn it."

Mary Schneider of P&J Oysters is one of the suppliers who has learned firsthand about Uglesich's standards. "We started working with Mr. Anthony about eleven years ago," she says. "Just before his longtime provider (David Cvintanovich) retired, he came into our shop and explained that he'd like us to take over Mr. Anthony's account. Since then, we've supplied all his product. But it hasn't been easy.

"Every morning, I'll personally taste the different lots of oysters for the day," Schneider says. "About five o'clock, he'll call me before he's had his coffee and ask me what they taste like. He's looking for size, flavor, and shell size. We know which ones he wants, and he's willing to pay a premium for the best product. He'll pay extra for the big shells, because he knows his clientele, and that's how he likes to present them. And he always gets what he wants. He's one of my favorite people, but he's picky, picky, picky."

The day's first customers—lone tourists toting guidebooks and bracing against the cold—arrive dutifully at 10:30 A.M. sharp, the official opening time. Each wears blue jeans, a black leather jacket, and a puzzled expression.

A few straggling deliveries—a huge brown bag filled with Leidenheimer po-boy loaves, several cases of wine—come through the door as the customers get their instructions from Uglesich. "Take a menu and find a table," he says with a somewhat distracted smile. "We'll be over to help you in a second."

He shakes his head slowly. "The forecast says we got cold drizzle all day. The weather's gonna be bad for the fishermen and it's gonna be bad for business today."

After signing for the wine and bread, Uglesich grabs his pad and edges past Rogers, still shucking at the oyster bar. He moves a little hesitantly, with a limp that comes from fifty years of walking on the room's unforgiving concrete floors. "I stay on my feet too much, and it's given me bad knee problems," he says. "The only two days of work I missed in forty-five years were because of my knees. I had them 'scoped on Friday, and I was back on the Monday. But they've been getting worse lately."

Add to that a history of arthritis and bone spurs in his feet, and you've got a snapshot of the classic restaurant lifer. His ailments match those of his long-time colleagues such as Susan Spicer. "When I go in, we talk about travel, new ingredients and flavors, but just as often swap stories about the restaurant business and compare our battle scars," she says. "Bad knees, bad feet. We got it all."

The first customers sit at separate tables, and Uglesich limps over to lead them one by one through the menu's two-dozen appetizers and thirty entries. He poses a series of questions that borders on interrogation. "What are you in the mood for today?" is a common opener, along with "You like spicy food?" and "Tell me what seafood you like and whether you want a sandwich or a plate." Whether delivered tableside or from behind the counter, Uglesich's voice carries a distinctly serious tone—as if there's a single right answer that the customer could give in a lunch order.

Within minutes, plates emerge from the kitchen and the affable Rea carts them over to the waiting diners. One contains a crispy, deep-fried patty made of tender shrimp and salty country sausage drizzled with a creamy Creole mustard sauce. Spicy but well balanced, it's one of Uglesich's many successful (and often unlikely) ingredient combinations that become house standards.

"I'm not scared of blending things together," he says. "Take the crawfish ball appetizer—fried crawfish balls with a spicy Thai dipping sauce and a little rice on the side. It's a mix of Creole and Asian. Some people don't like it, other people love it."

On the plate, that appetizer is a study in flavor and texture. Plump Louisiana crawfish tails in a sweetish egg-and-bread-crumb binder are deep-fried to a crispy consistency then served with a tangy, thin-bodied mixture flavored with fish sauce, rice vinegar and, a time-delayed chili/garlic afterburn.

By 11:30 A.M., the restaurant is standing room only. Fifteen minutes later, there's hardly any standing room left. The tables are packed, most for the second time, and new groups jostle to get in from the cold.

Gail arrived a half-hour earlier, dressed in her trademark uniform—an oversized denim shirt embroidered with Warner Brothers cartoon characters. With the crowds swirling around the main counter, she takes orders, works the cash register, and keeps track of new arrivals. Every so often, she states the house rules with an authoritative tone left over from her classroom teaching days ("Place your order up front first, please!").

Group after group approaches Anthony, hoping to gain a little insight into the dense, often confusing menu. One customer points to a handwritten sign on the wall: FRESH TROUT—MARKET PRICE. "How are the trout?" he asks. "Naaaaahhh, I don't have any," Anthony tells him. "I can't get fresh, and I won't buy frozen." He laughs and shakes his head. "Tell you what, I'll get you a nice catfish from Des Allemandes, Louisiana. You won't know the difference. When I tell you the catfish is good, the catfish is good. You should listen to me."

Behind the kitchen's half-wall, the action ratchets up to full speed and stays there. The cooks work elbow to elbow, staring up at the active tickets as their hands assemble and double-check outgoing orders. The full griddle hisses in the background as Cooper tends five orders of grilled catfish, two orders of shrimp in the fry pots, and four sauté pans. Anthony Rogers works all three sections of the stainless steel sink, keeping the shelves filled with clean dishes and utensils. It's a lot of action for a ten-foot square, but it's executed plate after plate, check after check, without missing a beat.

Judging from the conversations, today's crowd is mostly made up of tourists. Two couples from Memphis squeal over a chance meeting 400 miles from home. A Bay Area business traveler, menu and cell phone in hand, reads his options to his San Francisco connection. Gail mixes a round of super-strength cocktails from the cluttered tabletop bar. A couple of petite Uptown ladies stop in for an early lunch without bothering to consult the menu: "Mama will have a Sam's Favorite, and I'll just have the half-and-half po-boy."

"It used to be my customers were 80 percent local and 20 percent tourists," Uglesich says. "Now it's the other way around."

Paul Varisco, one of Uglesich's most consistent customers, has watched these changes for more than thirty years. "I started coming in here about 1972, and the business was about 90 percent local. When the menu started expanding, they got a write-up in *USA Today* about the time the Republican convention came to town in 1988. The reputation built from there. People would come into town and ask me for a real local place, and I'd bring them here. Ahmet Ertegun, the CEO of Atlantic Records, became a big fan and always brought people in. Then the chefs—Frank, Susan, Emeril—came in and brought their friends."

The early connection to Lagasse resulted in several television appearances for Uglesich on the chef's popular TV shows *Essence of Emeril* and *Emeril Live*. Whenever Lagasse was asked about his favorite underground eating establishments, Uglesich's would pop to the top of the list. "Emeril's been real good to me," Uglesich acknowledges. "He's brought a lot of people in here in the early days, and he always treats me well at his restaurants."

Since then, magazines from *Travel and Leisure* to *Cigar Aficionado* to *Bon Appetit* and *Gourmet* have raved about New Orleans's unlikely "fine dining dive." Television producers looking for the seamy-yet-safe underbelly of local cuisine gravitate toward the place. Even Martha Stewart shot a segment in which Gail and Anthony demonstrated a recipe for their famous "oyster shooters."

"For people outside New Orleans, it's like Lourdes," says *Gourmet*'s Gold. "If you're a tourist, you have certain expectations about New Orleans, and it fills them all—an exceptional, funky restaurant in a bad neighborhood run by a charming curmudgeon. There's a sense of civility among the decay. People always immediately understand what the big deal is."

Uglesich's reputation—and the attendant out-of-town crowds—grows larger every year. During peak seasons such as Jazz Fest and Mardi Gras, the line can start forming at the start of the early morning prep shift. Over time, the national following has pretty much replaced the local lunch traffic. Both lines and wait times are unpredictable, making Uglesich's a perfect illustration of Yogi Berra's classic line: "Nobody goes there anymore. It's too crowded."

Uglesich recognizes the regional differences of his customers. "Locals are more likely to order a simple lunch like a po-boy. But tourists tend to be a lot more adventurous. They'll come down, wait for an hour, and then eat for two more."

The out-of-towners have also shaped Uglesich's offerings over the years.

When asked about his unusually deep beverage list of twenty-one different wines and eighteen beer brands, he replies, "Customers started coming in and asking for different wines—people from California suggested their favorites, so we started carrying them. We listen to our customers."

The tables are still packed at 2:30 P.M. and the line has gone from three deep at the bar to a few couples clutching tiny yellow Post-It notes and waiting for Gail to call their number. Anthony has a little more time to chat with his customers. "You have a nice weekend. Need a cab? The streetcar's on St. Charles, two short blocks down Erato. You're gonna need the exercise after lunch," he laughs. "Come back and see us."

Rogers alternates between his shucking duties and backing up a busy Rea. In between calls for "dozen raw for the gentleman," he quickly buses and cleans vacant tables, delivers hot plates from the kitchen to their assigned tables, and poses for pictures with customers.

It hasn't been a good day for the raw bar, partially because Uglesich does his best to discourage would-be raw oyster patrons. "Nah, get 'em from the kitchen, but not from the bar," he tells them with disappointment, bemoaning the effects of Hurricanes Isidore and Lili on coastal oyster beds. "This is the weakest December I can remember."

As the front bar clears a bit, Uglesich takes a breather to talk about the business end of things. "I'm glad I stayed small," he says. "If you get big, you can't always get your ingredients like you want them. I remember talking to my daddy about this. If I get big, I gotta do what other people do—use imported or farm-raised products, and those just don't have the flavors I like."

"We had a chance to move close to the convention center in the 1980s, but my kids weren't interested in taking over, so we didn't do it. I've had some offers, but nobody who really sounds serious. People want to buy the business and hire somebody else to run it. And you can't do it like that."

"I've learned a lot over the years from people right here. Frank Brigtsen is always good. You know what I respect? That he stays on the premises and does his own cooking. Anne (Kearney) and Susan (Spicer), those women working in the kitchen, they put in some *real* hard work."

Talk turns to the impending transition. "This place is my life, it's my love," he says. "But I'm getting old. I've been having knee problems, and I just can't keep going. We've got Gail's parents at home, too, and they've got to have twenty-four-hour care. We just can't do it all. I'd like to have more time to travel, maybe put these recipes in a book."

The exact timing of Uglesich's retirement remains a guessing game even for those closest to him. "Anthony's always said that he'd work until he was sixty-five, but I'm not really sure beyond that." Gail says. "I really like to cook, and I like talkin' to people. That's what I'm really going to miss."

Friends and colleagues still hold out hope that something can breathe new life into the institution. "He first started talking about closing about ten years ago," says Spicer. "Everybody has a view in their mind of the perfect heir—one of their sous chefs who could take the place over."

"The vacations have been getting longer—they started out as two weeks a year, then four, and last year it was ten weeks," says Varisco. "Two years ago, there was some talk about his closing, and this year it's more serious."

"He's talked that way for years," Brigtsen echoes. "Business is either so bad it's killin' him or it's so good it's killin' him. They've got a lot going on right now with the family, so you never know."

As for life in a post-Uggie era, Spicer says, "I don't like to think about it."

Whether their run ends this year or next, Gail and Anthony will have left an enduring legacy on the New Orleans restaurant scene.

"I've met a lot of wonderful chefs in my time, but Anthony is my hero," says Brigtsen. "It's amazing to see that kind of dedication to the customers and their love of food. Anthony and Gail make it their 24/7 occupation, and that's why Uglesich's is what it is. They serve the best seafood in New Orleans in a neighborhood restaurant, and his care for his food and guests is beyond par-allel. Uglesich's is the epitome of the New Orleans neighborhood restaurant—and there ain't that many of them left."

Lagasse also considers the Uglesiches to be role models. "They developed such a personal cuisine that you really can't duplicate it. They're just trying to do their own thing," he says. "Over the years, I've seen them evolve. They'll go through times when they're doing a lot of testing, and there's new things com-ing out of the kitchen. They're not resting on their laurels; they're trying to be great cooks."

"He's been a hero of mine for years. He's a smart man, he's a great cook, he's a smart business guy. It's unfortunate that he hasn't been able to find someone to take over for him. But that would be pretty hard for somebody to do, because it's so personal for him and Gail. And so we'll end up losing a great institution. It'll be a sad day."

It's 4:30 P.M., official closing time. One straggling table—a returning group of event planners from Washington, D.C.—calls for another bottle of wine as they finish up their second round of appetizers.

"You get to try a little thing I'm working on," Uglesich says as he pushes the bacon-wrapped shrimp to the center of the table. Half the plate is covered with what Uglesich called a "sweet potato cream sauce," a flash-broiled custard with a smooth, souffle-like texture. Not surprisingly, the dish—with well-balanced sea-and-pig flavors and sweet finish—is a hit.

The last entrees leave the kitchen. The line crew breathes a sigh of relief. Cooper emerges to talk with Gail for a few minutes, glad to take a break from the superheated kitchen strewn with a day's worth of bread crumbs and sauce splatters. A warm afternoon light bathes the nearly empty room in a peaceful, golden glow. The hurricane fence shielding the front window casts a diamond pattern on the empty tabletops.

"Well, that's it," sighs Rea. "A quiet Friday. Just about as busy as a good Thursday. But that's not so bad." After a quick sip of water, he turns to stack the empty tables. Michelle Rogers adjusts her do-rag before shifting into cleanup mode.

Gail says her good-byes and gathers her purse, along with zip-top bags of pre-prepped ingredients for her next early morning shift. Anthony walks her to the curb. As he returns to tally out the register, the pay phone rings yet again.

"Uglesich." he says, leaning in to accommodate the short, braided cord. "Uglesich. It's pronounced YOU, GULL like a seagull, SITCH. No, ma'am, we don't serve dinner. We're closed now. Closed on weekends, too."

Then, as if to give his caller a little hope: "We'll be open on Monday, though. You gonna be in town? Good. C'mon by and see us."

EPILOGUE: MARDI GRAS 2004

"John, bring us some of the Purgatory Shrimp." It's a full year later, and Anthony sits down for a late afternoon break, smiling but rubbing his knees.

With another Mardi Gras only weeks away, it's the calm before yet another springtime storm—after carnival season comes the Jazzfest flurry, and beyond that, the long summer break.

"We're not sure what's gonna happen this year," he says. "Gail needs a break, so we're talking about it now. We might go down to four days a week, might take a longer vacation . . ." He trails off and shrugs. "But I can't do this without her."

A few other projects are humming along: a website, a cookbook due out in October of 2004, and of course, new dishes for the menu. What happens in 2005 is anybody's guess.

The steaming plate of Purgatory Shrimp seems simple enough—crispy fried shrimp topped with a buttery hot sauce. A tiny metal ramekin of creamy mystery dip seems to be ranch dressing, but on the tongue, it opens up a world of intense, earthy flavor.

"That's Gorgonzola sauce," Anthony says. "I think the cheese works well with the hot sauce. What do you think?"

Every bite sings. Crunchy crust gives way to tender seafood, infused with buttery flavor and a zing of tart cayenne heat. Seconds later, the creamy gorgonzola cools the palate and fills sinuses with a pleasing cheesy funk.

"Yeah," he smiles, "we couldn't get that one in the book. Maybe I'll save it for the next one . . ."

Catfish People

EARL SHERMAN BRAGGS

They eat mostly catfish, this lowly crowd
Of Mississippi River mud people.

I, the lonely stranger do not know this darkly handsome breed
Of wild house cats that do not take kindly to new faces

prowling back rooms, where fat cat men gamble away
tomorrow's catch for a good time tonight

down at Jake Hardy's place. Barely clad in steamy heat
fresh catfish women dance in smoky slow motion.

"Look at those yellow cat-eyed gals" waiting to see
which one of the black cat men will win.

Tonight I am floating in the musty arms of muddy water
blues. Any news you lose when you get caught.

stealing sugar water blues from a yellow cat-eyed gal.
"You better watch out, her man might come in through the back.

door before you know," an old man's eyes say
without turning to look beyond his private corner.

"Take me to church tomorrow morning," her hot breath whispers
softly. Sunday is a kind day. Everything is forgiven on Sunday.

Saturday nights are cruel, purple black and haunting
as a full moon that refuses to reflect.

their little cat children sucking stewed onions and fish heads
from walking age until they walk away from this catman town.

Around her anything that moves is stalked by a prowl of lowly feet that do
   not trust the suit I wear

that do not care for my pointed stacy shoes
too shiny to waltz to a muddy water blues. Always

three steps behind the sultry beat of a yellow gal,
pulling me deeper and deeper into the mouth of her river,

drowning me then pulling me out with a net
full of catfish men smelling of last night's gin.

THE PLACES

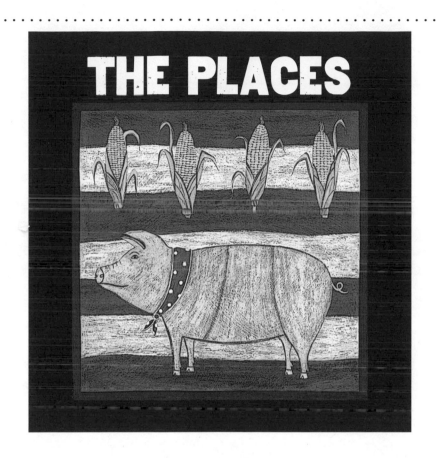

And the Band Played On
Taylor Grocery, Mississippi

SARAH THOMAS

It isn't a sinking ship, exactly.
The liquor flows free and the talk freer
and the fried catfish would make Jesus
rethink that whole loaves situation.
It might be dinner on the ground
except for the tin roof, the pine floor
and the music that wears us down,
down to a place where bourbon
and French fries make us wonder
how milk and honey ever made the cut.

Texas ladies smoking in the parking lot
talk Taylor's boy into a side trip
to a cotton gin where ghosts of the South
rise, billow towards a constellation
no one recognizes—
but maybe we can see double.
And back in that dirt packed lot,
not one but two mongrel dogs wait
in the dark where we can hear the music
say something about going down to a well . . .
but not anymore, oh no, not anymore.
We keep watch for Faulkner.
He may not show, but he's welcome
and rumor has it that boy can dance.

You see,
We're the purest distillation you can get.
Even when the mixture's off,

once we've been mashed through this sieve
called the South, fed on deep fried fiction
and rolled in fresh red clay while
the sounds some ole boy pulls
from out his soul wash over us, well . . .
You might as well kick off your shoes
and watch this hurricane come ashore.
If you're lucky, you'll wash on out to sea.

Open House

JOHN T. EDGE

I arrived at the University of Georgia as a seventeen-year-old freshman in September of 1980. The night before classes began, I pledged a fraternity, shot-
gunned a six-pack of Country Club malt liquor, and gulped down a pint of
Pepe Lopez tequila. Around two that morning, in the company of my new
brothers, I went carousing through the narrow streets of Athens, bound for an
all-night diner known as Blanche's Open House. Once there, I scarfed a platter of eggs and grits before excusing myself to vomit in the direction of the toi-
let. I missed. When I walked to the counter to tell someone what I had done,
a middle-aged woman with a tight henna bouffant threw me a rag and
screamed, "Don't give me that; I don't want to hear it. Clean up your own
shit!" This, I learned, was Blanche Guest.

Set on the seedy side of downtown, between a tire plant and a coin-oper-
ated Laundromat, Blanche's Open House was the place to be late at night.
Though Blanche opened at nine each evening, the real action started around
one or two in the morning, after the bars closed, after the frat parties began to
peter out.

The floor was a checkerboard of red and white tiles. At one time the interior walls had probably been painted white, but years of cigarette smoke had
rendered the bricks a dull beige. If there were posters or paintings, I can't recall them. A jukebox stocked with George Jones and Parliament Funkadelic
hunkered by the front window. Seven red vinyl stools faced a scarred linoleum
counter, behind which Blanche worked the grill and the cash register. On a
typical Friday night the wait for one of the eight tables approached an hour,
and on football Saturdays the line stretched out the door and onto the sidewalk. The food, as I recall, was greasy but generous.

Blanche fascinated me. I remember her as a cross between Minnie Pearl
and Daisy Mae, with a fondness for wearing silk tops and a tremulous voice
that sounded like a buzz saw. I never recall seeing her without a lit cigarette
dangling from her bottom lip. And I swear that I never heard her utter a sen-

tence that was not punctuated by an expletive. Yet strange as it may seem, there was something maternal about her manner: when a friend of mine, for reasons I still cannot fathom, tried to climb on top of the glass-fronted jukebox, she screamed, "Get down, goddamn it, or you'll cut your damn fool legs off."

For my fraternity brothers and a host of other university students, Blanche's Open House served as a kind of late-night purgatory, a holding tank where young drunks loaded up on grease and caffeine in an effort to ward off a hangover or stymie a Breathalyzer test. Sure, we'd heard that Blanche's husband, Herbert Guest, had a troubled past, that he had been somehow implicated in a murder back in the 1960s, but the word was he had never been convicted. When we caught wind of rumors that Herbert was once active in the Klan and that the Open House had functioned as a gathering place for the local Klavern, we just turned a deaf ear and ordered another cheeseburger. What right did we have to stir up the past?

Six or eight years back, I read a book, *The Great Good Place*, by Ray Oldenburg. The author examines how communal bonds are fostered not at work, not at home, but at "third places" like taverns and coffeehouses and cafés, where unrelated people relate as equals. I have a peculiar affinity for such institutions, but until I read *The Great Good Place*, I had never been quite sure why. Emboldened by his theories and a budding interest in the civil rights movement, I began exploring the role of third places in the public life of the South. In the name of research, I ate smoke-charred ribs at Aleck's Barbecue Heaven in Atlanta, where Martin Luther King Jr. and his lieutenants plotted marches and sit-ins, kneel-ins, and wade-ins. I wolfed a pig-ear sandwich at Jackson, Mississippi's Big Apple Inn and listened as the owner regaled me with stories of the days when the NAACP field secretary Medgar Evers kept his office upstairs. And I made a trip to Washington, D.C., to sup at Ben's Chili Bowl, the U Street hot dog joint that served as a de facto community center and Student Nonviolent Coordinating Committee command post during the riots that followed King's 1968 assassination.

It took me a while, however, to warm to the idea of exploring the dark side of the South's third places. But there was no getting around it. Third places take on the attributes of the regulars who populate them, and if a third place could serve as a staging ground for the civil rights movement, as a home away from home for the Beloved Community, then a different kind of third place with a different kind of clientele could serve as an incubator of opposition, as an incubator of violence. In January of this year, with all this top of mind, I went back to Athens in search of the truth about my old haunt, Blanche's Open House.

JOHN T. EDGE

I did not have to wait long for answers. Early into my research at the University of Georgia library, I find a photocopy of an FBI teletype dated July 19, 1964: "Investigation to date has placed suspects Guest, Phillips, Lackey, Myers, and Sims as frequenting the Open House restaurant, hangout for rabid Klansmen located at 234 West Hancock Street at various times between twelve zero one a.m. and five thirty a.m., July eleven last." The matter being investigated was the murder of Lemuel Penn, a black Army Reserve officer. During the early morning hours of July 11, 1964, Penn, en route from Fort Benning in Georgia to his home in Washington, D.C., was killed near a bridge twenty-two miles north of Athens. A shotgun blast blew out the back of his head. According to newspaper accounts of the day, he was singled out by the Klan for the color of his skin and the out-of-state license plate bolted to the bumper of his car.

Inspired by my discovery, I spent the next few days hunched over a microfilm viewer in the library basement, scanning contemporary newspaper accounts and a newly declassified 5,600-page FBI file on the Penn murder. Once in a while, I surfaced from the depths to comb through city directories, tracing the lineage of the businesses that have occupied the two hundred block of West Hancock Street, and to read memoirs of the civil rights movement.

My life in Athens took on an ascetic quality: I passed way too much time, book in hand, at the Varsity, a storied chili dog drive-in that, during the spring and summer of 1964, was a site of nonviolent demonstrations by black youth and a target of violent counterdemonstrations by hooded white thugs from Clarke County Klavern 244, United Klans of America, Knights of the Ku Klux Klan. When my body cried out for something green and crunchy, I dined at the Grit, a hipster vegetarian restaurant of more recent vintage. But the summer of 1964 hounds me: during the course of my research, I learned that the space above what is now the Grit had, during that same fateful summer, served as the meeting place for the local Klavern.

Accounts of the summer of 1964 almost invariably mention the Open House. In June, Klansmen from the local 244 terrorized the residents of an Athens housing complex, firing shotguns, first into the air and then later into the back door of an apartment, striking a nineteen-year-old black man in the eye and a thirteen-year-old black girl in the lip. Herbert Guest—described by the journalist William Bradford Huie as a "282-pound garage operator with a first grade education . . . blackhaired, with several front teeth missing"—was arrested in the first round of shootings and charged with disorderly conduct. He paid a $105 fine. Paul Strickland, one of the triggerman, dredged up an alibi: he claimed to be drinking coffee at the Open House when the shots were fired.

Almost eighty FBI agents descended on Athens during late July 1964. They canvassed residents of rural Madison County, where Penn was shot. They questioned college students who claimed to have purchased amphetamines from Guest's Garage. They interviewed a man who spoke of buying bootleg whiskey from Guest and another man who claimed that the garage was involved in the white slavery trade, specifically the transport of prostitutes from Athens to Jacksonville, Florida. Guest's Garage was also the alleged home base for the Klan security patrol, a group of four to six men, some of whom were known to wear side arms and drive about town with KKK placards fixed to the sides of their cars. A July 14 FBI memo described them as "a terror group, ostensibly operating without the knowledge or approval of Klavern officials."

The FBI knew Herbert Guest to be a Klansman, and they listed Blanche as one of eight members of the Ladies Auxiliary of the Ku Klux Klan. At the time of Penn's murder, Blanche and Herbert worked together at Guest's Garage, four blocks away from the Open House on West Hancock Street. The Open House was a regular stakeout sight. On the evening of July 19, FBI informants observed the following patrons at the restaurant: a filling station employee, a drive-in theater worker, several college students, a midget, two state patrolmen, one Athens policeman, and a man who bragged of "hitting and killing a nigger with his car."

It was a fairly typical night.

The Guests were under constant surveillance. On July 31, Herbert's thirty-seventh birthday, two FBI agents delivered a cake to Guest's Garage. "Herbert wanted to sit down and eat it," Blanche told *Atlanta Constitution* reporter Bill Shipp. "But I wouldn't let him. I told him he didn't know what the FBI might have put in that cake." Frosted with white icing and topped with the appropriate number of candles, the coconut cake was understood to be a message: "I believe it was just their way of letting Herbert know they knew all about him," said a friend.

On August 6, suspect James Lackey cracked under FBI questioning. According to his confession, Howard Sims, Cecil Myers, and he were on "security patrol" the morning of Lemuel Penn's death. Lackey was driving, with Myers in the passenger seat and Sims in the back. Sims and Meyers were armed. According to witness interviews, they spent the majority of the evening shuttling back and forth between the Open House and Guest's Garage until around four in the morning, when they spotted Penn's car. "The original reason for our following the colored men," Lackey told investigators, "was because we had heard that Martin Luther King might make Georgia a testing ground with the new Civil Rights bill. We thought some out-of-town niggers might stir up some trouble in Athens. . . . I had no idea they would really shoot the Negro."

That same day, on the strength of Lackey's confession, FBI agents arrested him along with Sims, Myers, and Herbert Guest—who at the time was pegged as the ringleader of the group—on federal charges of violating Penn's civil rights. A state murder indictment followed for Lackey, Sims, and Meyers. Guest, who was arrested as an accessory after the fact, corroborated Lackey's statement. Conviction seemed inevitable. But by the time of the murder trial, Lackey and Guest repudiated their testimonies. On September 4, an all-white jury found the defendants not guilty of murder. Almost two years later Sims and Myers were convicted on the civil rights charges, but as far as the courts are concerned, the murder of Lemuel Penn remains unsolved.

Though Herbert Guest was never convicted in the Penn case, he did serve time for the sale of amphetamines—a turn of events that compelled Blanche to try a new career. When Herbert headed for the federal penitentiary in late 1966, she closed the garage and bought the restaurant that her husband and his cronies had called home. She dubbed it Blanche's Open House. Assisted by Herbert after his release from prison, Blanche operated the Open House until 1985, when she sold her lease to a man named Herbie Abroms, recently retired from a career in the ladies' apparel industry.

Before I departed for home on Sunday, I drove by Blanche's old spot on Hancock Street one more time. There were no reminders of her tenure in the red-brick building. No beer cans littered the parking lot like they once did. Gone was the Coca-Cola sign that advertised "Open All Night." Instead, a hand-painted sign hung above the entrance. It read: "Fountain of Life Ministries." It was around eleven o'clock in the morning when I drove up in front of the adjacent beauty shop and climbed out. There was a crowd milling about in the parking lot of the storefront church. As I moved closer, I heard music. Every face I saw was black. Since I was a little underdressed for church, I hung back at the edge of the crowd, unsure if I should join them inside.

A pickup soon pulled alongside me, and when the driver emerged, we fell into conversation. I told him I'm writing about the restaurant that used to be here. He told me that he doesn't remember it as a restaurant. "They used to sell hub caps out of here," he said. "Least that's what it was before we moved in a couple of years back."

When I told him about the Guests and the Klan, he squinted into the morning sun and shook his head. I stammered an attempt at explanation, but he cut me off. I tried to tell him about third places, but he just kept shaking his head. "I don't care what it was before," he says, his voice rising, "It's a church now."

A few days into my research on the 1964 murder of Lemuel Penn, I think to ask a rather elemental question: What happened to Blanche and Herbert Guest, proprietors of the late-night diner in Athens, Georgia, that hosted Klansmen in the 1960s and drunken frat boys like me in the 1980s? I had pegged Blanche as ancient when I met her twenty-plus years ago. Had she and Herbert passed away?

A quick check of the phone book tells me they are both alive. When I call Blanche to set up an interview, I am rather vague about my intentions. I am not disingenuous, but I also am not keen on letting Blanche and Herbert know that this reformed frat boy has been leafing through their old FBI files, trying to make sense of their past and, by extension, my own.

Early one afternoon, I drive out Prince Avenue to Whitehead Road, where Blanche and Herbert live in a brick, ranch-style house. Blanche is vacuuming when I knock. Her face is now deeply lined, and her hair has turned ashen, but she looks spry for a seventy-one-year-old. Herbert hasn't fared as well. His already formidable weight has ballooned, and he wheezes when he walks.

Soon after I take a seat at the dining room table, Blanche hands me a tumbler of sweet tea and launches into a serial recollection: "We were known for our barbecue goat omelets." And, "Did you realize that I always bought fresh eggs, I never did take to store bought eggs." And, "I can't remember when we installed bars on the men's bathroom window, but we had to do it. There were just too damn many drunks crawling out and not paying."

On two separate occasions Herbert begins a story about a past indiscretion, only to have Blanche cut him off, redirect my line of questioning, and plunge headlong into another tale. As she talks, my mind begins to wander. I concoct a daydream in which I return to my car, grab my file of FBI clippings, dump them on the walnut tabletop, and shout something akin to "J'accuse!"

Instead, I smile and nod and swallow hard. This is not one of my prouder moments: rather than give Blanche and Herbert a chance to explain themselves, rather than lay claim to the bully pulpit for myself, I defile the hospitality of my hosts and deny the empirical truth of my research.

Later that afternoon, I return home from the library to find that Blanche has left a message on my answering machine. "I found an old matchbook from the restaurant," she says. "Stop by the house tomorrow and I'll give it to you as a souvenir. Ain't too many of these left, you know."

Learning and Loafing at Tennessee's Oldest Business

FRED W. SAUCEMAN

Ron Dawson demonstrates his favorite magic trick as he stands behind the cash register at St. John Milling Company. Dimes and quarters disappear and reappear in quick succession. Then, unlike television or tableside magicians, he explains the mechanics of the trick. Gives the whole thing away gladly. No secrets. Despite his dexterity with the coins, he knows that deception has no place in the milling business. It's a line of work based on honesty, a trait handed down for nearly 225 years through the families that have run the oldest business in Tennessee. A sign on the building reads, "Please weigh with driver off truck."

On the banks of north-flowing Brush Creek in Northeast Tennessee, St. John Milling survived Yankee raids in 1862 and the coming of the discount stores a century later. It escaped the domination of cheaper Kansas wheat by milling animal feeds instead. Still, the owners have yet to buy a computer. Ron Dawson says, "It's coming," but adds quickly that if such a machine is purchased, he wouldn't want it to show.

Yet Ron and his eighty-nine-year-old father-in-law, George St. John, don't fight technology. Ron is trained to be an audiovisual communication specialist. George took a decaying, out-of-date mill, applied his newly acquired engineering knowledge from the University of Tennessee, and began modernizing the business during the pain of the Great Depression in the 1930s. The census of 1900 reported over forty mills in operation in Washington County. By mid-century, most all of them were boarded up. Seeing a dim future in grinding corn and wheat, Dawson and St. John bought equipment from some of those closed mills and created a farm store and feed mill. Ten years ago, the bulk of their business was cattle feed, but today, it's sweet feed for horses, a combination of cut corn, crimped oats, wheat bran, protein, soybean meal, minerals, and vitamins which is then run through a molasses blender. It nourishes 200-

pound ponies, 2,000-pound draft horses, and all sizes between. Vestiges of the mill's original purpose sit on the shelves today as biscuit mixes purchased from North Carolina.

The earthy smell and creaky floors of the Southern feed store, the rush of the cool creek just outside the back door, and a hot pork-tenderloin biscuit from the neighbors at T and S Country Kitchen make the St. John Mill one of East Tennessee's most beloved places. Farmers know they can come by and find a new T-post for fence-mending or a pulley for the barn. There's Grape Balm Hoof Healer, too. Gopher bait and apple-flavored horse treats. Along with each purchase comes the timeless wisdom of the feed store proprietor. Buy the Have-a-Heart trap and you learn the best way to catch raccoons. The folks at St. John were battling an unusually large population of the animals one year when a customer suggested baiting the traps with marshmallows.

"The next morning, we had two 'coons in one trap," Dawson says. More good advice: take a trip with the catch and transport the animals a minimum of seven miles from where they were caught. Make it only six, Dawson says, and they'll revisit.

It's the age-old exchange of information and stories, opinions and predictions that has taken place on courthouse benches and in country stores in these Appalachian Mountains ever since settlers got together in 1772 to organize the Watauga Association, America's first independent government. It wasn't long after that when Jeremiah Dungan, chased off a British hunting preserve in Bucks County, Pennsylvania, found a small, falling stream with a sixteen-foot gradient that could be harnessed for milling, unlike the nearby Watauga River. By 1778, he was in business on Brush Creek. Farmers shelled their corn by hand and brought their "turn" in special cotton sacks. "The miller dipped his toll box into the grain to get his share, usually about seven or eight pounds per bushel," says George St. John. When fall harvest time came, settlers and their families camped outside the mill and talked politics with their neighbors until it was time to grind their wheat or corn.

St. John Mill may well be the oldest manufacturing company in the United States. Tennessee governor Don Sundquist chose it for the opening of the state's bicentennial celebration in 1996. "No one was wanting money, no one wanting favors," George remembers. He enjoyed the party so much that he's planning another one for the spring of 2003, when he turns 90 and the mill 225. His grandfather bought the mill in 1866.

"I've been very lucky," he notes. "I've been my own boss for sixty-six years. I make my own decisions, handle my own problems. Something would break and I'd be here nearly all night fixing it. Or maybe a cow would be out on our adjoining farm and the police would be after me. Two o'clock in the morning and I'm out hunting a cow."

With a book of deeds, letters, and tax records dating back to 1784, George has become an amateur historian. He and Ron Dawson, who purchased the business from his father-in-law in 1975, have thought long and hard about how the mill made it through the Civil War, especially the bullets and the flames of Carter's Raid the day before New Year's Eve, 1862.

Brigadier General Samuel P. Carter had taken a leave of absence from the U.S. navy to fight the Confederates on land. In 1861, his warmongering retired Presbyterian minister brother William had met with President Lincoln and his staff to describe a plan for the destruction of all the bridges on the East Tennessee and Virginia Railroad between Bristol, Virginia, and Bridgeport, Alabama. Lincoln readily gave Carter an audience because the plan meshed well with the Federal strategy of using East Tennesseans' Union loyalty to its best, most deadly advantage against their Confederate neighbors. The bridge spanning the Watauga River, at Carter's Station, was on the hit list. According to Jim Maddox, in the *History of Washington County, Tennessee,* published in 2001, "a Federal cavalry force of Michigan, Ohio, and Pennsylvania troopers, some armed with Colt revolving carbines and led by General Samuel P. Carter, came down from Kentucky to attack the railroad bridges. . . . Destroying the bridge there (at Zollicoffer), the Federal cavalry went on to attack the Confederate garrison at Carter's Depot, and after a brisk fight there, captured most of them, paroling the prisoners, and destroying the bridge there as well as some ten railroad cars filled with lumber and other military supplies." One account says Carter drove a locomotive into the river.

Robert Tipton Nave, in the same publication, describes yet another assault in September of 1864, when Union men attacked the enemy at Carter's Depot, forced a retreat, but left before a larger Confederate contingent could come to defend the bridge. The Barnes house on Brush Creek, near the mill, was rattling with crossfire, and Mrs. Barnes packed her baby and three small children into the chimney while she crouched inside the fireplace for protection.

Ron Dawson and George St. John believe the only reason the mill escaped the raiders' torches is because it was run, during the Civil War, by Henry Bashor, a Dunkard minister who led Sunday services in the building. Bashor had purchased the mill in 1846, and his accounts were scattered throughout the South—Savannah, Atlanta, Birmingham, Huntsville—after the completion of the railroad from Bristol to Knoxville in 1856 opened up a whole new market.

"It's hard to conceive how this mill survived, being 500 yards from where

Carter's Raid happened, and being an established mill grinding wheat and corn when soldiers from both sides were frantically trying to cut supply lines for food and ammunition," Dawson says. "The only theory we find plausible is that it was used as a house of the Lord and therefore spared."

A highway bridge wasn't built over the river until 1913. To reach the mill from the other side of the Watauga, customers had to use a ferry or risk a dangerous crossing on foot at a swift and rocky ford. Still, the mill survived.

East Tennessee, immediately after the Civil War, was considered the "bread basket of the South," says George St. John. "While much of the South was torn up during the war, there was very little damage here, and the mill's customer base expanded." The Read House in downtown Chattanooga, once an army hospital during the Civil War, baked with cornmeal and flour from the St. John Mill.

Today, even St. John's competitors are customers, and they often pool their money to buy truckloads of goods, such as fenceposts, to get a better price break. Back in the middle of July, two of Dawson's four employees had to miss work because of illness. Instead of turning to the want ads or temporary employment services, he was aided by a competitor. Mike Galloway, at Galloway's Mill in Sullivan County, sent one of his employees over to St. John for two days and would accept no pay.

"Back thirty years ago, Galloway's had a building burn," Dawson explained. "George St. John sent over a truck and men to help them get back on their feet, and they never forgot it. You don't see that in business today."

The majority of the nation's oldest businesses, like St. John Milling, exist in rural areas, and Dawson believes they are organizations that have gotten past the idea that the only reason for their existence is to make money.

"We're working to give service, to help others. We've arrived when you have a businessman come in and you see him reach up and get his tie and loosen it. That action says I don't have to put up a front for anyone. I can be myself. I think it's the way the Good Lord wanted us to be."

I take yet another drive out Highway 400 to refine my loafing skills at the best place I know to do it. Shirley Casey slips me a country-ham-and-egg biscuit through the window of T and S Country Kitchen. There are fifteen different kinds of biscuits, ready around 6:35 in the morning. I find a seat at one of the old stone picnic tables on the banks of Brush Creek, right between the mill and the restaurant. I listen to the creekwater and hear cattle around the corn crib in the pasture just across the road. I step inside the mill for a good story and the smell of oats. And an even slicker magic trick. I overhear a customer telling about how the real estate agents are bringing too many Floridians through Roan Mountain. I pick up one of David Cretsinger's cypress wood buckets, at a third of the Dollywood price, and contemplate buying one of his butter churns on the next visit. Today I learn what the percentage figure means on the horse feed. I find out what made a good buhrstone. I hear George St. John speculate about where the original Fort Watauga could have been. Maybe right across the road. I hear Ron Dawson count his blessings for never taking that job in Chicago or the one way out in Stockton, California. And I come to appreciate, even more, the richness of life in East Tennessee, thanks to the wisdom within these old walls.

Pitmaster James Willis, Memphis, Tennessee

Al Clayton of Jasper, Georgia, shot the photographs in this section.
Some were originally published in John Egerton's *Southern Food: At Home,
on the Road, in History*; some were published in magazine articles and in
other books. Over the course of a long and distinguished career, Clayton
has had a profound influence on how we see the South. During the 1960s,
he took photographs for a U.S. Senate investigation on hunger. Those
images were a catalyst for passage of the food stamp program.
(Photographs used by permission of the photographer)

Doug Mahan, oyster smoker, Bowens Island, South Carolina

Church dinner on the ground, Buena Vista, Georgia

International Barbecue Cooking Contest and Festival, Memphis, Tennessee

Roadside vendors, rural Georgia

Lucille "Mama" Cole, Panama City, Florida

Oyster shucker, Mobile, Alabama

Willie Brown, oyster shucker, Mobile, Alabama

THE TRADITION

Roadside Table

MICHAEL McFEE

It was an ugly slab of rough concrete
or warped green boards carved and stained
by greasy sticky previous picnickers

but still we'd pack the creaking station wagon
with hungry relatives and cardboard boxes
full of deviled-egg luster under wax paper

and fried chicken's golden warm aroma
and the moist strata of granny's coconut cake
then drive for what felt like forever, starving,

till dad saw a blue sign for one just ahead
and pulled off into a shady dirt turnout
between the busy highway and some river

where we all waited while meticulous aunts
brushed off the crumby weathered surfaces
then unfolded a tablecloth of newspapers

which we held down with the now-cooled feast
before suffering through interminable grace
and loading our flimsy plates with layers

of food as if we never ate at home,
as if we didn't have our own picnic table
around which, anytime, we all could gather.

What Abby Fisher Knows

SARA ROAHEN

Every summer, Abby Fisher gathered just-ripe cling peaches and preserved them in brandy. I don't know how long she let the brandy peaches rest on the closet shelf before she spooned them over ice cream or served them with feather cake, but it was probably at least a few months, until the time when she was also baking apple pies, digging warmer clothes out of chests, and worrying about the imminent frost. I'll never know what occupied her mind while she put up those peaches, but because she included two recipes for brandy peaches in *What Mrs. Fisher Knows about Old Southern Cooking*, along with thirty other recipes for pickles and preserves, I do know a good bit about how she moved through the world and its seasons. The remainder of her recipes—all equally accessible to intuitive modern-day cooks (you have to wing temperatures and cooking times)—are for roasted and broiled meats, breakfast breads, cakes, croquettes, sweet and savory puddings and pies, salads, soups and gumbos, and home remedies. Cooking was the motion of Abby Fisher's life.

The handful of hard biographical facts we can know about Abby Fisher are contained in an invaluable afterword written by culinary historian Karen Hess, who culled bits of information from census reports, other historians, and her own extensive knowledge of Southern cooking. Fisher was probably born a slave in North Carolina, the offspring of a slave mother and a French slave-owner father. She married a mulatto from Alabama, had eleven children, and, sometime in the 1870s, moved from Mobile to San Francisco, where she opened a pickling and preserving business and later survived the earthquake of 1906. Hers is the first known cookbook by an African American, according to Hess, though subsequent findings suggest that another black woman, Melinda Russell, published *A Domestic Cookbook: Containing a Careful Selection of Useful Recipes for the Kitchen*, in 1866. The Women's Co-operative Printing Office in San Francisco published the book in 1881, "about forty years before women won the right to vote." As Abby Fisher could neither read nor write, prominent friends in San Francisco transcribed the recipes for her.

These tidbits of information are fascinating, even sensational. They drew me to the pocket-size book in the first place. But they are no competition for the reason I now hold it dear: the recipes.

A cookbook like this one is an intimate memoir. A collection of a cook's own recipes reveals her heart in the most visceral way, by laying down the particulars of how she feeds her family, herself, and, in some cases, her employers. The sure, feminine voice running throughout Abby Fisher's book divulges more about her attitude during her routine activities than we can sometimes learn about our own neighbors. Take her final recipe:

Pap for Infant Diet

Take one pint of flour, sift it and tie it up in a clean cloth securely tight, so that no water can get into it; and put it in boiling water and let it boil steady for two hours, then take it out of water, and when it gets cold take outside crust from it. Whenever you are ready to nurse or feed the child, grate one tablespoonful of the boiled flour, and stir it into half a pint of boiled milk while the milk is still boiling; sweeten the same with white sugar to taste. When the child has diarrhea, boil a two-inch stick of cinnamon in the pap. I have given birth to eleven children and raised them all, and nursed them with this diet. It is a Southern plantation preparation.

With few words, she shows us how she spent thousands of hours engaged in the primordial task of nursing her children. Reading these practical instructions, I imagine her uncorking a jar of cinnamon sticks with a sick child in one arm as the milk comes to a simmer nearby on the hearth; I imagine her in the rocking chair, or asking a relative to comfort the child while she finalizes the plantation's dinner preparations. But much more vital than my imaginings, I have her words. By following them by taking less than ten minutes to make pie pastry, say, rolling the dough "to the thickness of an egg-shell," I glimpse the mind of this meticulous, observant woman and the pride she took in her day-to-day occupations. No amount of historical trivia could replicate such insights.

As I chop away at the 160 recipes, republished in paperback by Applewood Books in 1995, I miss absolutely nothing. I enter Abby Fisher's world, and, just as in any captivating story, there's enough here to keep me busy for days. This is a world in which I "grate two or three sour pickles" for lamb croquettes and then "chop the whole up very fine indeed"; the world in which peaches "remain under sugar for twenty-four hours," bleeding every drop of their reddish pigment, before I add brandy, "cork the jars and put in closet." I lose myself in the chopping and in the waiting, the simple motions that Abby Fisher's legacy stirred me to perform. These motions aren't terribly unique. Thousands of people are performing similar tasks in their kitchens at this moment, which is exactly what holds me so rapt. At the end of the day, it's the basic commonalities between humans that let us begin to understand one another at all. I like to grate orange zest into sweet potato pie filling. So did Abby Fisher. I do it because someone once told me to, and because it made sense; she probably did it because citrus and sweet potatoes came into season around the same time, and because it made sense. Rather than accentuate our exotic differences, cooking from this ex-slave's recipes almost feels like knowing her.

There's a jar of brandy peaches on a shelf in my kitchen now. When I glance up at it, I don't think about all the unconfirmed facts and missing details, but rather I wonder which recipe I'll try next and what it will disclose about the seasons of Abby Fisher's life. I often recall one line in her "Preface and Apology": "Not being able to read or write myself, and my husband also being without the advantages of an education upon whom would devolve the writing of the book at my dictation caused me to doubt whether I would be able to present a work that would give perfect satisfaction." Abby Fisher's perfectly satisfying book teaches that, just as authoring her recipe memoir had little to do with the physical act of writing, so reading is just one step in the process of learning another person's story.

Ice Cream Dreams

EDDIE DEAN

I first discovered the power of a Fudge Bomb when I was surrounded by a family of Blue Ridge Mennonites who hadn't seen the ice-cream truck for a week. All their Fudge Bombs had run out days ago, and their Sno-Cones and Chocolate Chump Bars, too. Their sturdy white frame house sat on a hill in Greene County, Virginia, and I was parked before it in my truck, both of us coughing up dust after the long climb up the winding gravel driveway. These people were hurting badly. We were there to help them.

For generations, locals have found this rocky region as poor as a snake. But it's been a gold mine for interlopers—first the folk-song collectors and then the government men and the social workers and finally the movie stars here for peace of mind and land for their trotting horses. The movie stars didn't buy ice cream, not off a truck anyway. Just about everybody else did, though. At least, they did back then. This was twenty years ago, before gourmet ice cream and the culture of instant gratification. If you lived in Greene County, the only way you could get a Fudge Bomb was from my truck.

A Fudge Bomb is a brown and yellow "quiescently frozen confection" impaled on a stick and molded in the shape of a Sputnik-era nuclear warhead. It is infused with an equatorial stripe of artificially flavored banana that beads with tropical sweat when unveiled in the July heat by a Mennonite housewife in a gingham dress. At the time I was selling them, a Fudge Bomb cost sixty cents, a crucial dime more than its red-white-and-blue cousin, the Superstar Bomb Pop, but well worth the extra investment. No mere popsicle, a Fudge Bomb is a bona fide meal.

The Mennonites are a strict denomination. For them, every day is a holy day, and they dress and try to behave as such. But there is nothing in their rules that forbids the indulgence of sweets. And no visiting preacher ever inspired more joy than did the driver of the truck with the BIG LIK license plates. I would often linger in the shade as the family members gathered on the green lawn, becalmed by the sacrament of ice cream. The rippling folds of the Blue Ridge Mountains stretched to the horizon as big white clouds drifted by like so many covered wagons. At such a moment of a bright Sunday many summers ago, I understood why their ancestors decided to nestle here instead of pushing west. This perch would do fine until the Battle of Armageddon.

Those were good customers, that family, one of several Mennonite families on the route. They even bought ice cream for their livestock. They had a goat named Curly leashed to a tombstone in the family graveyard, a stone-walled plot near the driveway. His reward for keeping the grass trim was an ice-cream sandwich. The Mennonites were businesspeople themselves. I'd often pass roadside stands where they sold homemade peanut-butter pies to the weekend tourists from Washington, D.C.

They were better off than most of my customers, who had little in worldly possessions other than the junk accumulated on their ramshackle properties. Yet even the most destitute were no less faithful when that ice-cream bell came ringing. For them, the unbidden arrival of the BIG LIK truck was proof that even if they weren't among the affluent or the righteous, they would not be denied their just desserts—even if it meant scraping together a fistful of pennies for a 25-cent popsicle.

Behind the wheel of BIG LIK, in the shadow of the hazy, hallucinatory Blue Ridge, I believed I'd found my calling, though at twenty I would have never used such a word. All I knew was that it didn't seem like work, and it beat delivering pizza in a borrowed car. What began as a seasonal job during my time at the University of Virginia held me in Charlottesville well after graduation. It wasn't driving the truck that hooked me: I fell for the geography. I'd grown up in the lowland piedmont of Richmond, and there was something about this rugged landscape that moved me. Whatever the reason, the mountains cast a spell that I couldn't shake.

It was naïve, to be sure. Nonetheless, I knew in my gut that I was lucky to gain passage on this route, the only one of its kind in the history of the Shenandoah Valley, and perhaps in the entire United States. It was a foolhardy expedition from the start. No sane businessman would have even considered it, much less actually attempted it. The meandering circuit was carved out of the ridges and hollows three decades ago by hippie entrepreneurs who didn't know any better. (One later worked for a spell as a Wall Street commodities broker.) The route survived until the late eighties, and it was during those twilight years when I drove the truck.

I worked for a two-vehicle renegade independent without allegiance to the corporate-owned fleets that dominate the industry. My truck was a converted '71 GMC step van weighted down by a lead-lined, coffin-sized freezer. On the filthy, battered exterior, a painted tin plate promised "Happy Time Ice Cream." The truck was customized well beyond the BIG LIK tags, down to a Radio Shack cassette tape deck and a photo of a stoned Sly Stone above the rearview mirror. Sly sported a floppy, rhinestone-studded pimp's hat and a baked expression of grim weariness that gave warning to all who would pursue the perpetual buzz.

The road of excess leads to the palace of wisdom, sayeth William Blake, and Sly was our road-wizened guru. More than that, he was our very own *orisha*, our guardian spirit against the highway patrol, our patron saint of Hot Fun and Weird Shit in the Summertime. He was also the source of countless queries from customers demanding to know who in the hell he was. The sixties counterculture was little more than a rumor in these parts. If you said Woodstock, you were talking about a town off Lee Highway where the only long-hairs were a breed of pig. The heroes around here were bad dudes on TV who drove fast and talked trash and kicked ass: Richard Petty and Wahoo McDaniel and Mr. T and the Dukes of Hazzard.

The county routes, as we called them, traversed the farthest reaches of Greene and Page Counties, southern Appalachian outbacks little changed since the depression. Just two hours drive from the nation's capital, it was a world away in every other respect. No maps of the routes exist except the one in my head. The journey began near an abandoned woolen mill in Charlottesville and ended twelve hours later and a hundred miles away in a synesthesia of smoldering asbestos brake pads and melted Dreamsicles on the hot floorboard steps. It was a grueling ride for the driver and eventually a money drain for the company, but the route gave a taste of a bygone era when hauling ice cream by truck lived up to its mythic status as a vital American ritual.

At the time, the ice-cream truck was still a unifying force that transcended class lines and social status: the haves and the have-nots alike hailed down BIG LIK for a quick fix. Besides the county routes, there were the town and city routes, our big moneymakers. The town route included some well-to-do suburbs where some people patronized the truck every so often for the kick of some half-remembered nostalgia. They deemed it proper parenting to make selections for their kids: ice-cream sandwiches and "healthy" items. Like the children, who craved adventurous fare like cherry Screwballs and Elephant Ears, I despised these parents for their well-meaning stupidity.

The most lucrative stops on the town and city runs were in the poorer neighborhoods, where dogs and kids roamed unsupervised. From May until past Halloween, we trolled these anarchic projects and trailer parks every day of the week, sometimes twice a day, as ubiquitous as the cops and the drug dealers. Some parents decided we were another Pusherman on the prowl; one irate mother yanked the arm of a BIG LIK passenger to check for needle marks. For many children, the constant dose of Bomb Pops really did become an ugly habit. Some groveled and begged for a freebie, ice cream smeared on their angry, squinched faces. I couldn't much blame them, because it was our relentless hard sell that fed their addiction.

Even so, BIG LIK provided balm when needed. Once, on the edge of the town route, not far from the house of a devout female customer who had the same sprout of chin whiskers you see in photographs of Confederate president Jefferson Davis, I came upon a cat writhing in the hot tar road, struck down moments before the truck rolled up. A man appeared from a nearby house and identified the dying animal. He went back home and returned carrying a pistol. As his daughter and her friends stood by shrieking, he walked a few paces off the road behind some bramble. One shot rang out, and another. Then he ambled over to the truck and bought a Sno-Cone for his daughter.

Next to the mercenary grind of the city and town routines, the county routes were a revelation. A few miles outside Charlottesville, the manicured, fenced-in spreads of gentrified horse farms gave way to the great wide-open of hardcore ice cream country. Heading west of Ruckersville on Route 33, I welcomed the sight of the hog pens and the A-frame coops for fighting chickens and rusted cars half-buried in the ground. These were the tell-tale signs of serious ice-cream customers. Some houses were strictly for shelter and barely that. One family, faithful and longtime patrons, resided in an abandoned school bus parked permanently a few feet off the road.

Out in these green hills and dark hollows, the people were always happy to see BIG LIK. For generations, most outsiders seen in these parts came only to plunder. In 1916 and 1918, British musicologist Cecil Sharp made several trips to the area, collecting folk songs that had survived for centuries. These were bloody murder ballads and songs about dead babies and assorted domestic tragedies. From Florence Puckett he got "The Shooting of His Dear" and "The Cuckoo"; from Horton Barker came "Hares of The Mountains," and from Leila Yowell, "The Farmer's Curst Wife." From Lizzie Gibson, who Sharp recalled as "a fine woman and regular type of mountaineer who sang very well," he got "Pretty Saro" and "Earl Brand." Sharp collected hundreds of tunes, many dating back to Elizabethan times, and published them in *English Folk Songs from the Southern Appalachians.*

At first locals had taken Sharp for a German spy, but it was their own government who proved to be the enemy. In the mid-thirties, federal authorities evicted hundreds of mountain families to make way for the newly created

Shenandoah National Park, the so-called "Playground for Washingtonians." Popular opinion of the time had little sympathy for their plight.

Some locals did not leave willingly. Melancthon Cliser ran a filling station and diner called Blue Ridge Lunch at the top of Panorama Gap, a few miles north from where our ice-cream route cut west through the mountains. Lawmen nabbed the sixty-two-year-old in front of his business; Cliser stood in handcuffs and delivered a quavering rendition of "The Star-Spangled Banner," and then gave a speech declaring himself a free man defending his constitutional rights. It took four deputies to wrestle Cliser into the sheriff's car; meanwhile, his wife and the couple's dog, Boodgy, sat defiantly on the front porch, even after authorities had boarded up the building to prevent reentry.

There were other ugly altercations. John Mace owned a place near Madison Run. From a spring on his property, he bottled his own brand of "Health Mineral Water," which he recommended to "all suffering from Eczema, Pimples, Tettor, or other skin diseases, Stomach Trouble, Kidney Trouble, Nervousness, or Loss of Appetite." Like Cliser, he refused all offers for his property. After deputies talked him out of his house, they piled his furniture and belongings in the yard. Then, with Mace standing by, they burned the place down.

Before it was over, authorities had conducted a forced removal that left century-old homesteads in charred ruins. Some of my customers were among the displaced, and they still lived in the shabby prefab houses the government built for them in resettlement areas. Not a few carried a bitterness against the feds that time only deepened. It was probably just as well they didn't know that our ice cream came from a wholesale supplier in Washington.

So BIG LIK was something altogether new here, an intruder come to peddle instead of pillage. We came only once or twice a week, so the people never got tired of us. On the county routes, politeness was the rule, and the barter system was often in effect. A carton of watermelon-flavored Italian ice for a fresh mulberry pie; a Chipwich for a clay-encrusted can of Pabst Blue Ribbon buried for God knows how long in some secret hiding place. They bestowed their own names on favorite items. A Nutty Buddy was a drumstick, an Eskimo Pie a chocolate cover, and a Neapolitan ice-cream sandwich a Napoleon.

The locals showed a genuine concern for the truck's well-being. They sympathized with its dilapidated condition and greeted a flat tire with the swift attention of those who know what it is to be in need. The men who helped with a tow or a tool kit refused any offers of free ice cream as thanks. They were poor but fiercely proud, and they were quick to forgive as well. One BIG LIK driver got his kicks swerving at jaywalking animals instead of around them. Wild or domesticated, all God's creatures were potential roadkill to him. The owner of a dog run down by this assassin had only a stern reprimand for the driver the next time through: "You could have at least cleaned it up."

Some events could never be forgotten, even if they happened more than a century ago. One man stopped patronizing the truck after he discovered that a driver was a descendant of a Union officer in the Civil War. You often hear how mountain people refused to fight for the South, but around here they did fight, and they remembered. The town of Earlysville was named for Rebel general Jubal Early, and battle reenactments were part of the local social calendar. The Shenandoah Valley, the Breadbasket of the Confederacy, was a crucial strategic stronghold during the war. Our route followed many of the same mountain passes where Stonewall Jackson's troops zigzagged on the all-night marches that so beleaguered the Yanks.

Out here, the ice-cream bell was no mere prop but a signal I depended on when I entered a hollow. The sound of the electric bell hung in the air for miles around, alerting my customers of BIG LIK's arrival. (Once, the far-flung ringing wooed a calf that mistook the sound for its mother, broke free from a fenced field, and followed the truck a half-mile.) Leaning hard on the bell, I would make a high-speed run to the dead end of a hollow where the state road hits gravel. On the ride back out, my customers waited in anxious clumps, sometimes three generations strong. They stood next to battered mailboxes with hand-scrawled names: Morris, Roach, Shifflett. That last surname was by far the most prevalent in the region. There must have been several hundred members of this clan in every nook and cranny of the upper Blue Ridge. The Shiffletts spelled their name every conceivable way, but they all liked ice cream.

The beauty of the land spoiled me as surely as did the free ice cream. The variety of vistas, from roadside cliffs strung with kudzu beards to boulder-strewn, stubbled fields, seemed infinite. Sometimes a thunderstorm would dance across a valley half-lit by a blazing sun, and the scampering downpour reeled off a succession of rainbows I would chase but never catch. And always the Blue Ridge framed the view, with humble names like Brokenback Mountain, old as the continent. These were no majestic peaks to conquer, but worn-down, welcoming hills to burrow into.

My boss refused to bother with the county routes, which he'd inherited when he bought the business. His pride and joy was the one he developed, the highly profitable city route, the twice-a-day circuit through Charlottesville's poorest neighborhoods. He usually spent the off-season globe-trotting in exotic realms such as India and Tibet, taking photos of Buddhist monks and their prayer flags high in the Eastern sky. I would tell him he was missing out on some mystical terrain right in his own backyard. The Blue Ridge had its own ancient spirits, even if they lacked the faintest whiff of patchouli.

One of the drivers, Dave Brooks, understood my affinities. He was raised in Bath County near the West Virginia line, so he was no stranger to the mountains. It was Brooks who taught me the county routes, and his enthusiasm for the people and places stoked my youthful enthusiasm. He truly loved the Greene and Page runs, and he drove them more often than any other driver. It was only years later that I discovered that Brooks had been documenting the routes with his camera.

Looking at his photos two decades hence, I can remember every face, though I never knew their names, and they didn't know mine. The photos remind me how sharply the bucolic setting contrasted with the dire poverty of the locals. They came to the truck barefoot and bandaged and black-eyed, in threadbare clothes and in metal curlers. They rarely displayed jewelry of any kind—instead a necklace of fresh, red hickeys on the pale neck of a teenage girl, or the raw insect bites on the spindly, hairy legs of some crone with an unfiltered Camel smoldering in her sun-blistered lips as she counted out pennies for a popsicle, or the hardened scab on the bloodshot, bulbous nose of an old farmer who always received his purchase on a cast-iron skillet. (He said the ice cream was too cold for his gnarled, trembling hands.) It was obvious many of the children were hungry for more than ice cream, and when the adults would flash a gap-toothed smile, I could see the years of Bomb Pops had done their work.

For friends who joined me on the route, this scenario could make for some unsettling encounters. Those expecting to meet the Waltons were in for a rude awakening; the amount of roadkill alone proved daunting enough for some. Not long into the journey, they quietly set aside their cameras and huddled in a corner away from the sales window when the customers clamored around. Others used chemicals to try to commiserate with the surroundings. One day-tripper ate some psychedelic mushrooms along with his ice cream. Somewhere outside Earlysville, he said he needed some fresh air and bolted from the truck as it rounded a curve.

As for myself, I got used to the hard lot of the BIG LIK customers. After a long day on the truck, I didn't spend much time pondering the harsh economic conditions. One of the drivers said we were exploiting these people, but I couldn't see the injustice. All I saw was my customers happy to see the truck every week, grateful that somebody hadn't forgotten them. I'd take my cut of grimy, sweat-stained bills from the money box, buy a six-pack of Black Label, and give thanks that I didn't have to work a real job. For me, the county route was a paid adventure that I knew wouldn't last, so I relished it.

The truck gave me entry into places otherwise off-limits to outsiders. Bacon Hollow abutted the Appalachian Trail and the Shenandoah National Park. It was poor and insular even by Greene County standards, shunned by most beer-drinking Christians. Bacon Hollow earned its reputation as a place unfriendly to strangers, especially the county social workers meddling in their domestic affairs.

They had their own way of talking in Bacon Hollow. They had their own ways, period. It was not uncommon to see crude effigies nailed to trees. In the late seventies, a driver got embroiled in a local family feud when a Shifflett gunned down a Morris. He'd recently had a run-in with this same Shifflett, who'd invited the driver to join a roadside corn-liquor party. "If you don't have a drink with us," he said, "You ain't getting out of the hollow this evening." The driver thought it wise to be polite and partake. The victim's family wanted him to testify as a character witness in the trial. His refusal to take sides earned him death threats and the enmity of both clans. He was forced to quit the route lest he become another casualty.

Bacon Hollow hadn't changed by the time I came through. Here you might get a kid paying with a swiped jarful of old rare coins, and you'd accept the money even if it probably meant he'd get a whipping. Sometimes, pranksters would set out boards with nails to give drivers an obstacle course on the way out. One homestead boasted fearsome-looking deer antlers on its porch roof. Like many of the houses here, it lay across a creek from the main road. To get to it, you had to cross a rickety bridge, and there was always some sort of gathering that could number a couple dozen revelers. But there was never a problem. The exiled driver notwithstanding, BIG LIK was always welcome here, and on a good day this was a $100 hollow. It was a prime example of how the best customers were inevitably the ones who could least afford it.

More ice-cream hotbeds were over in Page County. An offshoot that included a chunk of the Greene route, this route was typically a Sunday run that pushed further north into the valley. Brown Hollow was an all-black enclave with a baseball field dug out of a hillside with a backhoe. The players, ranging from kids to stooping gray-hairs, were arrayed in their Sunday best, coats off and shirtsleeves rolled up. Upon hearing the bell, they'd stop the game, and for a half-hour, BIG LIK was the center of the community.

On the county routes, the ice-cream truck really mattered to people, and they responded in kind, with courtesy and heartfelt thanks. Out here, the sins of the city and town routes were redeemed. Out here, the ritual hadn't gone rotten. There was still room for magic, like when I'd reach into the freezer and toss a handful of ice shavings at a group of toddlers—a little touch of snow in summer.

As it turns out, the BIG LIK expedition wasn't able to pay its own way. The truck simply couldn't take the hairpin curves and billy-goat slopes anymore. Barreling back across Swift Run Gap with an empty freezer, the top-heavy rig was always nearly out of control. With a few beers and the high altitude going to my head, I'd ride the brakes hard and BIG LIK would howl like some beast of burden in pain. Eventually our mechanic, Race, had to install new brake pads and other replacement parts every couple weeks. The truck rarely grossed more than a few hundred dollars, and my 25 percent take wasn't much after you added up the hours.

And so, by the end of the eighties, the county routes vanished, gone the way of traveling medicine shows and knife peddlers and professional hoboes. Even before its demise, I had already returned to Richmond. Several bad omens helped hasten my retirement. Coming back from Greene County at dark, I ran over a black cat a block from the boss's house, where we usually kept the trucks. My driving record was spotless until then, but that didn't matter much to the pet's owners. Not long after, I backed the truck into a dogwood in my boss's yard, damaging the truck and the state tree of Virginia.

A few years ago, I paid a return visit to ice-cream country. With the exception of the more remote places like Bacon Hollow, I found the area changed almost beyond recognition. Hordes of the middle-class and the newly rich had fled the suburbs to join celebrity homesteaders such as Jessica Lange and Sissy Spacek in the promised land. They had satellite dishes and spacious tract houses and, no doubt, refrigerators full of grocery-store gourmet ice cream.

The transformation was as sad as it was inevitable. No doubt the poorest of my former customers, like those in Bacon Hollow, were stranded more than ever before, left further and further behind by the tide of prosperity flooding the mountains. BIG LIK wouldn't be much help to them now. No amount of Bomb Pops could bridge the ever-widening gap.

It was a writing project that brought me back, a story on the displaced mountain people. My old route beckoned me deeper into the Blue Ridge, and I found myself parked in front of one of the regular stops. It was a cold, gray winter day, and the scene was bleak. I barely recognized the house without its usual curtain of green vegetation. It was now revealed as the bare shack it was, not a drape on a window, no smoke curling from the stone chimney. At first, I thought maybe the place was abandoned. Where were the strutting chickens and the yapping dogs? Most important, where were the kids who'd clamored for BIG LIK so many years ago?

Then I spotted a couple of gangly teens behind the house, taking turns on a cigarette. They said when they were younger, they were devoted customers of the truck. But ice cream didn't interest them much anymore. They were standing in the bitter mountain air, they explained, because it was even colder inside the house. The firewood had run out that morning. We had a laugh recalling some favorites from the truck; they said they were hooked on Screwballs, cherry-flavored ice crammed into a clear plastic cone and packed with bubble gum at the bottom. I have watched many a wild-eyed kid chuck the whole thing to get to that buried treasure.

A beat-up Honda compact pulled up into the dirt driveway and whimpered to a stop. A woman emerged in untied high-top sneakers, a thin, faded coat thrown over her nightgown. She had soft, prematurely graying hair bundled over her worry-lined face. It was the boys' mother. She told them to get the firewood out of the trunk—some pine scraps from a nearby lumberyard.

Greeting a stranger warmly, she said she remembered the ice-cream truck, but it hadn't come by for years. That was the least of her worries. She had recently been laid off from her job at the textile mill, and somebody had burned down the old family home over on Hightop Mountain.

She watched her sons carry the scraps into the house: "Those boys loved that ice cream." She pulled the coat tight around her and apologized for not inviting me inside. "Next time you come by, I'll have heat in the house," she said in her soft singsong voice. Then she forced a smile and shut the door.

For the Love of Mullet

DIANE ROBERTS

Ten thousand pounds of mullet. Five tons of mullet: netted, beheaded, scaled, gutted, battered, fried. It's not all the fish in the Gulf of Mexico, but it sure looks like it, as five laughing, sweating guys work their huge propane-fired fry- ers like pinball wizards with delicate, taut, subtle turns of the wrist, moving the fish in and out of the spitting oil.

In this booth, marked "Boggy Boys Sportsman's Club," a Boggy Boy in a T-shirt that proclaims, "All You Can Do Is All You Can Do"—obviously some kind of West Florida Zen slogan—takes over at the fryer from another Boggy Boy. The first one goes to the back, out of range of the hush puppy batter, to fire up a Marlboro.

That fish needs to pile up fast; there's line of people all the way down to the funnel cake stand and beyond. They've been waiting since the Boggy Bayou Mullet Festival opened its gates, swatting at mosquitoes who ought to be gone by now—it's October—and watching the billion-dollar jets from Eglin Air Force Base arc like comets in the sunset sky. Sure, some of the crowd of fifty thousand have come to the festival to hear Rhett Akins sing "That Ain't My Truck," some have come to see NASCAR demigod Geoff Bodine's genetically enhanced Ford Taurus, and some have come to drink more beer than they can hide from Daddy back home. But most have come to eat mullet.

Along the Gulf, mullet used to be poor people's fish, trash fish, rarely sold to the fancy restaurants and seafood markets in New Orleans, Pensacola, or Mobile. The fish can get up to eighteen inches long, but most will fit comfort- ably on a paper plate. Mullet started at campaign fish fries in the swamp ham- lets of North Florida and Lower Alabama, where a politico could demonstrate that he was the goodest of good ole boys, untainted by the linen-tablecloth- and-fancy-bourbon, fat-cat world in Tallahassee or Montgomery, just by sucking mullet bones in public.

In lean times, mullet was subsistence food (like possum or squirrel). Peo- ple would net them or catch them with a baited hook, maybe "chumming" the water by sprinkling rabbit food or bread crumbs on the surface to seduce them. Between October and Christmas, you'd get the bonus of white or red roe. The red is the mullet caviar, deliciously oleaginous by itself or forked up in scrambled eggs and grits. The white isn't roe at all but mullet sperm. In our house, this unmentionable feature of fresh-caught mullet was discreetly turned over to the cats, but Walk Spence of Niceville, Florida, whose father, Francis, founded the Boggy Bayou Mullet Festival in 1977, says, "I like to eat that white roe. I fry it or smoke it; it's milder than the red roe."

Roe is increasingly hard to get. The Japanese and the Taiwanese have taken to paying big money, maybe fifteen dollars a pound, for red roe. Some claim it enhances sexual performance.

As you might expect, if people are prepared to pay top dollar for fish eggs to help them, as Marvin Gaye would say, get it on, then the fish themselves start getting scarce. "You never," says Florida State University marine biologist Felicia Coleman, "want to be considered an aphrodisiac. It's a disaster for a species."

In 1995 the state of Florida banned the use of nets larger than five hundred square feet. This isn't just a state law now but an actual constitutional amendment, approved by 72 percent of the voters. Why this happened and whether it's a good thing depends on whom you ask. The state's official line is that mullet stocks were depleted, with large-scale abortions performed on mullet mothers in the name of jump-starting Asian love lives, and replacement of the fish slowed. So the state made it much harder to catch mullet. Dr. Coleman allows that "any time you hammer a species during the height of its reproductive season, you are asking for trouble. It severely reduces the replacement capacity of the population."

Advocates of the fisherman say that the real battle wasn't humans versus fish, but commercial fishermen versus "sport" fishermen, poor-but-proud entrepreneurs with shabby boats and proletarian tans versus real estate pirates and corporate lawyers with thirty-two-foot Parkers powered by twin 200-horsepower engines—Old Florida versus New Florida.

The coastal communities from Homosassa Springs to Perdido Key fought against the net ban down to almost every man, woman, and yard dog. Fisherman Lee Spears of Spring Creek, Florida, a tiny village in the wetlands off Ochlockonee Bay, does not understand why the gradual measures the state began to take years before—no fishing on weekends, the increasing of net-mesh size—were not enough. He calls the net ban "too drastic." The Spears family has been fishing for seventy-five years, father and sons. Now they live mostly from crabbing, getting only "a little bit" of mullet.

Walt Spence is careful to point out that the mullet for the Boggy Bayou jubilee comes from the Alabama end of Perdido Bay, where the big net is still legal. He admits there has been overfishing in some spots but thinks that the problem should have been addressed on a case-by-case basis, not with a generic ban. "The sport fishermen helped create a scare," he says. They were mad because mullet fishermen kept catching speckled trout.

Sportfishermen are never trying to catch mullet; they want trout, grouper, red drum snapper—the glamour fish of the Gulf, not the country cousin that many think of as mere bait.

Felicia Coleman says the net ban was sold to the public as an environmental issue—"check this little box on the ballot, and you've done your green thing for the year"—but was always a sportfishing issue. The Florida Conservation Association (now the Coastal Conservation Association), an environmental lobbying group with oceans of dollars, helped mount the petition drive that got the craftily worded measure on the ballot in the first place. They were aided not just by virtuous environmentalists but also by charter boat operators and the tourist industry. Dr. Coleman acknowledges that "there clearly has been a positive effect on marine resources," but adds that the method was "Machiavellian" and that "fishery management is a complex issue that should be based on good science, both biological and socioeconomic, not politics and emotion."

Yet it's hard for Lee Spears to keep the emotion out of his voice when he talks about the huge public relations campaign, largely waged in the magazine *Florida Sportsman*, for the net ban. The fishermen feel the magazine distorted the truth. "They said we tangled up porpoises and such as that catching mullet. If you just looked at their side of the story, we should have been hung instead of banned."

The striped mullet, *Mugilidae cephalus*, which translates literally, but inelegantly, as "suckerhead," has become a cause célèbre. As I sit here in Niceville (the town's original, more descriptive name was Boggy Bayou), picking delicately textured mullet flesh, sweet as a pecan, off its many bones, I am aware that I and all the other people exclaiming over the Boys' speed-frying technique and the subtle flavor of the fish aren't just having dinner, we are committing a political act. We are not precisely defiant (though fishermen have been defying the net ban by casting plastic tarps or other creative material not covered by the amendment), but we do resist what Florida is becoming: rich, Republican, urban, un-Southern. A place where mullet, like grits, is an embarrassment or a joke. Eating mullet is an assertion of the old ways, homage to a time before Disney and developers. Mullet has become the coastal Cracker poster-fish, a badge of proud redneckery.

Mullet has always had a vexed relationship with the apparatus of state in Florida. There's this story, which has taken on the status of myth, about the time mullet was declared a bird. In *Mulletheads*, a wonderful disquisition on mullet and mullet culture, author Michael Swindle puts the date at some time in the 1920s, but up and down the coast I've heard people variously claim that this happened just after the Civil War, in the 1950s, and about ten years ago. It doesn't matter. Seems these three guys were arrested for fishing mullet out of season. In court, their lawyer had a biologist testify that since mullet have gizzards (which is perfectly true, because mullet live mostly on hard-shelled algae and need to grind off the hard layer to get at the oil inside), then mullet are ipso facto chickens. The judge bought it, and the three guys got off.

In the mid-1960s, the state of Florida decided that it was too hard to market mullet as mullet, irrevocably associated as it was with bottom-feeding and the backwoods. So the state renamed the fish "lisa," the Spanish word for mullet, and tried canning it like tuna. One day at my weird little hippie prep school (I think I was in the fourth grade), we were informed that the governor was having lunch with us. With grins like the prison guards in Cool Hand Luke, the lunch ladies served us lisa pizza. It smelled like an old metal garbage can and had a sort of butane aftertaste. The governor ate all of his, but we figured that's why he got the big bucks. It is understating the case to say that canned lisa did not fly.

Mullet in Florida is, as they say in the philosophy department, a multiple signifier. There's the mullet haircut, favored by the fourteen-year-old boys you see hanging around the skating rink on the south side of Tallahassee and, less attractively, by the thirty-five-year-olds in Ron Jon surf shop pastels who offer to buy you a Mai Tai at Fudpucker's in Destin or the Spinnaker II in Panama City. Mark Hinson, a Tallahassee cartoonist and writer who admits to having sported a mullet in the early eighties, describes it as "a shag-style 'do, short on the sides, long rattail in the back, and porcupine on top."

Hinson blames Billy Ray Cyrus, the country crooner culpable for "Achy Breaky Heart"—he popularized the mullet for the head of the South. I believe it: next to me at the picnic table, crunching fried mullet tails and spooning up baked beans, sits a whole mullet-cut family: Mama, Daddy, and Junior—he's cross-cultural, sporting a T-shirt with the "Yo quiero Taco Bell" Chihuahua superimposed on a large Confederate battle flag.

Florida's most important fish celebrity has to be Henry the Pole-Vaulting Mullet at Wakulla Springs. Along with the tree Johnny Weissmuller swung from in the Tarzan movies and the patch of swamp where they filmed *Creature from the Black Lagoon*, Henry is a big attraction. And he's a good little jumper

DIANE ROBERTS

for a fish, though Felicia Coleman points out that all Henry's doing when he back-flips over the stick, dramatically rubbing his scale's on it, is scraping off ectoparasites. Still, the one thing in this world mullet like to do (insofar as they can be said to like to do anything) is jump. Schools of them leap in the Gulf, their little fish bodies going rigid for a second, then belly flopping back into the waves. It may be that this disposition to hop gave some genius the idea for the most famous mullet event of all—the mullet-toss.

The Flora-Bama Lounge bestrides the border between Florida and Alabama like a drunken colossus. It incorporates ten bars, and it claims that the mullet-toss, in which people stand in Florida and hunk a mullet (deceased) as far as they can into Alabama, was invented here circa 1985. Maybe, maybe not: there are people on St. George Island who swear they've been tossing mullet there for twenty years, and one Alligator Point friend of mine says she's tossed mullet at least since Armstrong walked on the moon.

Mullet-tossing probably has no single point of origin. When people get liquored up, they just want to throw something. But why mullet? "They're much lighter than dwarves," says Dr. Coleman.

Walt Spence, on the other hand, is dumbfounded. "Lord, I don't know why," he says. "People who have messed with mullet have always tossed them. They're barbed, too, and can hurt your hands as bad as picking cotton."

For whatever reason, mullet-tossing now happens in bars up and down the Gulf, or informally on the beach, once the Wild Turkey reaches a certain level in the bloodstream. (There are even protests against mullet-tossing—always a sign that a sport has come of age.) The 1996 Interstate Mullet Toss at the Flora-Bama drew Kenny "the Snake" Stabler, the former University of Alabama and Oakland Raiders quarterback, to toss the first fish but also got the attention of Nanci Alexander of the Animal Rights Foundation of Florida (ARFF). She was quoted in an *UP!* story from April 1996: "Mullet tossing? That's pretty gross. Living creatures weren't made to be thrown around. It would be worse if they were still alive, but it's still not right."

I'm driving down Highway 98, the Gulf coast road in Florida, past little Holiness churches, country stores called Register's, and a rent-a-sign in front of a closed motel reading "Red Nek Riv-era." From Panacea to Mexico Beach, 98 always washes out in big storms: in some places it barely hangs on to the edge of high tide. A couple more years and the pale green water will take it back. The coastline will change shape again; the dunes will disappear in one place and reappear in another. Who knows what will become of the old fish houses in places like Carrabelle and Eastpoint? If the traditional fishermen give up, the condos will move in.

In Panacea, I stop at Metcalf Seafood, My Way Seafood, and Crum's to ask if they've caught any mullet today. Only My Way has, and I buy some whole fish to take back to Tallahassee in the ice chest. Mullet are still cheap, maybe two or three bucks a pound, when you can find them.

The war over mullet isn't over. The state of Florida is still trying to refine fishery regulations, while fishermen are still angry. Every month of so a commercial operation gets fined, or a crew arrested, for deploying an illegal gill net or using forbidden mesh. In March, fisherman Van Lewis confronted the governor and his cabinet while they discussed further tinkering with mesh sizes. Van Lewis was draped in netting with a few aromatic dead young mullet secreted about his person to protest what he called "crimes against fish."

I stop for a gin and tonic at the Gibson Inn, a nice sea-breezy place in Apalachicola, built in 1907. Old tourist brochures promise "Botanical Gardens" and an "Ice Machine Museum." Dr. John Gorrie invented the first ice maker in 1845, a piece of technology that would make fresh Florida seafood available to the world. But not mullet, of course: frozen mullet tastes muddy; you have to eat it within a short time of taking it from the sea. The Gibson has oysters, blue crab, and grouper. No mullet today. "We usually have it," says the bar lady, standing in front of the "Smoking Permitted" sign. "But you can't count on it these days."

At Angelo's on Ochlockonee Bay, I eat grouper (they don't have mullet today, either) and watch the sun make zigzag patterns on the water like heavy, dark-blue silk. Pelicans swoop, and I see, out in the bay, a little storm of jumping fish sailing over one another like stunt motorcyclists. It's a school of mullet, jumping to beat even Henry the pole-vaulter. It's somebody's dinner somewhere, but not mine.

Boiled Peanuts

JOHN MARTIN TAYLOR

I never eat boiled peanuts except when they are in season
(July through September), because they are only good when made from freshly
dug "green" peanuts—and the small, redskinned Valencias are the best.

When I wrote my first book about the cooking of the South Carolina coastal plain (*Hoppin' John's Lowcountry Cooking*, 1992), I was trying to present as honest a survey of our traditional foods as I could without sacrificing the integrity of a single dish or ingredient. At the time, I would no more have eaten a boiled, previously peeled jumbo peanut from Virginia or North Carolina than I would have eaten local oysters in July or peaches in February.

I was also trying to be as scholarly as possible, with solid historical documentation of what I was calling traditional. It was not always possible. For example, stories of Thomas Jefferson's single-handed importation of many of the foods that were South Carolina favorites just didn't ring true to me. Surely eggplant had been here in the subtropical low country before it had been in Virginia. Combing through plantation journals, diaries, shipping records, and newspapers hadn't proved my theory, however, until I found several mentions of "guinea squash," still a common name for *Solanum melongena* among old-timers here.

You won't find eggplant called "Guinea squash" in the *Oxford English Dictionary*, the *American Heritage Dictionary of the English Language*, *Hortus Third Cornucopia II*, or *Sturtevant's Edible Plants of the World*. But I found the term—and, hence, the plant—in numerous unpublished colonial papers. Encouraged, I soon thereafter stumbled on Henry Lauren's mention of tomatoes growing in his downtown Charleston garden, twenty years before Jefferson's. But peanuts—particularly boiled—still refuse to give up their roots.

I had always assumed that you could define the South as boiled peanut territory, but, in fact, there are many Southerners who have never even heard of them. For those of us who know and love them, boiled peanuts have probably always been a part of our lives. We do not recall a first tasting, but the thought of boiled peanuts conjures profound memories of places and people that we always associate with them. It has been suggested to me that perhaps boiled peanuts aren't really about taste but about those memories, but I don't think that's true either. I love them whether I'm eating them salty and warm on a brisk autumn day near the shore, or cold, right out of the refrigerator, as a left-over snack.

I've often said that the South is more emotion than nation—that describing the boundaries of the region is all but impossible. I've been asked to join "Southern" organizations that include only the states of the Confederacy, but I know lots of folks from Kentucky, Arkansas, and Oklahoma who consider themselves Southern. Few may think of northern Virginia as truly Southern, though most West Virginians would be insulted if I called them anything else. Some writers have tried to define the South as where you are automatically served grits with breakfast, but there are pockets throughout the region where corn has never been ground for use as a hot breakfast cereal. So grits aren't any more typical than boiled peanuts. But both of those Southern foods do evoke profound memories.

I think of the late fifties, before interstate highways and air-conditioning brought the hordes of people "from off" to the South Carolina low country where I was reared. When I was in the sixth grade, I would go waterskiing with the Salleys. Their daughters, Walton, Ding, and Sam (E.D., their father, must have really wanted boys!), taught me how to ski. They had a black cook who would boil up big batches of peanuts and put them in plastic Sunbeam bread loaf wrappers. We'd take them to Lake Murray, and E.D. would pick out a de-serted island in the middle of the lake to use as a base for our daylong adven-ture. We'd toss the bags of peanuts overboard to float on the water and then take turns skiing until our arms and knees hurt. I remember trying to time our stops so that we'd land by one of the floating bags of peanuts. We'd just drop the rope and slowly sink down into the muddy water. The Salley girls could lean over and pick up a bag from their slaloms. I could barely get within ten feet of them. But no one loved the boiled peanuts more than I, and I always re-call those floating bags of the warm, salty snacks whenever I eat them today.

Memories like those may simply come as a response to the inevitable ques-tions about boiled peanuts that arise these days at the outdoor events where peanuts are served. Invariably there is now someone who has moved here from off and who wants to know more about them.

Salley is an old Orangeburg County name. Settled by Germans and Swiss in 1730, the county is still largely populated by descendants of its original settlers, though by the time we moved there, it was 70 percent black. (Salley, South Carolina, home of the annual Chitlin' Strut Festival is in nearby Aiken County.) We weren't Old Orangeburg; we weren't even South Carolinians. We had moved there when I was three from the bayous of Louisiana, where my father worked in the chemical industry. He and Mother were both from Tennessee; she, from the western part of the state—McNairy County, later of *Walking Tall* fame; and he from the hills around Knoxville.

Recently, I asked Dad (who is a great cook and who, in the fifties, was a member of les Amis du Vin and had a wine cellar in Orangeburg) when he first remembered tasting boiled peanuts.

"Never heard of them till a trip to South Carolina in 1950. *Everybody* in Orangeburg ate them! In the Cajun country, *everybody* ate sausages—*rouge et blanc*—and tried to outdo each other with the intensity of the pepper."

My father has a summer house in the mountains of North Carolina now, so he's back near his childhood home. But he says he never saw boiled peanuts in the mountains when he first started going back up there about nine or ten years ago.

"Now," he says, "all the roadside stands have them!"

"We grew peanuts for our own consumption when I was a lad. Granny would soak them in brine, dry them, and then roast them in the oven. Salted in the shell. Of course, those were not green peanuts."

Green peanuts. That's the real key to understanding boiled peanuts. They've got to be freshly dug. I used to not eat boiled peanuts except in late summer, though these days I'm not as picky. There are so many good hybrids being grown now that taste pretty good (though I have never had a Virginia peanut—a variety known as "jumbo" in South Carolina—that tasted as good as the small ones) and that are available fresh ("green") from spring through fall. Of course, we never get green Virginias down here; they're always dried. The difference between fresh and dried is the same for all legumes, and a legume is, after all, what a peanut is.

Kathi Purvis, food editor of the *Charlotte Observer*, says she comes from a family, Georgians all, who are "boiled peanut fanatics."

"When I was a small child in eastern North Carolina, people treated my family like we were odd because we boiled our peanuts," she recently confided. "Parched and roasted peanuts are much more common in North Carolina and Virginia. I've long maintained (and had to, having spent much of my life in a non–boiled peanut state) that boiling peanuts makes much more sense than roasting them. They are, after all, a legume, and we would certainly never consider not boiling a kidney bean or a Great Northern."

The current trendiness of sushi bars throughout the country might help popularize boiled peanuts. Soybeans boiled in the shell—*edamame*—are becoming a very popular appetizer. I have a Japanese friend who visited Charleston, where I live, one summer, and when I offered her boiled peanuts, she took to them immediately, saying, "These taste very much like edamame. We eat them with beer at baseball games." Which is exactly when a lot of southerners eat them.

John T. Edge, director of the Southern Foodways Alliance at the Center for the Study of Southern Culture at the University of Mississippi, admits that they are, "bar none," his favorite snack. He admits to having "fond memories" of going to the South Carolina State Farmer's Market in Columbia and buying them there. It always seemed that was the epicenter of boiled peanut culture for my family.

Columbia is about forty miles from Orangeburg. It's real peanut country. But when I went to college in Georgia, half the people I met, it seemed, came from South Georgia, where there are fifteen thousand peanut farmers. But not all Southerners, much less Georgians, are fond of boiled peanuts. Some well-known authorities on Southern cooking are loath to enjoy them.

The *Atlanta Journal-Constitution*'s Jim Auchmutey, a native of the big city, hates them. "I have tried to like them. Every year, when we're driving up to the mountains to see some leaves, my wife Pam, a Savannah native, makes me stop beside a boiling cauldron to buy a bag. She eats a bunch of them—suck, swallow, spit—and then I try one to see if my taste buds have changed in the past year, the way I suddenly liked cheese when I became a senior in high school. Boiled peanuts haven't happened for me yet. They always taste like those salt pills the coaches told you to take in track to keep from throwing up."

I prefer boiled peanuts that aren't all the same size, so that some of the smaller ones are cooked so soft that you can eat the shell as well as the peanuts. I asked Lucille Grant, one of Charleston's great cooks and the granddaughter of a slave, if she had always eaten boiled peanuts.

"Oh, yes," she mused. "Boiled peanuts were one of my granddaddy's things. He really prided himself on his peanuts, and he would only grow those little Spanish ones. He'd come from the fields with some dug-up bushes and he'd boil them up and they were always so good! But you can hardly find those little peanuts any more, and they really do taste the best."

Peanuts are grown in nine states, but only about 1 percent of them are those little Valencias—and most of those are grown in New Mexico, far from boiled peanut territory. Nearly half of the peanuts grown in this country go into peanut butter.

Growing up in Orangeburg, I heard peanuts called "ground-nuts," "goobers," "goober-peas," and "pindars," but the dictionaries and usual sources haven't helped much with those words, either. Sir Hans Sloan published a natural history of Jamaica in 1707 in which he described the "pindal," or Indian Earth-nut, but the first citation the *Oxford English Dictionary* lists for "goober" is 1887. We know that the words "goober" and "pindal," like "okra," "gumbo," and "yam," are of West African origin. Though peanuts are native to the New World, they came to be known in America through slaves from West Africa. Food writers mostly avoid any mention of boiled peanuts, but Jessica Harris, the eminent scholar of the African diaspora, has found boiled peanuts in Ghana, whence the recipe probably arrived in South Carolina, and in Brazil. In Ghana, the peanuts were simply boiled and eaten as a snack or with boiled ears of corn on the cob; in Brazil they were served as part of a Candomble spiritual ceremony.

There are a lot of websites about peanuts on the internet, but I'm still at a loss to find much recorded history about boiled ones. Peanuts are still grown primarily in coastal southern states—Virginia, North Carolina, South Carolina, Georgia, Florida, Alabama, and Texas—as well as in Oklahoma and New Mexico. They require a long growing season and are very sensitive to frost. It's no wonder the recipe for boiled green peanuts didn't travel inland—the green peanuts didn't either. I've found no mention of boiled peanuts in the many eighteenth- and nineteenth-century sources I've relied on for years in my research on the foods of the South, but I'm not surprised. There are also very few written recipes for some of the most basic dishes of the coastal South—especially those for fish and vegetables. I do think it's telling that peanuts continue to be grown mostly in the coastal areas where West Africans were the majority prior to the Civil War. Nevertheless, culinary experts from New Orleans admit to knowing nothing about them. It's just not a Mississippi Delta thing.

It's apparently not a Virginia thing, either. Robert Waldrop is a Virginia writer whom I've known since our college days in Athens, Georgia. "First off," he told me, "Virginians abhor the thought of boiled peanuts. My mom, from Richmond, never heard of them till my family all started sharing an old beach cottage on Fernandina Beach, Florida, in the 1950s. I asked Shelby and Polly, neighbors of mine, if they had boiled peanuts growing up. All one of them said was a very direct, 'Lord, no, I'm from Richmond!'

"We got the old beach cottage each summer with my Uncle Hardy, Aunt Babs, and my cousins who lived in Blackshear, Georgia. I remember the peanuts getting boiled being a big occasion all by itself with the same mystique as crabs and shrimp.

"My mom says when she first saw Hardy eating them, he was on the veranda in a rocking chair all by himself. She asked him what they were. He said, 'Sex food.'"

"My mom said she asked to taste one, and Hardy said, 'No!'"

"And he ate them right in front of her!"

Perfectly boiled southern-style peanuts are always salty, but not overly so. They should perfectly accompany a beer, iced tea, or soft drink, though lately I've seen people eating them with white wine. It's best to eat them outside where it doesn't matter if wet shells are tossed on the ground. I think most boiled peanuts are probably purchased from roadside stands and eaten in the car while they're still hot, the shells tossed out the window. Those stands may now be appearing in places where they never were before as Southerners move to other parts of the country, but the popularity of boiled peanuts still seems very localized.

Fran McCullough, who edited my first two books on Southern cooking, tells me that "there's a funny little urban gardenish place up in Harlem that often has a very excited sign saying something like, 'We Got 'Em! Boiled Peanuts!' and I always think of you because I know you'd scream 'STOP!' and run right in."

I know exactly where she's talking about. It's the same place I'd go for my collards and "butt's meat" (smoked hog jowl) when I used to live in Manhattan. Some folks from South Carolina drive trucks up to New York once a week during the late summer and fall, full of old-time Southern specialties that just aren't available elsewhere, like just-picked okra without a hint of black on it, and thin porto rico sweet potatoes, no more than two inches in diameter and pointed at both ends. They get green peanuts, the little Valencias, before they dry up and lose that fresh beany flavor. They boil them in salted water for a couple of hours, then let them soak in the water until they've reached the right degree of saltiness, just like back home. They usually sell out, right from the kettle, before they cool off.

I was at a dinner party recently with some friends from Alabama. He's from Mobile—Ole Mobile—and she's from Opelika, near the Georgia border. He never ate boiled peanuts when he was growing up and wasn't introduced to them in college, either (he went to Washington and Lee, in Virginia). She knew them well, from summers spent in the Florida Panhandle—about as deep in the South as you can get. They are both fond of them now and try to offer them amidst the pistachios and almonds they serve in their home in the Hollywood Hills (if for no other reason than to assert their *Southernness*).

A new Southerner standing near us at the bar overheard our conversation and screwed up her face in disgust.

"I just don't see how you can eat those things," she said. "I can't stand the texture."

She proceeded to eat olives and a black bean dip with gusto, and I just smiled and said, "Fine, that means more for us."

I knew that if she had liked them, she would have used the plural, "y'all."

The Fruits of Memory

AMY E. WELDON

Each fall I receive an exact intimation of how far away I have become. Such signs are not always dramatic, the Old Testament notwithstanding. When God, or memory, or the past, or any stern force wants to get your attention, the ways are legion. Ravens shriek over Ezekiel's cowering head, branches burn and are not consumed, a child turns in a ninety-year-old womb. There's a secular version too: a taste of a coming season in the wind can sweep your whole life past you, rich in portent. Elizabeth Spencer, in *The Voice at the Back Door*, describes this as "the dusty stir of autumn in the twilight, with the indescribable quality beneath the eagerness and color that tried to speak and could not." Such thoughts are designed to haunt, in one way or another.

But there are different kinds of haunting. And different kinds of ghosts, which live in different places. The most powerful ghost that reaches for me in early fall, here in Chapel Hill, lives in a grocery store, in neat ranks of plastic snap-top boxes with stickers bearing the name of an orchard in Wadesboro, North Carolina. The phone number is included on the sticker, in a shade of green that almost matches the contents. Antiseptically, rebelliously, inside the box nestle thick-skinned globes of golden-green, sprinkled with microscopic brown freckles and sometimes wide, harmless liver spots, like those on the hands of a beloved elder. Scuppernongs.

The folksy humor that such a name encourages, popularized in tiresome public-radio commentaries about Mama-n-them, should be fiercely resisted. This name is a rich briar patch of syllables, strange with the forbidding strangeness of ancestor stories that terrify when viewed with humility. Trivializing the name because of its link to the memories of individual and collective rural pasts means trivializing the namers. It means trivializing Southern rural life, and it means scoffing at the darkness from which the stories reach for you, opening their scarred palms. The words of those stories taste as dark and rich as any fruit. Your great-great-uncle stuck a knife in a man's back when he cut in front of him in line at the cotton gin. Your great-aunt, the youngest child of a family that included six older brothers and a mother who beat them all with a mule bridle, struck out in the middle of the night to elope with a traveling salesman. Your grandfather, her second- or third-oldest brother, was still cursing the spot, forty years later, where the salesman's car outdistanced the Hupmobile bristling with father, brothers, and shotguns. You imagine that girl's frightened anger and shudder, but you lean into the touch of the stories on your shoulder, amazed at how gentle those long, rough hands can feel.

And there is no way now to explain or relive to yourself that gentleness — the paradoxical draw of the way of life that can produce such violence — except to lift that clamshell box from the grocery store shelf and take it home, and once home to eat them, one at a time, remembering how far away the time was when you ate them where they, and you, belonged. Twenty minutes into the country from the Alabama town where he maintained the controlled chaos of a small-town doctor's life, near the tiny, lyrically named settlement of Oak Bowery, your grandfather kept a farm — a farm your family has sworn will be the last of its holdings to go in times of depression. Here he maintained a herd of Angus and Hereford cattle, and a lake of catfish, and an orchard of plum and peach trees in which you were forbidden to climb but did anyway, and a rustling, purple-smelling fig tree, and a well of pure water that tasted like the tin dipper on its nail above the wooden well lid, and a scuppernong arbor.

High summer was the time of peaches and plums, yellow jackets glutted into harmlessness, and your grandmother in pedal pushers and not-yet-white hair posing happily above bushel baskets and scarred plastic buckets brimming with rosy fruit. You were happy that your mother was recording all this bounty with her camera. It was the time to run in the long grass of the orchard without fear, knowing snakes would flee before the commotion of picking, and to plant a small sneaker-shod foot on the tempting low branches and climb. Propped in the gnarled branches, you could eat plum after plum, trying to pinpoint the exact moment at which your teeth — innocent of braces or cavities or the adult yellowing of coffee and cigarettes — cracked the taut, burgundy skin and flooded your mouth with the savage, red essence of joy. Vaguely thrilling, vaguely frightening. Did the two go together? Does something always have to break?

The scuppernong time was wiser. It was September, the time of your own birthday and your sister's (which you hated because it drew attention from yours), the time of resigned re-bondage to school, the time that would drive you mad even then trying to name the wistful, mica-hard cast to the golden light in the sky. Something was different, although it all looked the same. The orchard was still hot, still rustling and green, still haunted by the terror of snake bodies writhing to life under your feet. It was all about to end. To ignore that, you walked under the low, rough timbers of the scuppernong arbor (the same kind of hand-broken cedar posts from which your father and his brothers made the wire gaps on this farm twenty years before) and reached into the galaxy of palm-sized, five-starred leaves over your head and ate scuppernongs. You ate and ate of that fruit of the knowledge of what exactly was behind the wise, melancholy light over the pastures and the catfish lake and the red clapboard sharecropper's cabin next to the orchard. Eventually you learned that the quiet man who had always worked in your grandmother's yard and was the only black mourner at your grandfather's funeral had been born in that cabin, where his family had lived since no one could remember. "They were there when we bought the place," you were told. "We inherited them." Always after that, you imagined the histories of these other children laid like a quilt over the same ground that held your own history: the quiet man and his brothers and sisters running barefoot as you did in the sun-hot dirt of the garden around the squash and collard plants; fearing what he has always called "no-shoulders" underfoot in the grass, just as you did; drinking from the same burnished tin dipper at the well. You learned what "inherit" meant, and it seemed much too small a word for people.

There is a care and a delicacy to the eating of scuppernongs that sounds sloppy when described. But then any good ritual does sound, at first, alarming. *My body and my blood, take and eat.* Choose a scuppernong for the right balance of gold and green, weighted toward gold, in the skin. Holding the scuppernong firmly between your thumb and forefinger, set it carefully between your teeth, stem end first, so that when you bite it, it bursts into your mouth. (If the other end has become overripe, it will burst in the wrong direction, and then you'll have scuppernong all over your shirt.) In one motion, you can scrape the seeds out against your teeth with your tongue and be Emily Dickinson's happy little tippler, leaning against your own innocent, perfect sun. Then, if you are so inclined, you can slip the thick, cracked rind over the tip of your tongue—thick and velvety on the inside, it fits your tongue like a red clown nose fits—and make faces at your sister, who is doing the same to you. And you can lie back in the grass beside a growing, boozy-smelling pile of seeds and husked scuppernong shells, shoo away yellow jackets, look at the sky, and feel at least a little closer to the mystery, pleasantly hypnotized into a sort of understanding. Ritual is hypnotic. That's why it lasts.

I tried to write a poem about all of this seven years ago, before I had learned I was not a poet, and although the poem was unsuccessful, the occasion of it was not. It helped to crystallize my awareness of a ritual as enduring as that of eating the fruit of the vine in the rueful light of fall—organizing in words the yearning blend of sensation, story, and memory that this place and others like it stir up in me. I began to learn that the shape a story assumes in your mind and the way it is transmuted into words can become parts of your life that you are unwilling to trade for anything. The touch of that lean, scarred hand on your shoulder, whenever it comes, should be heeded, as the seller of donkey colts in Jerusalem knew to heed the disciples' plea. When the call comes, you offer yourself to carry, or to be carried, without knowing where you will be going, whether you will be abandoned, or whether there is anything in the rush of that first flood of taste in the bitten grape beyond the taste itself. The sadness of scuppernongs in their antiseptic box in a grocery store in North Carolina, the sadness of eating them from that box at your desk in a world that seems antiseptic compared to the orchard twenty years before, the sadness of knowing that the era that produced the family stories you try to recreate is now beyond you—all of these come from the same place, as the richness of the scuppernong taste and the richness of the stories in your ears and the gentleness of that touch on your shoulder come from the same place. This is a place to struggle for, to keep alive in a strange land, as you have to do now. As we all have to do.

Missing Links
In Praise of the Cajun Foodstuff
That Doesn't Get Around

CALVIN TRILLIN

Of all the things I've eaten in the Cajun parishes of Louisiana—an array of foodstuffs which has been characterized as somewhere between extensive and deplorable—I yearn most often for boudin. When people in Breaux Bridge or Opelousas or Jeanerette talk about boudin (pronounced "boo-DAN"), they mean a soft, spicy mixture of rice and pork and liver and seasoning which is squeezed hot into the mouth from a sausage casing, usually in the parking lot of a grocery store and preferably while leaning against a pickup.

("Boudin" means blood sausage to the French, most of whom would probably line up for immigration visas if they ever tasted the Cajun version.) I figure that about 80 percent of the boudin purchased in Louisiana is consumed before the purchaser has left the parking lot, and most of the rest of it is polished off in the car. In other words, Cajun boudin not only doesn't get outside the state; it usually doesn't even get home. For Americans who haven't been to South Louisiana, boudin remains as foreign as *gado-gado* or *cheb*; for them, the word "Cajun" on a menu is simply a synonym for burnt fish or too much pepper. When I am daydreaming of boudin, it sometimes occurs to me that of all the indignities the Acadians of Louisiana have had visited upon them— being booted out of Nova Scotia, being ridiculed as rubes and swamp rats by neighboring Anglophones for a couple of centuries, being punished for speaking their own language in the schoolyard—nothing has been as deeply insulting as what restaurants outside South Louisiana present as Cajun food.

The scarcity of boudin in the rest of the country makes it all the more pleasurable to have a Louisiana friend who likes to travel and occasionally carries along an ice chest full of local ingredients, just in case. I happen to have such a friend in James Edmunds, of New Iberia, Louisiana. Over the past twenty years or so, James's visits to New York have regularly included the ritualistic unpacking of an ice chest on my kitchen table. His custom has been to bring the ice chest if he plans to cook a meal during the visit—crawfish étouffée, for instance, or gumbo, or his signature shrimp stew. On those trips, the ice chest would also hold some boudin. I was so eager to get my hands on the boudin that I often ate it right in the kitchen, as soon as we heated it through, rather than trying to make the experience more authentic by searching for something appropriate to lean against. In lower Manhattan, after all, it could take a while to find a pickup truck.

Then there came the day when I was sentenced to what I think of as medium-security cholesterol prison. (Once the cholesterol penal system was concessioned out to the manufacturers of statin drugs, medium-security cholesterol prison came to mean that the inmate could eat the occasional bit of bacon from the plate of a generous luncheon companion but could not order his own BLT) James stopped bringing boudin, the warders having summarily dismissed my argument that the kind I particularly like—Cajun boudin varies greatly from maker to maker—was mostly just rice anyway.

I did not despair. James is inventive, and he's flexible. Several years ago, he decided that an architect friend of his who lives just outside New Iberia made the best crawfish étouffée in the area, and, like one of those research-and-development hot shots who are always interested in ways of improving the product, he took the trouble to look into the recipe, which had been handed down to the architect by forebears of unadulterated Cajunness. James was prepared for the possibility that one of the secret ingredients of the architect's blissful étouffée was, say, some herb available only at certain times of year in the swamps of the Atchafalaya Basin Spillway. As it turned out, one of the secret ingredients was Campbell's cream of mushroom soup. (Although crawfish étouffée, which means smothered crawfish, is one the best-known Cajun dishes, it emerged only in the fifties, when a lot of people assumed that just about any recipe was enhanced by a can of Campbell's cream of mushroom soup.) During ensuing étouffée preparations in New York, there would come a moment when James said, in his soft South Louisiana accent, "I think this might be a good time for certain sensitive people to leave the kitchen for just a little while." Then we'd hear the whine of the can opener, followed by an unmistakable *glub-glub-glub*.

A few years after my sentence was imposed, James and I were talking on the telephone about an imminent New York visit that was to include the preparation of one of his dinner specialties, and he told me not to worry about the problem of items rattling around in his ice chest. I told him that I actually hadn't given that problem much thought, what with global warming and nuclear proliferation and all. As if he hadn't heard me, he went on to say that he'd stopped the rattling with what he called packing-boudin.

"Packing-boudin?

"That's right," James said.

I thought about that for a moment or two. "Well, it's got bubble wrap beat," I finally said. "And we wouldn't have to worry about adding to this country's solid-waste-disposal problem. Except for the casing." The habit of tossing aside the casing of a spent link of boudin is so ingrained in some parts of Louisiana that there is a bumper sticker reading, "Caution: Driver Eating Boudin" — a way of warning the cars that follow about the possibility of their windshields being splattered with what appear to be odd-looking insects. From that visit on, I took charge of packing-boudin disposal whenever James was carrying his ice chest, and I tried not to dwell on my disappointment when he wasn't.

Not long ago, I got a call from James before a business trip to New York which was not scheduled to include the preparation of a Louisiana meal — that is, a trip that would ordinarily not include boudin. He asked if he could store a turducken in my freezer for a couple of days; he was making a delivery for a friend. I hesitated. I was trying to remember precisely what a turducken is, other than something Cajuns make that seems to go against the laws of nature.

James, perhaps thinking that my hesitancy reflected some reluctance to take on the storage job, said, "There'd be rental-boudin involved, of course."

"Fair's fair," I said.

What led to my being in Louisiana a couple of weeks later for something that James insisted on calling a boudin blitzkrieg is rather complicated. As a matter of convenience, James had picked up the rental-boudin at the same place he'd bought the turducken, Hebert's Specialty Meats, in Maurice, Louisiana. Hebert's is a leading purveyor to turducken, which it makes by taking the bones out of a chicken and a duck and a turkey, stuffing the stuffed chicken into a similarly stuffed duck, and stuffing all that, along with a third kind of stuffing, into the turkey. The result cannot be criticized for lacking complexity, and it presents a challenge to the holiday carver almost precisely as daunting as meat loaf.

The emergence of turducken, eight or ten years ago, did not surprise Cajuns. When it comes to eating, they take improvisation for granted. Some people in New Iberia, for instance, collect the sludge left over from mashing peppers at the McIlhenny Tabasco plant and use it to spice up the huge pots of water they employ to boil crawfish. When Thanksgiving approaches, they fill the same huge pots with five or six gallons of lard instead of water and produce deep-fried turkey—a dish that is related to the traditional roast turkey in the way that *soupe au pistou* in Provence or *ribollita* in Tuscany is related to the vegetable soup that was served in your high school cafeteria. James's wife, Susan Hester, who works at the Iberia Parish Library, once heard a deputy sheriff who was lecturing on personal defense recommend buying water-based rather than oil-based pepper spray not only because it comes off the clothing easier but because it is preferable for flavoring the meat being grilled at a cookout.

Although I didn't want to appear ungrateful for the rental-boudin, I reminded James that his buying boudin in Maurice, which is more than twenty miles from New Iberia, flies in the face of the rule promulgated by his old friend Barry Jean Ancelet, a folklorist and French professor at the University of Louisiana at Lafayette: in the Cajun country of Louisiana, the best boudin is always the boudin closest to where you live, and the best place to eat boiled crawfish is always extraordinarily inconvenient to your house. James is aware that this theory has a problem with internal consistency—it means, for instance, that for him the best boudin is at Bonin's meat market, in New Iberia, and for Barry Jean Ancelet it's at The Best Stop Supermarket, in Scott—but he reconciles that by saying that Barry, being a folklorist, has a different notion of objective truth than some other people.

We had never talked much about the source of the boudin James brought to New York, except that I knew it had changed once, some years ago, when a purveyor named Dud Breaux retired. Once his purchase of boudin in Maurice raised the subject, though, James assured me that under ordinary circumstances he follows the Ancelet Dictum: before leaving for New York, he stocks up at Bonin's, assuming that the proprietor happens to be in what James called "a Period of non-retirement." The proprietor's name is Waldo Bonin, but he is known in New Iberia as Nook. He is a magisterial man with white hair and a white mustache and a white T-shirt and a white apron. Nook Bonin has not retired as many times as Frank Sinatra did, but he is about even with Michael Jordan.

Like one of those boxers who bid farewell to the ring with some regularity, Bonin comes back every time with a little less in his repertoire. For nearly fifty years, he and his wife, Delores, ran a full-service meat market that also included a lot of Cajun specialties. The first time they came out of retirement, they had dropped everything but boudin and cracklins (crunchy pieces of fatback that are produced by rendering lard from a hog) and hogshead cheese, plus soft drinks for those who weren't going to make it back to their cars with their purchases intact. The second time, when the Bonins started appearing only on Friday afternoons and Saturday mornings, they had dropped the cracklins. As a matter of policy, James doesn't actually eat cracklins—"I just think it's good to know that there's a line out there you're not going to cross," he has said—but, as someone who depends on Nook Bonin's boudin, he had to be disturbed by what appeared to be a trend. "I wouldn't mind losing the Cokes," he has said, when envisioning what might be dropped in the Bonins' next comeback. "But it is getting kind of scary."

The recipe for the boudin sold at Bonin's is a secret. In fact, it has occurred to James that the proprietor himself may not know the secret: people customarily speak of Nook Bonin's boudin, but it is actually made by Delores Bonin, who goes heavy on the rice and uses an array of spices that, I would be prepared to testify under oath, owe nothing to the test kitchens of the Campbell's Soup Company. Although the Bonins have two daughters, neither of them chose to go into the family business. Anna is an administrator in a special-education program, and Melissa is an artist. James and Susan happen to be longtime admirers of Melissa's work—some years ago, they bought the first painting she ever sold—but James can't help thinking that if she had chosen to put her creative energies into boudin-making rather than art, the community would not now be beset by the tension brought on by her parents' stair-step retirements. At this point, James and Susan have pinned their hopes on the Bonins' only grandchild—Melissa's son, Emile, unfortunately, Emile is only ten years old. James was cheered, though, when we walked into the Bonins' store on a Saturday morning and Delores Bonin reached over the meat case to hand us a photograph of Emile posing behind the device that stuffs boudin into sausage casing. Emile was smiling.

Even assuming that Emile decides to cast his lot with boudin, though, it will be a number of years before he's old enough to take over the business. James and I discussed that situation in the sort of conversation I can imagine a working team from State and Defense having about whether sufficient steps have been taken to guarantee that this country maintains a secure and unbroken supply of cobalt in the face of any contingency. We decided that, just in case the Bonin family line of succession does get broken, I should sample some of the possibilities for what I suppose you'd have to call replacement-boudin. This is why Susan, who was carrying a cutting board and a kitchen knife, and James and I were driving around on a sunny weekend, tasting what Nook Bonin had to offer and testing out, in a judicious way, the work of other purveyors. At least, that's what I would tell the penal authorities if the question ever came up.

By Sunday night, we had tried the boudin from, among other places, Legnon's Boucherie, in New Iberia, and Bruce's U-Need-A-Butcher, in Lafayette, and Poche's Meat Market and Restaurant, in Poche Bridge, and Heleaux's Grocery, also in Lafayette, and, of course, The Best Stop, in Scott. We hadn't by any measure exhausted the supply of even highly recommended boudin purveyors. For instance, we hadn't tried Johnson's Grocery, in Eunice, or Billeaud's, in Broussard, a town near Lafayette that used to have an annual boudin festival. A friend of mine in New Orleans, Randy Fertel, after tracking down the source of the boudin that he looks forward to eating every year at the New Orleans Jazz Fest, had recommended Abe's Cajun Market, in Lake Charles, which is practically in Texas, but there hadn't been time. Still, I had tasted enough contenders for replacement-boudin to tell James that I hoped Nook and Delores Bonin truly understood that for people who have been active all their lives retirement can be a trap.

I had to admit to Barry Jean Ancelet, who joined us at The Best Stop, that his local purveyor makes a distinguished link of boudin—moderate, shading toward meaty, when it comes to the all-important rice/meat ratio. Lawrence Menard, who opened The Best Stop in 1986, told us that he now sells between sixty-five hundred and seven thousand pounds of boudin a week. In a conversation that began, appropriately, at The Best Stop and continued later that evening in a restaurant called Bubba Frey's, Barry explained the Ancelet Dictum to us in more detail. A link of boudin, he said, is a clean food, essentially treated by Cajuns as "an enclosed lunch"; it's even cleaner if you eat the casing, which Lawrence Menard himself always does. Boiled crawfish, on the other hand, is notoriously messy, leaving a table piled with shells and crawfish heads. It stands to reason that you'd want to leave that kind of mess far from the lair. He pointed out that for boiled crawfish he and James both favor a place called Hawk's, whose location is inconvenient to both of them and to practically everybody else. In a book called *Cajun Country Guide*, Macon Fry and Julie Posner wrote that the reason Hawk's is so good is that Hawk Arceneaux puts his crawfish through a twenty-four-hour freshwater purging process, but, then again, they're not folklorists.

Since the "e" in Frey is silent, Bubba Frey's sounds at first like a succinct description of Southern cooking rather than a restaurant. It is a restaurant, though—a bright, knotty-pine place with a Cajun combo that, on the night we were there, included Bubba Frey himself as one of its fiddlers. We went there after a performance of "Rendezvous des Cadiens," a Cajun radio show that Barry emcees every Saturday at the Liberty Theatre in Eunice—a town in an area known as the Cajun Prairies. For some time, Bubba Frey has run a general store in a nearby hamlet called Mowata—a name I don't intend to investigate, just in case it is unconnected with a flood or the discovery of a particularly capacious well—and not long ago he decided to add a restaurant next door. Boudin balls were listed as an appetizer. Boudin isn't commonly served by restaurants, although Café des Amis, in Breaux Bridge, offers something called *Oreille de cochon*—beignet dough that is baked in the shape of pigs' ears, covered with powdered sugar, and, for an extra dollar, stuffed with boudin. It's a dollar well spent.

Boudin balls are made by rolling boudin into balls, coating them with something like Zatarain's Fish Fry, and frying away. At Bubba Frey's, they were delicious, and the proprietor, who came over to our table between sets, told us that the boudin was made at his store next door. I told James that the next time he happened to be on the Cajun Prairies he might consider finding out what Bubba's boudin tasted like unfried. Then it occurred to me that if James liked it better than he liked Nook Bonin's boudin he might feel obligated to move to Mowata. James did not seem enthusiastic about that prospect. He and Susan have both lived in New Iberia virtually all their lives, and have a lot of friends there. Also, James subscribes to the theory that, perhaps because the French settlement of the Cajun Prairies included a strong admixture of Germans, people there are a bit stiffer than the people who live in the Cajun bayous. I don't know how stiffness in Cajuns would manifest itself. Maybe they use only two kinds of stuffing in their turduckens.

A couple of weeks later, I heard from James: the boudin at Bubba Frey's store was, as we suspected, excellent—"a commendable second place to Nook," James wrote, "but still not with the transcendent special taste." Moving to Mowata was not on the table. Also, he and Susan and the Bonin's daughter Melissa had gone to dinner together and, as it happened, had fallen into a little chat about the future. "I told her that if Emile learned the recipe and learned how to make boudin he'd never starve," James said. "And neither, it goes without saying, would we."

Women Who Eat Dirt

SUSAN ALLPORT

Not too long ago, I received a package from a village in Nepal, high in the foothills of the Himalayas. It was from the brother of the shipping clerk in my husband's office, and it contained, as clearly written on the outside, two kinds of mud: red and white. These are the muds that the inhabitants of that faraway village use to plaster their houses, red for the bottom and white for the top. They are also the muds that the women of that village are known to snack on, especially during pregnancy. Victor Ghale, my husband's shipping clerk, knew I was interested in people who include dirt or clay in their diet, and so he asked his brother to send samples of these muds to me in New York.

The package arrived, fortunately, before fears of anthrax had made us all suspicious of envelopes containing powdery substances. So I had no reservations about opening it and decided to give these two chunks of hardened clay a try. The first was the white one, which was gritty and gummy-tasting as it dissolved, very slowly, in my mouth. It was hard to swallow and seemed to give me an almost instantaneous allergic reaction, since I itched all over for about an hour. The red mud, which I waited a day to try, was also gritty and gummy-tasting. But in some ways, it was like a good wine. While it dissolved, I sensed on the back of my palate the smell of fresh earth just after a rain.

As I savored the smell, I remembered the words that Victor had used when he told me about this gastronomic habit from Nepal. "The clays smell so good when it rains," he had said almost enviously.

"How handy to be able to snack on your own house," I had joked. "Every woman has her own twenty-four–hour convenience store.

"Nobody gives it much thought," he said with a shrug. "It's just something women do."

But the first thing that everyone should know about these women who eat dirt—and about this widespread habit of snacking on special clays or muds that has been reported among women in almost every part of the world—is that it's not just women who eat dirt. Dirt- or clay-eating is more usual among women, especially pregnant women, in many parts of the world—in Nepal, Africa, India, Central America, and the American South. But in other parts of the world, and at other times in history, entire populations have been known to consume dirt. In northern California and in Sardinia, where acorns used to be the dietary staple, the traditional bread was made by mixing acorn flour with clay and water, then baking the mixture in a slow oven. In Germany in the last century, some of the poorer workers and their families used very fine clays to "butter" their bread. In China, as in other parts of the world, clay was eaten by much of the population during times of severe want. Some clays, such as mectite, have a tendency to swell when they take up water, and these clays are present in famine food samples from China.

The list goes on and on and should make those with a peculiarly "female" explanation of dirt-eating ("geophagy," as it is known in scientific circles) question their assumptions. Geophagy has often been attributed to mood swings, hormonal rushes, magical and superstitious beliefs, and/or beliefs in the fertility of the earth—causes more closely associated with the distaff population. But any cogent explanation of this behavior, any explanation that pretends to make real and lasting sense, must also account for these examples of universal consumption.

The second thing that everyone should know is that it's not just humans—men, women, and children—who eat dirt. Dirt-eating is also widespread among animals. It's been reported in many species of birds; many species of herbivores (antelopes, elk, bison, elephants, and the like); and many species of omnivores (porcupines, bears, rats, gorillas, and chimpanzees). No strict carnivores have ever been reported eating dirt (for reasons I will come to), but carnivores do hang around the dirt sites used by other animals because of the hunting opportunities they present.

Many of us are familiar with dirt-eating in the animal kingdom, at least with such descriptive place-names as Licking Hollow, Elk Lick, and Three Bed Lick, which portray the activity of animals at specific dirt sites. So many of us don't find anything surprising about this behavior in other animals. But dirt-eating in animals can shed a lot of light on dirt-eating in humans. And it can help us to question our assumptions about diet and the nature of what should and should not be eaten.

Like humans, animals are very selective about the dirt they eat. No adult animal, it seems, eats just any dirt—a kind of indiscriminate, exploratory behavior seen only in very young animals, including children. A troop of gorillas or a herd of elephants concentrates on just a few sites that they return to again and again. East African elephants routinely excavate the caves of certain hillsides where they are able to access iodine-rich salt deposits. According to some scientists, elephants are particularly prone to iodine deficiency, and even their familiar, elephantine habits of wallowing in mud and throwing dirt on their hides are attempts to absorb iodine through the rich blood supply in their skin.

Mountain gorillas in Rwanda are not the regular dirt-eaters that elephants are, but they do visit sites five or six times a year where all the members of a group occupy themselves in digging and eating soil for about thirty minutes at a time. This soil, located high up in the side of a volcano, is rich in both salt and iron, and observers suspect that the gorillas may be after those two important nutrients. Mountain vegetation, after all, is usually very low in sodium, and gorillas, like all mammals living at high altitudes, need extra iron for the extra red-blood-cell production that is required at those altitudes. The easiest way for gorillas to get this extra iron may be these volcanic soils

And here's another insight into human geophagy that animals help us to see. Just as strict carnivores do not eat dirt or clay, human populations that include a lot of animal products in their diet also do not eat dirt or clay. Clay-eating is rare, even nonexistent, among the Masai of Kenya, cattle-herders whose diet consists largely of milk and blood. But it is extremely common among the neighboring Kikuya, agriculturalists whose diet is based largely upon plants.

Animal products are important both for what they have and what they don't have. They have most of the minerals that humans and other animals need to survive, including sodium, iron, phosphorus, zinc, selenium, and calcium (but only if the bones are chewed, since meat itself is low in calcium). And they don't have the many toxins that plant foods have: the tannins in acorns, the glycoalkaloids in potatoes, the phytates in soybeans. Because so many of the plants we eat in the United States have been bred to lessen their toxic load, we have the luxury of knowing very little about these chemicals, which were designed to protect plants from being attacked by funguses as well as animals. But they can cause severe and sometimes fatal damage. Some limit the nutrients available for growth, while others act as poisons, releasing cyanides, carcinogens, and other dangerous substances, bursting red blood cells and damaging neurons, kidneys, and the endocrine system.

Plant-eaters are not entirely at the mercy of the plants, though, and many find ways around these toxins. Some plant-eaters process plants to remove the most toxic parts, and some have become specialists in handling certain toxins, like the koala, which eats only eucalyptus. Others consume clay along with toxic plants so that the clay particles can absorb most of the toxins. Clays are ideal antitoxins for several reasons. Their very fine particles give them a large surface area and make it likely that those particles will come into contact with the toxins in foods. And their crystalline structure is layered with positively charged ions, primarily of silicon and aluminum. Since many organic toxins are also positively charged particles, they essentially trade places with the ions in the clays then pass harmlessly through the digestive system.

Animals seem to be aware of the benefits of adding clay to a plant-based diet, and in some animals, detoxification of plant foods seems to be the primary reason for eating dirt. In the study of the daily, dirt-eating behavior of tropical, plant-eating birds in New Guinea, Jared Diamond found that the soil chosen by these birds (cockatoos, parrots, and pigeons) is particularly good at binding the positively charged molecules of strychnine, quinine, and tannic acid that lace their diet of seeds and unripe fruits. The soil is not rich in any minerals that the birds might need, but it binds one-tenth of its own weight in toxins and has 50 percent more binding capacity than the surrounding soils that the birds do not eat.

Dirt-eating in animals also allows us to see how irrational we can be about dirt-eating in humans and how differently we regard the behavior of our own species. While few scientists question the underlying functionality of this behavior in animals, in humans, such arguments have usually been dismissed. Dirt-eating is seen as a sensible, instinctive way that animals can compensate for deficiencies in their diet and/or remove toxins from their foods. In humans, it is a perverse activity that few educated persons would ever admit to.

Which brings me to the third thing that we need to know in order to understand the human practice of geophagy. In fact, most of us are geophagists in that we seek salt from the earth or the oceans to add to our diet. We usually don't think of salt as dirt, but salt is a deposit found in rocks, and clay and dirt are nothing more than weathered rocks. Animals that are carnivores don't need to add salt to their diet because the muscles and guts of their prey have sodium enough to meet their needs. But most herbivores and omnivores— and that includes humans—cannot rely on diet alone for adequate amounts of this nutrient, essential to nerve transmission, muscle contraction, and the maintenance of fluid balance. Because salt is scarce in many parts of the planet, and hence in the plants that grow in those places, many animals must seek out salt licks or salt mines. The problem is particularly acute for inland vegetarians, such as the mountain gorillas of Rwanda, or much of the population of India. Because of this inverse correlation between meat consumption and salt requirements, a poor man, in general, needs more salt than a rich one. And a poor country needs more salt per head than a rich one, a fact of nature that led Gandhi to protest the British policy of salt taxation and take his followers on a "salt march" to the sea.

We so take for granted this almost universal form of geophagy—the salt-shaker—that we don't even see it as geophagy. And, therefore, we don't understand that geophagy is neither an uncommon nor an abnormal behavior, but a reflection of the fact that being an omnivore is a tricky business in many parts of the world. Humans need forty or fifty different nutrients to stay healthy, and sometimes we have to go outside the bounds of what is considered food to find them. Or we have to add things such as clay to our diet in order to turn toxic foods into nutritious ones. Since women, especially pregnant women, have a harder time meeting their nutritional needs, and since pregnant women must also protect the child that is growing inside them from the toxins in food, women tend to eat more dirt.

Calcium and iron present two of the biggest nutritional problems that women face over the course of their lives. A woman's need for calcium increases dramatically during pregnancy, from 800 to 1,200 milligrams per day, a challenge everywhere on earth, but especially in places where calcium levels in the soil are naturally low and/or in cultures where milk and milk products are not a part of the diet. A woman's ability to absorb calcium from the foods she eats increases during pregnancy, but to get the same amount of calcium as in one glass of milk, she would have to eat two and one-half cups of beans or two cups of cooked collards. Tofu is almost as good a source of calcium as dairy products, so Asian women have no harder time meeting their calcium needs than women in cultures where dairy is consumed, but women all over the world can easily consume too little calcium during pregnancy and lactation, shortfalls that they will pay for later with bone fractures and other signs of osteoporosis.

Some of the clays eaten by pregnant women in Africa provide large amounts of calcium, up to 80 percent of a pregnant woman's RDA, assuming a consumption pattern of 100 grams per day (the equivalent of a stick of butter). Others, however, provide only trace amounts of calcium. But, as Andrea Wiley and Solomon Katz point out in a theoretical paper on the role that calcium might play in geophagy, clay consumption can help a woman's calcium balance in ways other than by actually providing her with calcium. Clays can slow down the motility of the gastrointestinal system and thereby increase the time during which calcium can be absorbed from foodstuffs. And by binding with secondary compounds in plant foods, clays can also release minerals, including calcium, with which these compounds often form complexes. The traditional method of preparing corn tortillas in much of Mexico and Central

America by boiling the corn with limestone markedly improves the calcium, as well as the protein, content of the tortillas and is probably the reason for the low incidence of osteoporosis in those same areas.

Iron presents an even longer-term problem for women, from the onset of puberty until menopause, from around age fifteen to fifty-one. Women have higher iron requirements than men, but they consume fewer calories. So even Western diets—diets that include many more iron-rich types of meat than those in less-developed countries—can leave women with shortages of iron. Iron deficiency, not surprisingly, is the most common nutrient of deficiency in the world.

In the United States, women make up for shortages of iron with supplements and fortified foods (and by consuming more food than they need—a subject for another article). Elsewhere, they might visit clay pits or termite mounds. The clays of termite mounds are rich in both calcium and iron and supply a woman who eats at least twenty grams a day with more than 100 percent of her RDA for iron. It has never been proved that women eat these clays in order to obtain extra calcium and iron, but it is telling that, in certain parts of Africa at least, most of the pregnant population makes it a habit of visiting termite mounds. And telling, too, that women must compete for these same clays with many other animals, including giraffes, chimpanzees, and cattle. The cattle, in their rush for these mineral-rich clays, have been known to knock women and children down.

Another problem that becomes more difficult for women during pregnancy—and one that also inclines them toward dirt-eating—is the problem of plant toxins. Many substances that are mildly toxic to adults are extremely toxic to developing embryos. Some researchers have speculated that the nausea and food aversions that plague women during the first trimester help women to avoid the ingestion of these harmful substances, but for women who have no choice but to eat foods that are loaded with toxins, a daily dose of clay could help to minimize their effects. Small amounts of clay might also directly relieve the symptoms of pregnancy by changing the acidity of the stomach and/or by absorbing excessive amounts of saliva. Whatever the actual reasons why pregnant women eat dirt, dirt-eating is an integral part of the behavior of pregnant women in many parts of the world. "That's how you know when you are pregnant," as one African informant says.

With all the examples I've given of dirt-eating in humans and other animals, with all the possible benefits that dirt-eating can provide, especially to pregnant women, I'm not arguing that all dirt-eating in our species serves a clear nutritional purpose. Nor that all dirt-eating is benign. Humans can abuse clay just like anything else they put into their mouths, and eating too much clay can cause intestinal blockages that may have to be surgically removed and can sometimes result in death. Clay-eating also causes tooth abrasion (some dentists are able to pick out the geophagists in their patient population by the amount of wear on their teeth), and it's suspected of causing, not curing, nutrient deficiencies, especially iron-deficiency anemia, a suspicion that has been around since ancient times.

The relationship between clay-eating and anemia is a complex one that has never been clearly resolved. Physicians have long observed that many of their patients who eat dirt are anemic, but is clay-eating a cause of anemia or a consequence? Part of the confusion, investigators are beginning to realize, stems from the fact that different clays have very different effects on a person's nutritional status. Certain clays are rich in easily absorbable mineral, but others actually rob the body of nutrients and minerals. When clays are ingested with food, the cations in the clays trade places with the cations in the food. So there can be a net gain or loss of mineral nutrition depending on the clay and the food. A clay may pick up an iron particle and leave behind an aluminum particle, a net loss for the consumer. Or it may pick up a toxic particle and leave behind an iron particle, a substantial gain. Human and animal populations presumably learn what clays to eat through trial and error, and over many generations, but if that knowledge is interrupted through voluntary or forced dislocation, new clays that may be substituted by these populations can do more harm than good.

The experience of slaves in the New World may be an example of this. When slaves were forcibly removed from Africa, they brought their well-established clay-eating traditions with them, and plantation owners were soon commenting on their "mania for eating dirt." Owners came to blame this practice for much of the illness they saw in the black population and for a new and often fatal syndrome they called "Cachexia Africana," or "mal d'estomac," a syndrome characterized by sluggishness, anemia, and mental insensibility as well as dirt-eating.

"The only appreciable signs of mental activity exhibited during the course of this disease," wrote F. W. Cragin, a physician who described the syndrome of Cachexia Africana in 1835, "are the crafty and cunning plans which the patient most subtily [sic] matures, and as stealthily executes, to procures his desired repast . . . of charcoal, chalk, dried mortar, mud, clay, sand, shells, rotten wood, shreds of cloth or paper, hair, or occasionally some other unnatural substance." Slave owners attributed these unnatural appetites to willfulness on the part of their slaves and viewed geophagy as a slow method of suicide. And they tried, largely unsuccessfully, to break their slaves of the habit (and to protect their economic investment) by chaining perpetrators or by forcing them to wear cone-shaped mouth locks, tin masks that covered the entire face.

In recent years, several researchers have revisited this once-common syndrome, second only to yellow fever as a cause of death among slaves in parts of the South. Some have suggested that a deficiency of B vitamins, along with hookworm infestation and intestinal parasites, brought on the symptoms of earth-eating, as well as those of weakness, anemia, edema, and heart failure; others, that the clays eaten by the slaves acted to bind dietary potassium and iron and cause all the symptoms of the disease. But dirt-eating is still very common in the South, and physicians see very few patients with symptoms similar to those described by pre–Civil War physicians. So though it is conceivable that the specific clays the slaves ate in the New World initiated a new and often fatal medical syndrome, it is more likely that slaves ate more and more clay when their circumstances and diet left them malnourished, overworked, and unable to fight infections.

Questions about the cause and the nature of this syndrome still remain, though, and they underscore the lack of solid information that accompanies almost every instance of human geophagy. In the South, as in most places where dirt-eating has been observed, the usual reaction has been to repress, not study, the habit. From the earliest writings on the subject of geophagy, a term used by Aristotle in the fourth century B.C., medical practitioners have regarded the practice with a skepticism bordering on contempt. Many recognized the usefulness of clay in treating cases of poisoning. But as to the daily consumption of dirt, one physician who lived in A.D. 1000 wrote of the necessity of controlling it, "in boys by use of the whip, in older patients by restraints, prison and medical exhibits, while incorrigible ones are abandoned to the grave." Clay-eating until recently has been synonymous with pica, a perversion of appetite that causes one to ingest strange and unsuitable substances.

Perhaps part of this negative attitude toward geophagy has been due to the misconception that dirt-eaters eat surface dirt, a truly inappropriate food loaded with bacteria, parasites, and other potentially harmful substances. In truth, most edible clays are taken from the band of clay-enriched soil ten to thirty inches below the surface, and the fact that they are usually dried or baked further reduces the possibility of contamination. Perhaps part of the attitude comes from a population that has always had enough meat and dairy in their diet to make geophagy less vital and necessary. Whatever the cause, the effect has been to cover up an aspect of human gastronomy that has been extremely important to the survival of the human omnivore—and extremely long-lived. Edible clays have been found at archaeological sites once occupied by early man, and the fact that chimpanzees regularly ingest clays suggests that this practice predates our evolution as a species.

Attitudes toward geophagy have been changing, though, largely as the result of the work of two scientists, Donald Vermeer and Timothy Johns, who both "stumbled across" the practice of dirt-eating in the course of other research. Vermeer, a geographer with Louisiana State University and George Washington University before he retired in 1996, was the first researcher to recognize the great similarity between edible clays sold all over West Africa and the commercial pharmaceutical Kaopectate. Johns is a plant biologist at McGill University in Canada, best known for his work on the role that plant toxins have played in shaping human diet and medicine.

In 1960, when Vermeer was preparing for his first trip to Africa, he came across occasional references to the practice of geophagy in the scientific and medical literature and assumed that dirt-eating must play a persistent but fairly insignificant role in the dietary habits of the people of West Africa. When he actually got to Nigeria, though, he found evidence of the habit everywhere: in pestles full of clay pieces outside almost every home, in the pouches of edible clays that women wore around their waists, in the marketplaces where clay was sold and sometimes consumed in public. He once watched a woman eat about 150 grams of clay in five minutes. But the usual amount, he learned, was a small handful of clay (30 to 50 grams), consumed over the course of a day.

Vermeer began to wonder if geophagy might in fact be almost universal in West Africa, at least among pregnant women, and he decided to investigate the mining, processing, and marketing of geophagical clays. He found that four hundred to five hundred tons of eko, a clay from the village of Uzalla, in Nigeria, were being produced each year and sold in markets as far away as Liberia, Ghana, and Togo. Irregular blocks of these clays were sun-dried, then smoked and hardened for two to three days over a smoldering fire. In the process, they were transformed from their original, gray-shale color into the rich chocolate color and sheen of eko, the final product.

Vermeer also reported on how West Africans use this clay medicinally, and he was the first, as I've said, to demonstrate the striking similarity between eko and Kaopectate, widely used in the United States to counteract gastric upset and diarrhea. Kaopectate is made of pectin and kaolin, a type of clay that forms a protective coating on the mucous membranes of the digestive tract and is capable of absorbing bacterial and plant toxins. Both eko and Kaopectate have X-ray diffraction patterns that reveal an almost identical quantity and size of kaolin particles; not surprisingly, eleven of the nineteen preparations that village medicine men make out of eko are intended for stomach and intestinal problems, including diarrhea. The other eight are for problems associated with pregnancy.

"The extent to which the many different ethnic groups in West Africa are aware of the antidiarrheal properties of eko is uncertain," Vermeer concludes in a paper in the journal *Science*. "The fact that so many medicinal preparations in the village of Uzalla use eko, however, supports the notion that the therapeutic qualities of the clay are recognized by those who supply it to the West African market system and possibly by those who purchase it."

Why was he the first Westerner to document the uses and composition of eko? I once put this question to Vermeer, a tall, unassuming, and very genial geographer. We were having lunch one day when he was in New York to attend the annual meeting of the Association of American Geographers, and I was struck by the fact that so many tons of this clay are produced and sold every year, yet only west Africans had been aware of its existence.

"I don't know," Vermeer answered in a soft, raspy voice he has acquired from his ongoing treatments for throat cancer. "People must have had blinders on. They must have automatically condemned this practice."

"And why didn't you?" I pursued.

Then Vermeer told me about a childhood spent largely outdoors, in the hills outside of Oakland, California, where he grew up, and in the deserts of New Mexico, where he visited his missionary uncle and played and rode bareback with Navaho children. He has been looking at rocks and soils all his life, he said, so he couldn't not see them in the markets of Africa. In order to better understand the practice of geophagy, Vermeer also began sampling clays in Africa, and the good ones, he says, dissolve like a piece of chocolate in the mouth. He has tried hundreds of different clays, and most taste like chalk. He has yet to detect the pleasant "sour" taste that so many women say they enjoy about eating clay.

Eko is not the only clay consumed in West Africa, and as Vermeer continued to investigate the practice of geophagy, he found numerous examples that do not paint as neat a picture as eko and Kaopectate. There were coastal groups in Ghana that regularly consumed sand, a totally inert substance—a practice for which he has yet to come up with any kind of plausible explanation other than that it was a habit that formerly interior-living people took with them to the coast. There were groups for which clay clearly seemed to serve a nutritive purpose, such as the Tiv of Nigeria, where women eat clay that is very high in calcium. But they live right next door, so to speak, to groups where the same explanation doesn't hold. The Igbo people live near the Tiv, and theirs is also a nondairy culture. Igbo women have the same need for calcium as Tiv women, yet the clay they routinely consume has very little of this mineral.

The mystery of why people eat clay continued to expand with Vermeer's work in the American South, where the habit was once so widespread that clay removal caused considerable damage to roads, and some states posted signs requesting that local inhabitants not dig into the banks. Since most of the Southerners who eat clay are blacks, the usual explanation for the clay-eating habit in America is that slaves brought it to this country from Africa. But clay-eating has never been an exclusively black habit—in Africa or in the South. In Africa, Europeans used to carry their stashes of edible clays in little silver cases; David Livingstone once observed that both slaves and rich men were affected. In the South, the appellations "sand lickers," "sand lappers," and "sand hillers" refer to the practice among poor whites. During the course of his research, Vermeer has also come across numerous examples of whites eating clay, such as the nurse in Holmes County, Mississippi, with a Master of Science degree in public health. She pulled Vermeer aside one day to say, "I just wanted you to know that I am also a practitioner."

Clay-eating in the South is more prevalent, though, in the black population, and in the 1970s, 50 percent of black women admitted to eating clay, about four times the frequency among white women. The percentage of blacks admitting to clay-eating has dropped since then, as clay-eaters have become increasingly aware of the stigma attached to their practice and have either broken their habit or switched to eating cornstarch or laundry starch (a switch, by the way, that spares women from the humiliation of being known as a dirt-eater, but adds only calories to their diets). Nevertheless, the practice is still widespread.

As in Africa, the clays commonly eaten in the South are dug from clay deposits below the surface. And, as in Africa, clays are usually dried before they are eaten, either in the oven or on top of the stove. Clay consumption averages one to two ounces (thirty to fifty grams) daily, and clay-eating among blacks often occurs under social conditions such as watching TV; the habits of white women, on the other hand, are much more private and covert.

As Vermeer began to look into the reasons why Southern women consume dirt, however, he could find no consistent mineral content in clays that could explain the habit. Nor could he find any consistent medical or nutritional problems, such as anemia, diarrhea, toxins in foods, parasite infection, etc., associated with eating clay. He concluded that eating dirt in the South does not stem from either a physiological or nutritional need but is, rather, "a common custom arising from traditional values and attitudes."

"Millions around the world practice geophagy, and I hope I've encouraged the medical establishment to approach geophagy with a more open mind," says Vermeer. Yet all that he can say with certainty about the practice is that it is "neither good nor bad." It has the chance for being beneficial in some settings; in other settings, it seems to serve a purely psychological or cultural purpose, transferred from one generation to the next, like smoking or dipping snuff. And he warned me, as I began my research, that I will get as many answers about why people eat dirt as people I ask.

Timothy Johns, on the other hand, is much more convinced of the underlying nutritional and medical reason for most dirt-eating, a conviction that stems in part from his knowledge of the ubiquitousness of plant toxins.

Like Vermeer, Johns saw his first edible clays in a market, but a market in the mountains of Peru where the clays were being sold alongside potatoes. Johns was in South America to study the domestication of the potato. So he was, of course, curious. He knew that wild potatoes growing at high altitudes are full of toxic, bitter-tasting chemicals called glycoalkaloids, which can cause stomach pains, vomiting, and even death if consumed in sufficient quantity. But he had always assumed that Indians living in the Andes ate a domesticated and less toxic version of that wild and bitter food. So it was an eye-opening experience for him to learn that the clays were being sold alongside the potatoes because the Indians ate the clays with their potatoes in order to take the bitterness out. They boil the potatoes, then dip them into a slurry of clay and water before each bite.

"This sounds pretty awful," Johns said when we were discussing this novel gastronomic technique over the phone, "but the clays are very fine, and their texture isn't at all gritty. The taste is in fact quite pleasant, reminiscent of unsalted butter or margarine." Eating their potatoes in this way, the Indians consume several grams of clay at a meal, and that is enough, Johns has found through extensive absorption studies, to take up most of the toxic glycoalkaloids in the potatoes. The clays that the Andean Indians choose to consume with their potatoes are particularly fine, and they have cation-to-exchange qualities that make them magnets for positively charged substances, particularly glycoalkaloids.

Johns's experience in the Andes gave him a new perspective on geophagy and the role that geophagy probably played in human dietary history. "It's all very well to say that humans have reduced the toxic load of their plants through domestication, but what did they eat before domestication?" he asks. His findings suggest that clay-eating gave humans the flexibility to eat a broader range of plants, and this flexibility was important not just in the Andes, but all over the world. The use of clays in Africa had not before been linked to the detoxification of plants. Vermeer, for instance, had not considered the role of detoxification, because he had never seen clays being eaten in combination with specific foods. But when Johns tested edible clays from West Africa, as well as from California and Sardinia, he found that they all share this ability to absorb plant toxins.

According to Johns, then, clay-eating has allowed us to adapt to an ever-changing array of foods. It is an important part of the behavioral repertoire of experimental omnivores like us and is "a kind of buffer, or protective device, for quelling gastrointestinal stress induced by barely tolerable wild plants or pangs of hunger." It could also make a significant nutritional contribution to the diet, in terms of calcium, iron, or zinc, but this role of clays is harder to pin down because the mineral content of edible clays varies greatly from one clay to the next. Until researchers invest the time and the money to examine geophagy very thoroughly—an unlikely occurrence in this day of cheap mineral substitutes and many more pressing medical problems—we may never know all the reasons why people eat dirt. Perhaps it is enough to know that there are many good reasons, and that women, with the extra demands of pregnancy and lactation, have the most reason of all. "Earth," says Johns, "may not be to everyone's taste, but it is one of the oldest tastes known to humankind."

A few days after my conversations with Johns, I received a second sample of dirt in the mail, this time from the Down Home Georgia White Dirt Company in Griffin, Georgia. A company spokesman assured me that this dirt, kaoline from a private mine, is sold strictly as a novelty item (The label says, "Not Suggested for Human Consumption"). But the person who first told me about it, the owner of Mrs. Bea's Kitchen in Atlanta, said that all her customers for the dirt were women looking for edible clays. She stocks it behind the cash register, along with the candy and cigarettes, and charges $1.29 for a one-pound bag.

I broke open the bag that was sent to me and bit off a small piece of one of the white chunks. It was fine, not gritty at all, but very gummy and chalk-like. I can't imagine craving this stuff, and craving it more than food, a feeling that many dirt-eaters have reported. But, hey, I'm an omnivore (and a woman too), and so I will keep my dietary options open.

Rich and Famous

JULIA REED

In *Lady Baltimore*, Owen Wister's ornate 1906 novel of American manners set in the post–Civil War South, the protagonist, John Mayrant, is engaged to a "steel wasp" of dubious background. (She is from either Natchez or Mobile; her father, a Confederate general, is said to have fled the Battle of Chatta-nooga.) She smokes, drinks highballs, and consorts with other men, including a New York banker she uses to investigate the magnitude of her future hus-band's fortune. However, in the eyes of the narrator, the gravest of her sins is that she pretends to be so financially strapped that the prospective groom must arrange the details of the wedding himself. This includes ordering a cake — a Lady Baltimore — from the Woman's Exchange tea room.

Though the cake business takes place as the novel opens, John has already realized he may have made a mistake. But he is a man of honor, and this is turn-of-the-century Charleston (Wister changed the city's name to King's Port on the advice of his friend Henry James), where honor is pretty much all there is left. Finally, after a lot of tortured goings-on and some not-very-well-disguised lectures from the author on North-South relations and the wisdom of the Fifteenth Amendment, our hero finds a way to release himself from his previous engagement and marries the girl he really loves. It was the Lady Bal-timore cake that did it — the bride turns out to be the sweet plantation girl he ordered it from.

It is no wonder that this cake plays such a key role in the novel. It is really, really good, a fact that the narrator, a Yankee who eats a piece for lunch almost every day, comments on with frequency. ("Oh, my goodness! Did you ever taste it? It's all soft, and it's in layers, and it has nuts — but I can't write any more about it; my mouth waters too much.") It turns out that there really was a Woman's Exchange in Charleston, and legend has it that Owen Wister was served a piece of the cake there by its creator, Alicia Rhett Mayberry. But in the years since, its popularity has grown far beyond that city. A light, three-layer "silver" cake (meaning it is made with egg whites instead of yolks), it has a filling containing dried figs, pecans, raisins, and a bit of brandy or sherry. It is indeed grand enough for a wedding, and its fame spawned a Lord Baltimore cake (made with yolks instead of whites, and whose filling contains macaroon crumbs, toasted almonds, and candied cherries).

No one can tell me why Mrs. Mayberry, a native of Charleston, named the cake Lady Baltimore, but there was such a woman. Her name was Joan Calvert, second wife of George Calvert, the first Lord Baltimore, who founded the first religiously tolerant colony in North America (Avalon, a refuge for Catholics fleeing English penal laws, on the southern coat of Newfoundland) and whose heirs founded St. Mary's City, the first settlement in what is now Maryland. Mrs. Calvert, a rather homely woman with jet black ringlets, seems unlikely to have inspired such a rapturous cake. It's more likely there was a fad for using her title, which has been given to everything from a silver pattern to a species of African violet. And while her cake is probably the most famous one named after someone, there are plenty more.

Usually cakes are named for famous people who like them. There's a Robert E. Lee cake, a popular (during his lifetime) sponge cake with a citrusy filling the general is said to have loved, and a Robert Redford cake that the legendary baker Maida Heatter read about in *Chocolate News* magazine. (Redford was reported to have been wild about a chocolate cake sweetened with honey he ate in a Manhattan restaurant, so Heatter procured the recipe and gave it his name.) There's a flourless chocolate cake named after the late queen mother. (It was served to her once at tea in a private house, and, the story goes, she began featuring it at royal parties.) There is even a cake, a genoise layered with kirsch-flavored crème mousseline and strawberries, named after a bandleader, Ray Ventura, who was popular in France just after World War II.

A carrot cake is often called a Queen Anne's cake in England, but it is named after Queen Anne's lace, the flower, which is in fact a wild carrot. In France, there are Proust's famous madeleines and the cupcakes called marguerites. In this country, cakes are mass-produced and have the decidedly more down-market names of Little Debbie and Suzy Q. A whole company named after Dolley Madison makes a dreadful chocolate cream–filled version. Dolley was far more famous for introducing ice cream to the White House (introduced to her by Thomas Jefferson, who had enjoyed it in Paris) at her raucous Wednesday-night receptions. I'm sure there were plenty of cakes offered on those occasions, but they wouldn't have been anything like the too-sweet chocolate sponge cake that bears her name. In those pre–baking powder days, cakes were dense affairs, loaded with alcohol, dried fruits, and nuts.

In the mid to late nineteenth century, baking powder finally became reliable, so cooks deconstructed those Old English–style cakes, incorporating their booze and fruits and nuts into fillings that they then put between layers of the newly possible light and airy cakes. The Lady Baltimore and Robert E. Lee cakes are typical of Southern cakes invented in that period, as is Mrs. Emma Ryulander Lane's Prize Cake. Originally published in 1898 in *Some Good Things to Eat*, the recipe for Lane Cake, as it is now known, called for a rich white cake filled with an even richer custard containing "one wineglass full of good whiskey or brandy" and raisins. It is still popular in the South, but I've seen the recipes for it everywhere, including *James Beard's Menus for Entertaining*. He adds coconut, pecans, and cherries to the filling and inexplicably refers to poor departed Mrs. Lane as Glenna McGinnis Lane.

The Mrs. Lane of my day is almost certainly Mrs. Margaret Harling, the mother of my friend screenwriter Robert Harling and the maker of a coconut cake that is one of the best things I have ever eaten. Owen Wister would surely move to her hometown of Natchitoches, Louisiana, and come up with a novel to set there were he alive to taste it. I long to be the first person to publish its recipe, named, of course, Mrs. Margaret Harling's Prize Cake. Alas, though she makes it almost weekly for church bazaars and birthdays, the recipe is locked in her head and fails to work as soon as she puts it on paper. There is a long history of this problem among instinctive cooks, but I intend to persevere. Until then, I'll make do with generous gifts from Mrs. Harling and, of course, the luscious Lady Baltimore. Or perhaps, in honor of the patriotic spirit currently pervading our land, I'll switch to the Betsy Ross, a white sheet cake iced with white butter cream and decorated with strawberries and blueberries to form the Stars and Stripes.

Love, Death, and Macaroni

PAT CONROY

In 1962, I was playing the first baseball game of the season with Beaufort High School. Our best pitcher was the boy who sat next to me in Gene Norris's English class, Randy Randle, son of the school superintendent. Randy was a superb athlete and a delight for us other boys in the classroom — mouthy, irreverent, and extroverted.

Mr. Norris would get exasperated with Randy and say, "Sit down in your seat, Randy, you fool. And hush your mouth, boy."

"Norris," Randy would say sadly, "don't forget who my father is. Your job's hanging by a thread, Gene. One word from me, and you're in the unemployment line."

"Don't you dare call me Gene, you little scalawag," Mr. Norris would rage. "How dare you threaten me with my job!"

"No threat, Gene," Randy would say, grinning at the class. "I'm talking fact here, son."

Randy had asked me to go golfing with him on Easter weekend, when he and his parents were returning to his grandmother's house in Newberry, South Carolina. Because I was a military brat, I had never gone to anyone's house for a whole weekend in my life. Up until then my high school years had been excruciatingly lonely ones. My mother was thrilled that Randy had extended this invitation and gave me permission to go immediately.

At fifteen, Randy was six feet four inches tall and a true baseball talent. Already there was talk about his pitching in the major leagues one day. But that first game our coach started Jimmy Melvin, a lanky junior who was hit hard by the visiting Wade Hampton team in the first inning. Jimmy Melvin's name is now enshrined on the wall of black marble honoring those killed in action in Vietnam during that long, dispiriting war. The coach replaced Jimmy with Bruce Harper, who had a fastball I was afraid of, but Bruce was throwing wild that afternoon. Soon the coach had Randy warming up in what passed for a bull pen at Beaufort High. Bruce Harper would walk out of the history of that game and into the history of his time: He would serve with distinction as one of John Ehrlichman's lawyers during the Watergate trials.

Then it was Randy Randle's time, and he was called on to shut down the Wade Hampton Generals. Randy was going to prove that there was substance to all the talk about his chances in the majors. He struck out five of the first seven batters he faced, and the other two batters did not even get the ball out of the infield.

Randy Randle had not allowed a single hit when he fell suddenly to the ground after striking out his fifth batter. The ambulance finally arrived, and a girl named Pat Everette gave Randy mouth-to-mouth resuscitation until Dr. Herbert Keyserling moved her aside and injected a shot of pure adrenaline into Randy's heart. The doctor said that Randy had been dead when he hit the ground. In that moment, the lives of every witness to Randy Randle's fall to the earth had been changed, and changed for all time.

In Eugene Norris's English class the next day, Randy's empty seat exuded a disconsolate sense of loss. His seat's emptiness filled the room. The whole world seemed misplaced and ill-fitting. My class and I were in a state of shock when Gene Norris walked into the room, cleaning his glasses with his tie.

"I was just thinking about grief and how we express it. Or how we don't. Boys seem to have the toughest time showing how much they hurt, but don't be afraid to. Not in this room. Not among those who loved Randy with you."

The room came apart, and I cracked like an egg. I wept for two days and could do nothing to stop myself. I wrote my first poem about Randy's death and gave it to his mother and father after the funeral. Nor did I have to call off my trip to Newberry, because Randy was buried there with his mother's people in the Rosemont Cemetery. I rode to Newberry with Gene Norris and stayed in his Uncle John and Aunt Elizabeth's house, where I fell in love with Gene's pretty cousin, Liz, or "Cuz," as he called her.

I did not know then that love and death could find each other at the same dance. Liz was an uncommonly lovely freshman at Columbia College, and I was smitten the moment I walked into the room. She moved with a dreamy, sophisticated air that made me and the other high school boys who encountered her unsteady in our loafers.

On the way to Randy's burial service, I asked Mr. Norris, "Does Liz ever date high school boys, Mr. Norris?"

"Of course not," Gene said, dismissing the fact out of hand. "She wouldn't be caught dead with a high school Harry like you. Liz only dates the cream of the crop. College boys. From the very best fraternities. Her boyfriend's going to be a doctor. Yes, sir, a doctor."

"If she ever breaks up with her doctor friend, I'd sure be interested, Mr. Norris."

"Of course you'd be interested, boy," he said. "But she's got big plans with a Clemson man. She left you boys back in the playgrounds a long time ago. Now quit mooning over my cousin and start thinking about Randy."

When I got to Randy's grandmother's house, I could smell the food all the way up the hill on Main Street, where we parked the car. His grandmother, Mrs. Smith, who would soon become Mamaw to me, introduced me to Dunbar macaroni. She gave me the history, lore, and legend of the dish as she served me a large portion.

"No one knows who Mr. Dunbar was, but we are absolutely sure he was a Newberrian. The dish is native to this town. You'll never find another single soul eating this anywhere. And it's delicious. Though there are two or three versions, I'm letting you eat mine. I make it the classical way. No frills or fuss."

I knew so little about food and the way it was prepared that all I remember about her Dunbar macaroni was that she watched me closely as I ate her concoction of cheese and macaroni and onions. It was my first South Carolina funeral, and everything about that day remains bright, vivid, and profoundly sad.

Though I had never felt sadder, I had never eaten better in my whole life. There was something scandalous to me about combining mourning Randy with the exquisite pleasures of the Newberry table.

I did not eat Dunbar macaroni again for thirty years. I was in the middle of finishing the novel *Beach Music* when I got a call from my old English teacher, Gene Norris, late at night. He could hardly speak as he told me that his cousin, Liz, the one who had infatuated me as a boy, had died in her sleep at the age of forty-nine. Liz had followed her plan with immaculate precision and married that Clemson fraternity man, who then set about becoming a doctor. They had lived out their lives as important citizens of Newberry, raised two children, attended the Lutheran Church, and had some fine years before it began to go wrong with them. Their divorce was almost final when she was found dead in her bed.

Sadness had attached itself to her final years, and Gene would periodically ask me to call Liz to cheer her up when things were really bad. I tried to get her to come to a screening of *The Prince of Tides* in New York City with Gene, but her lawyer said it could be used against her in court. I sent her the bottle of champagne that Barbra Streisand had had delivered to my hotel room after that screening. Liz called me to tell me she and several of her girlfriends had made an elaborate ceremony out of drinking it. When I gathered with her family after her burial, I saw the note I had written when I sent her the champagne. It was hanging by a magnet on her refrigerator door.

I was reading my note to Liz when one of her friends tapped me lightly on the shoulder and said, handing me a plate, "You've got to eat this. It's a Newberry County specialty. We call it Dunbar macaroni."

I had never seen Liz Norris after that day of Randy's funeral. We had, of course, spoken on the phone, but our paths never crossed again. As I ate Dunbar macaroni for the second time in my life, I said a prayer for Liz and thought how strange it was that her high school Harry had finally caught up with her when it was far too late for either one of us.

CONTRIBUTORS

Susan Allport writes about food and the difficulties of being a human omnivore. Her most recent book is *The Primal Beast: Food, Sex, Foraging, and Love.*

Brett Anderson is the restaurant critic and a food feature writer at the *New Orleans Times-Picayune.*

Maude Andrews wrote about the importance of barbecue long before any of us were born, in 1896.

James Applewhite, a professor of English at Duke University, is the author of *Seas and Inland Journeys: Landscape and Consciousness from Wordsworth to Roethke* and seven books of poetry, including *Daytime and Starlight.*

Jim Auchmutey is a reporter for the *Atlanta Journal-Constitution* and author of two books on Southern food.

Earl Sherman Braggs is a professor of English at the University of Tennessee at Chattanooga. His publications include *Crossing Tecumseh Street, House on Fontanka, Walking Back from Woodstock, Hat Dancer Blue,* and *Hats.*

Max Brantley of Little Rock was a food writer for the *Arkansas Times.*

Bethany Ewald Bultman of New Orleans has written for *Town & Country* and *Elle Décor* and served as a contributing editor at *House & Garden.* She is the author of *Redneck Heaven: Portrait of a Vanishing Culture.*

Al Clayton of Jasper, Georgia, took photographs for a U.S. Senate committee investigation on hunger. His photographs aided in the passage of the food stamp program and were collected in Robert Coles's book, *Still Hungry in America.*

Pat Conroy is the author of seven books. In 2001, he was awarded a James Beard Foundation award for excellence in writing about food.

Eddie Dean is a contributing writer for *Washington City* paper. His work has appeared in *Harper's,* the *Wall Street Journal, SPIN,* and *Da Capo's Best Music Writing 2000,* among other publications.

John T. Edge is the director of the Southern Foodways Alliance. He writes for numerous magazines, including *Gourmet.* His latest book is *Fried Chicken: An American Story.*

Lolis Eric Elie, a columnist for the *New Orleans Times-Picayune,* is the author of *Smokestack Lightning: Adventures in the Heart of Barbecue Country.*

Amy Evans is a freelance photographer, painter, art instructor, and cofounder of PieceWorks, an arts and outreach organization for the Deep South. She is the oral history coordinator for the Southern Foodways Alliance.

Marcie Cohen Ferris is a visiting professor in American studies at the University of North Carolina at Chapel Hill. She is interested in the history of Jews in the American South and how their foodways bridge Southern and Jewish culture.

Randy Fertel, a writer and teacher based in New York and New Orleans, specializes in the literature of the Vietnam War. His forthcoming book, *The Gorilla Man and the Empress of Steaks*, is the tale of his parents and their fascinating worlds.

William Price Fox of Columbia, South Carolina, is the author of a number of books, including the comic classic, *Southern Fried Plus Six*, and, more recently, *Wild Blue Yonder*.

Bárbara Renaud González is a writer and journalist based in San Antonio, Texas. She is currently writing the novel, *"Golondrina," a Texas Story*, which inspired her essay in this anthology.

Juliana Gray teaches English at the University of Alabama in Tuscaloosa. She is the author of a poetry chapbook, *History in Bones*.

Jessica B. Harris is a food historian and cookbook author who lives in New York City and New Orleans. Her latest work is *Beyond Gumbo: Creole Fusion Food from the Atlantic Rim*.

Ripley Golovin Hathaway would like to thank Shirley Maul and Clyde Gritten for the help they gave her twenty-five years ago when she wrote her senior thesis, from which her essay is adapted.

Jenine Holmes is a poet whose work came to the editor's attention in *Literary Lunch*, a collection of food writing from the Knoxville Writers Guild.

Rufus Jarmon was a writer with a penchant for documenting the American South. His work appeared in the *Saturday Evening Post* and elsewhere.

Pableaux Johnson is a New Orleans–based food and travel writer. His essay, "End of the Lines?," received a 2004 James Beard Foundation nomination.

Peter Kaminsky writes about food and the outdoors. His work appears regularly in the *New York Times*, *New York Magazine*, and *Food & Wine*. His newest book is *Pig Perfect: Encounters with Remarkable Swine*, from which his essay is excerpted.

Jeff Daniel Marion's most recent books are *Letters Home* and *Ebbing and Flowing Springs: New and Selected Poems and Prose*. A native of Rogersville, Tennessee, he now lives down the road in Knoxville.

Linda Parsons Marion, a native of Nashville, Tennessee, is a widely published poet. She lives in Knoxville, where she is an editor at the University of Tennessee.

Michael McFee has published six poetry collections, most recently *Earthly*. He teaches at the University of North Carolina at Chapel Hill.

Matt McMillen is a Washington, D.C.–based freelance writer whose work has appeared in the *Washington Post* and *Gourmet*. His primary beats are food and health.

Molly O'Neill writes for the *New Yorker*. She was the longtime food columnist for the *New York Times Magazine*. She is the host of the PBS series *Great Food* and has published three cookbooks.

John Shelton Reed is William Rand Kenan, Jr., Professor Emeritus of Sociology at the University of North Carolina at Chapel Hill and coeditor of the journal *Southern Cultures*.

Julia Reed was born in Greenville, Mississippi. She is a senior writer at *Vogue* and writes about food for the *New York Times Magazine*.

Sara Roahen lives in New Orleans, where she writes about food and restaurants for, among other publications, *Gambit*.

Diane Roberts is an eighth-generation Floridian, a commentator for National Public Radio, and a university professor. Her new book is *Dream State*.

Fred W. Sauceman is executive assistant to the president for university relations at East Tennessee State University.

Stephen Smith is a native Arkansawyer, a certified trencherman, a professor of communication at the University of Arkansas, and author of *Myth, Media, and the Southern Mind*.

Vince Staten is a writer, author, and barbecue eater. He has eaten barbecue at more than 1,000 barbecue joints, more than any person alive and quite a few who aren't.

John Martin Taylor is the owner of ‹HoppinJohns.com›, a culinary website. He is the author of several cookbooks, including *Hoppin' John's Lowcountry Cooking*.

Saddler Taylor is curator of folklife and research at the University of South Carolina's McKissick Museum in Columbia.

Sarah Thomas works in public relations at Biltmore Estate in Asheville, North Carolina. Her husband and three dogs are her muses.

Mary V. Thompson is currently the research specialist at Mount Vernon, where she has worked since completing graduate school in 1980.

Calvin Trillin, a native of Kansas City, is a staff writer for the *New Yorker*. His most recent book is *Feeding a Yen: Savoring Local Specialties from Kansas City to Cuzco*.

Robb Walsh is the restaurant critic of the *Houston Press*. His newest book is *The Tex-Mex Cookbook: A History in Recipes and Photos*.

Amy E. Weldon, an Alabama native, is a Ph.D. candidate in nineteenth-century British literature at the University of North Carolina at Chapel Hill.

Jake Adam York's poems have appeared in the *Southern Review, Shenandoah, Crab Orchard Review*, and many other journals. He coedits *StorySouth*.

ACKNOWLEDGMENTS

A lot of individuals worked hard to put this book together. Someone had to get authors' permissions; someone had to keep the files in order; someone had to answer phone calls and write letters; someone had to make the editor look good when he failed to do so for himself. Almost all of those people were named Mary Beth Lasseter. We offer her a small thanks in lieu of the much larger compensation she deserves.

This, the second volume of the Southern Foodways Alliance's *Cornbread Nation*, owes much to the team who put together the first volume—John T. Edge, our director; John Egerton, our spiritual leader; David Perry, our editor at the University of North Carolina Press; and Mark Simpson-Vos, his assistant.

The Southern Foodways Alliance would also like to thank the Atticus Trust for their very generous financial support. We are also grateful to the writers and photographers whose works appear herein. Many contributors waived their reprint fees, and we are doubly thankful for that. We have made every effort to trace and contact copyright holders. If an error or omission is brought to our attention, we will make corrections in future editions.

If you wish to submit an essay for inclusion in *Cornbread Nation 3*, please write to John T. Edge in care of the Southern Foodways Alliance, Center for the Study of Southern Culture, P.O. Box 1848, University, MS 38677, or send an e-mail message to sfamail@olemiss.edu.

The following is a list of permissions to reprint the essays that appear in this book.

"The Land of Barbacoa" by Bárbara Renaud González. Printed by permission of the author.

"Barbecue Service" by James Applewhite. Originally published in Michael McFee, *The Language They Speak Is Things to Eat* (1994). Reprinted by permission of the author.

"Caribbean Connection" by Jessica B. Harris. Printed by permission of the author.

"George Washington and Barbecue" by Mary V. Thompson. Originally prepared for Mount Vernon. Reprinted by permission of the author.

"An Ode to the Pig: Assorted Thoughts on the World's Most Controversial Food" by Bethany Ewald Bultman. Originally published in *Louisiana Cultural Vistas* (Louisiana Endowment of the Humanities) 15, no. 2 (Summer 2004). Printed by permission of the author.

"The Georgia Barbecue" by Maude Andrews. Originally published in *Harper's Weekly*, October 24, 1896.

"Dixie's Most Disputed Dish" by Rufus Jarmon. Originally published in the *Saturday Evening Post*, July 3, 1954. Reprinted by permission of the *Saturday Evening Post*, © 1954 (renewed), BFL&MS, Inc., Indianapolis.

"Texas Barbecue in Black and White" by Robb Walsh. Originally published by ‹houstonpress.com›, May 1, 2003. Reprinted by permission of ‹houstonpress.com›.

"The Rhetoric of Barbecue: A Southern Rite and Ritual" by Stephen Smith. Originally published in *Studies in Popular Culture* 8, no. 1 (1985). Reprinted by permission of the author.

"Politics and Pork" by Jim Auchmutey. Originally presented at the 2002 Southern Foodways Symposium at the University of Mississippi. Printed by permission of the author.

"Barbecue Sociology: The Meat of the Matter" by John Shelton Reed. Portions of this essay originally appeared in *Chronicles: A Magazine of American Culture*, August and September 1992. Reprinted by permission of the author.

"In Xanadu Did Barbecue" by Ripley Golovin Hathaway. Excerpted from the author's senior thesis at Vassar College. Reprinted by permission of the author.

"We Didn't Know from Fatback: A Southern Jewish Perspective on Barbecue" by Marcie Cohen Ferris. Drawn from a forthcoming book to be published by the University of North Carolina Press. All rights reserved. Reprinted by permission of the author.

"By the Light of the Moon: The Hash Pot Runneth Over" by Saddler Taylor. Reprinted by permission of the author.

"The Ribs Hit the Fan" by Max Brantley. Originally published in the *Arkansas Gazette*, July 21, 1977. Reprinted by permission of the *Arkansas Democrat-Gazette*.

"Cheer Up Mama" by Peter Kaminsky. Excerpted from his forthcoming book *Pig Perfect: Encounters with Remarkable Swine*. Reprinted by permission of the author.

"When Pigs Fly West" by Lolis Eric Elie. Originally published in *Gourmet*, June 2002. Reprinted by permission of the author.

"Whole Hog" by Jeff Daniel Marion. The poem "Song for Wood's Barbeque Shack, McKenzie, Tennessee" was first published in *Crossroads: A Journal of Southern Culture* 1, no. 1 (Fall 1992) and later reprinted in *Lost & Found* (1994). Reprinted by permission of the author.

"Kicking Butt" by Matt McMillen. Originally published in the *Washington Post*, June 19, 2002. Reprinted by permission of the author.

"Real Barbecue Revisited" by Vince Staten. Reprinted by permission of the author.

"To the Unconverted" by Jake Adam York. Originally published in *Crab Orchard Review*, Spring 2003. Reprinted by permission of the author.

"In the Kitchen" by Linda Parsons Marion. Originally published in *Home Fires* (1997). Reprinted by permission of the author.

"Willodene" by Juliana Gray. Printed by permission of the author.

"Creole Contretemps" by Brett Anderson. Originally published in the *New Orleans Times-Picayune*, July 7, 2002. Reprinted by permission of the author.

"The Viking Invasion" by Molly O'Neill. Originally published in the *New Yorker*, July 29, 2002. Reprinted by permission of the author.

"Never Give a Child an Artichoke" by Jenine Holmes. Originally published in Knoxville Writers Guild, *Literary Lunch* (2002). Reprinted by permission of the author.

"The Power of Memory and Presence" by Randy Fertel. Excerpted from his forthcoming book *The Gorilla Man and the Empress of Steaks*. Reprinted by permission of the author.

"The Hamburger King" by William Price Fox. Originally published in *Free Times*, July 12–18, 2000. Reprinted by permission of the author.

"End of the Lines?" by Pableaux Johnson. Originally published in *Gambit Weekly*, March 4, 2003. Reprinted by permission of the author.

"Catfish People" by Earl Sherman Braggs. Originally published in his book *Hat Dancer Blue* (1993). Reprinted by permission of the author.

"And the Band Played On: Taylor Grocery, Mississippi" by Sarah Thomas. Printed by permission of the author.

"Open House" by John T. Edge. Originally published in the *Oxford American*, January/February 2003. Reprinted by permission of the author.

"Learning and Loafing at Tennessee's Oldest Business" by Fred W. Sauceman. Originally published in *Marquee* magazine, Autumn 2002. Reprinted by permission of the author.

"Roadside Table" by Michael McFee. Originally published in *Nantahala Review* 1 (2002). Reprinted by permission of the author.

"What Abby Fisher Knows" by Sara Roahen. Originally published in *Tin House* 4, no. 2 (2003). Reprinted by permission of the author.

"Ice Cream Dreams" by Eddie Dean. Originally published in *Arthur*, October 2002. Reprinted by permission of the author.

"For the Love of Mullet" by Diane Roberts. Originally published in the *Oxford American*, no. 25 (1998). Reprinted by permission of the author.

"Boiled Peanuts" by John Martin Taylor. Originally published in *Gastronomica*, Fall 2001. Reprinted by permission of the author.

"The Fruits of Memory" by Amy E. Weldon. Originally published in *Southern Cultures*, Summer 2003. Reprinted by permission of the author.

"Missing Links: In Praise of the Cajun Foodstuff That Doesn't Get Around" by Calvin Trillin. Copyright © 2002 by Calvin Trillin. Originally published in the *New Yorker*, January 26, 2002. Reprinted by permission of the author and Lescher & Lescher, Ltd. All rights reserved.

"Women Who Eat Dirt" by Susan Allport. Originally published in *Gastronomica*, Spring 2002. Reprinted by permission of the author.

"Rich and Famous" by Julia Reed. Originally published in *New York* magazine, April 21, 2002. Reprinted by permission of the author.

"Love, Death, and Macaroni" by Pat Conroy. Originally published in *Gourmet*, February 2003. Reprinted by permission of the author.

The Southern Foodways Alliance (SFA), an affiliated institute of the Center for the Study of Southern Culture at the University of Mississippi, celebrates, teaches, preserves, and promotes the diverse food cultures of the American South. Along with sponsoring the Southern Foodways Symposium and Southern Foodways Field Trips, we document Southern foodways through oral history collection and archival research.

Established in 1977 at the University of Mississippi, the Center for the Study of Southern Culture has become a focal point for innovative education and research by promoting scholarship on every aspect of Southern culture. The center offers both B.A. and M.A. degrees in Southern studies and is well known for its public programs, including the annual Faulkner and Yoknapatawpha conference and the Conference for the Book.

The fifty founding members of the SFA are a diverse bunch: they are cookbook authors and anthropologists, culinary historians and home cooks, chefs, organic gardeners and barbecue pit masters, food journalists and inquisitive eaters, native-born Southerners and outlanders too. For more information, point your browser to ‹www.southernfoodways.com› or call 662-915-5993.

SFA Founding Members

Ann Abadie, Oxford, Miss.
Kaye Adams, Birmingham, Ala.
Jim Auchmutey, Atlanta, Ga.
Marilou Awiakta, Memphis, Tenn.
Ben Barker, Durham, N.C.
Ella Brennan, New Orleans, La.
Ann Brewer, Covington, Ga.
Karen Cathey, Arlington, Va.
Leah Chase, New Orleans, La.
Al Clayton, Jasper, Ga.
Mary Ann Clayton, Jasper, Ga.
Shirley Corriher, Atlanta, Ga.
Norma Jean Darden, New York, N.Y.
Crescent Dragonwagon, Eureka Springs, Ark.
Nathalie Dupree, Social Circle, Ga.

John T. Edge, Oxford, Miss.
John Egerton, Nashville, Tenn.
Lolis Eric Elie, New Orleans, La.
John Folse, Donaldsonville, La.
Terry Ford, Ripley, Tenn.
Psyche Williams Forson, Beltsville, Md.
Damon Lee Fowler, Savannah, Ga.
Vertamae Grosvenor, Washington, D.C.
Jessica B. Harris, Brooklyn, N.Y.
Cynthia Hizer, Covington, Ga.
Portia James, Washington, D.C.
Martha Johnston, Birmingham, Ala.
Sally Belk King, Richmond, Va.
Sarah Labensky, Columbus, Miss.
Edna Lewis, Atlanta, Ga.
Rudy Lombard, Chicago, Ill.

Ronni Lundy, Louisville, Ky.
Louis Osteen, Charleston, S.C.
Marlene Osteen, Charleston, S.C.
Timothy W. Patridge, Atlanta, Ga.
Paul Prudhomme, New Orleans, La.
Joe Randall, Savannah, Ga.
Marie Rudisill, Hudson, Fla.
Dori Sanders, Clover, S.C.
Richard Schweid, Barcelona, Spain
Ned Shank, Eureka Springs, Ark.

Kathy Starr, Greenville, Miss.
Frank Stitt, Birmingham, Ala.
Pardis Stitt, Birmingham, Ala.
Marion Sullivan, Mt. Pleasant, S.C.
Van Sykes, Bessemer, Ala.
John Martin Taylor, Charleston, S.C.
Toni Tipton-Martin, Austin, Tex.
Jeanne Voltz, Pittsboro, N.C.
Charles Reagan Wilson, Oxford, Miss.